Hindsights

the autobiography of an unknown artist

Stan Erisman

Hindsights

Published by Stan Erisman
Publishing partner: Paragon Publishing, Rothersthorpe
First published 2020

© Stan Erisman 2020

The rights of Stan Erisman to be identified as the author of this work have been asserted by him in accordance with the Copyright, Designs and Patents Act of 1988.

All rights reserved; no part of this publication may be reproduced, stored in a retrieval system, or transmitted in any form or by any means, electronic, mechanical, photocopying, recording or otherwise without the prior written consent of the publisher or a licence permitting copying in the UK issued by the Copyright Licensing Agency Ltd.
www.cla.co.uk

ISBN 978-1-78222-776-2

Book design, layout and production management by Into Print
www.intoprint.net
+44 (0)1604 832149

Cover illustration: *The Animal in Me*, oil painting #11, by Stan Erisman, 1969

The Foreword to the *Hindsights* series can be found in Book 1, *Natural Shocks*.

To be, or not to be, that is the question:
Whether 'tis nobler in the mind to suffer
The ***slings and arrows*** of outrageous fortune,
Or to take Arms against ***a Sea of troubles***,
And by opposing end them: to die, to sleep
No more; and by a sleep, to say we end
The heart-ache, and the thousand ***natural shocks***
That Flesh is heir to? 'Tis a consummation
Devoutly to be wished. To die, to sleep,
To sleep, ***perchance to Dream***; aye, there's the rub,
For in that sleep of death, what dreams may come,
When we have shuffled off this mortal coil,
Must give us pause. There's the respect
That makes Calamity of so long life:
For who would bear the Whips and Scorns of time,
The Oppressor's wrong, the proud man's Contumely,
The pangs of despised Love, the Law's delay,
The insolence of Office, and the spurns
That patient merit of the unworthy takes,
When he himself might his Quietus make
With a bare Bodkin? Who would Fardels bear,
To grunt and sweat under a weary life,
But that the dread of something after death,
The undiscovered country, from whose bourn
No traveller returns, puzzles the will,
And makes us rather bear those ills we have,
Than fly to others that we know not of.
Thus conscience does make cowards of us all,
And thus the native hue of Resolution
Is sicklied o'er, with the pale cast of Thought,
And enterprises of great pitch and moment,
With this regard their Currents turn awry,
And lose the name of Action.

– William Shakespeare, Hamlet's soliloquy
from *Hamlet*, act III, scene I

The Undiscovered Country

Book two in the Hindsights series

Stan Erisman

CONTENTS

Chapter 1: The Tenderloin 1

How Norm and I adapted to a very new life and world in San Francisco, in the Tenderloin District, away from the brainwashing world of the Meeting and our parents (but not yet from religion as such); how our new life diverged from most of what had previously defined it; and how wonderful and scary it was not knowing what would replace it.

Chapter 2: The fall of '64 31

How Norm's life and mine began moving in separate directions; how my childhood outlook and values became foreign to me, even as I struggled to retain some vestiges of non-Meeting religion; how my introduction to university studies shook my foundations; and how I met Jeanette and fell in love.

Chapter 3: A different footing 46

How my foolishness abruptly brought my life with Norm to a foolish end; how my continued love for my parents caused me to try to appease them despite the success of my rebellion and escape, while at the same time trying to assure Jeanette of my love for her; and how my university studies continued to blow my mind.

Chapter 4: Off the deep end 69

How I put myself through college while working part-time; how my studies of literature and philosophy enthralled, stimulated and challenged me; how Jeanette came to love me despite my mom's active, underhanded and nearly successful attempts to sabotage our relationship; and how the specter of Vietnam began to color everything.

Chapter 5: Weddings and other problems 96

How the mental chaos of uncertainty about morality and religion, a wedding, a confrontation with Catholicism, Vietnam, politics and a bizarre but temporary reunion with Norm led to my chaotic and indefensible behavior; how Jeanette and I were lucky to survive our wedding.

Chapter 6: Escapades and other escapes 121

How my moral tumult nearly landed me in prison or worse; how Jeanette's and my growing love and the escalating War gave us the strength to survive; and how Jeanette and I encouraged each other to uproot our lives (me for the second time) to do the previously unthinkable: to leave our native land.

CHAPTER 7: Landed immigrants 163

How Jeanette and I sought to make a new life for ourselves in Canada (Vancouver), in a tiny basement apartment, with me in graduate school and her working as a part-time secretary; how debates with my brothers obliged me to continue questioning the foundations of religion; and how Jeanette and I learned to live in tranquility on a shoestring budget and plenty of love.

CHAPTER 8: Mario's dilemma 187

How Mario (our Italian landlord) embarrassingly informed us that our too-frequent visitors were a problem; and how Jeanette and I in a single afternoon (October 12th, 1968) reasoned our way from his discomfort and my disenchantment with graduate school, through an analysis of our options and Jeanette's desire for Europe, to a decision to move to the Swedish city of Malmö, a place we'd never even heard of.

CHAPTER 9: Inconclusive anticipation 194

How we attempted to prepare for a plunge into the great unknown; how I started to paint again, for the first time with a conscious focus and with the enthusiastic support of Jeanette; how our preparations for moving mostly took the form of divestments (material and otherwise); and how unafraid we were as we stood together on the deck of the ship in the Montreal harbor.

APPENDIX 1: MY HOMES, 1964-69 219
APPENDIX 2: PAINTINGS 9-12 222

CHAPTER 1

The Tenderloin

It was raining lightly when the Greyhound bus at last brought Norm and me to San Francisco, our unknown watershed destination. The depot was on 7th Street, just south of Market Street, in the downtown area, in the northeastern quadrant of the city. We'd been about ten long minutes late leaving the Chicago Loop. The first point of any import to us along the 52-hour ride was Des Moines, also the first of several transfer points along the way, only one of which required us to change from the Greyhound Scenicruiser in which we left Chicago to the mere Greyhound bus in which we arrived in San Francisco.

Seating on the Scenicruiser was up half a flight of stairs, in comfortable seats, with surprisingly little road or engine noise. More than half of the other passengers were "single old ladies", which to a couple of teenage guys like Norm and me probably meant any females over 30 traveling without accompanying males.

Norm's sisters and families were there to greet us in Des Moines (or to greet Norm; I stayed pretty much in the background) during the brief 20-minute stop in the early evening. Then we rolled on across the rest of Iowa towards Omaha. Sitting there in the upper level, heading into the American West, gave us a bizarre, surreal feeling. It was the dawn of a kind of freedom we'd never felt before, unlike any feeling we'd ever had. We couldn't yet fully recognize what it was.

From Omaha in the late evening, we dozed across southern Nebraska through the not-excessively-uncomfortable night, and reached Colorado in the morning. And the evening and the morning were the first day, and we saw that it was good.

Denver, the next transfer point we were aware of, entailed a longer stop. It also entailed glimpses of the Rockies in the distance. I don't remember what we did about meals on that trip, but presumably we took care of our hunger with burgers when the bus stopped long enough to allow it. The opportunity of finding anything resembling a well-balanced diet just wasn't available, if indeed teenage boys could be expected to have food-group priorities. However, a couple of the major stops and transfer points gave us anywhere from 20 minutes up to a full hour to stretch our legs.

Leaving Denver at around noon, we continued to enjoy our elegantly elevated vista as we headed north a couple of hours to Cheyenne, then west across

Wyoming. The boredom of the Great Plains began to give way to exciting views of prong-horned antelope, and at last the beautiful and sometimes spectacular views of the snow-covered peaks of the approaching Rockies. I thought of the stories of how buffalo used to roam the foothills in vast herds that blanketed the ground, turning the prairie grasses into a living brown tide, until heroic white men exterminated most of them, leaving a brown cesspool of rotting flesh instead, and in so doing also destroyed the entire culture, livelihood and sustenance of many an indigenous tribe. In the early evening, at a slightly longer stop in Evanston (Wyoming), I had time to get a postcard. I wrote my first short note home, assuring Mom and Dad that we were fine and that I loved them.

A couple of hours out of Evanston, we arrived in Salt Lake City, our longest stop along the way. Here we had to change buses. We were anxious to ascertain that our bags, including my big black trunk, would be duly joining us on the new bus. But we didn't get much of a chance to oversee the baggage handling, and besides, we needed food again. Not being seasoned travelers, we failed to realize that one of us should also have been concerned about securing good seats on the new bus, especially since we were unable to determine anything about our baggage anyway. But we gave more thought to filling our bellies, which ended up costing us anything resembling comfortable seats for the last leg of our Great Escape.

The new bus was older. It was no Scenicruiser, and thus had no upper-level vista. By the time we boarded, the only vacant seats next to each other were all the way at the back, in the aisle-less row that spanned the entire width of the bus, directly above the incessant din and inescapable vibrations of the engine. Our one last transfer point was in Reno in the morning, but there were only a few who didn't remain on our bus to San Francisco. No better seats became available.

The back-row seats out of Salt Lake City did have one thing in their favor for me, however: we were joined in the back row by a pretty girl our age – Sally P, a nursing student from England – who was going to be spending a couple of days in San Francisco as part of her US vacation tour. So of course we struck up a conversation, and as the lulling darkness put Norm to sleep and the droning engine wore on, producing a kind of numbing sensory deprivation, Sally and I hesitatingly began to kiss, then neck. I was hoping in vain for as much sensory depr*a*vation as might be achieved in the back of a crowded, noisy bus, but she had her limits. After Reno, we headed across the Sierra Nevadas and into California, arriving in Sacramento in mid-morning. From here it was just a two-hour stretch to the bustling, somewhat chaotic, totally foreign San Francisco bus terminal.

Sitting for over 50 hours on a bus, regardless of the color of the hound, is enough to make a person want to settle down for a while. Norm and I had just escaped from the suffocating environment of our Oak Park Plymouth Brethren upbringing, in which everything we found fun was strictly prohibited, and in which everything was about the Lord and separating ourselves from The World. None of it made much sense to us. For a time we both wanted to go to Hollywood and be discovered. But as the time for absconding approached, I developed a gnawing feeling that Hollywood could turn out to be some kind of prehensile theme park for deluded discoverees and dashed hopes. Aversionase (the not-yet-discovered enzyme that promotes aversion) began pouring into my bloodstream. The whole point, after all, was to get away, as far away as possible, and there was nowhere (in my world at least) where one could get farther away from Oak Park (Illinois) than California, was there? So why not try San Francisco?

In the warm gray drizzle of that midday Monday in June, Norm and I were looking all around, wide-eyed, having traveled so much farther and further than we could have imagined, to the polar opposite of Oak Park in terms of politics, climate, beauty, culture, vibrancy, pulse and attitude, in addition to all it meant and would come to mean for us in terms of freedom. But first we had to deal with a mild state of panic: our luggage had not arrived with us on the bus from Salt Lake City.

We asked one of the handlers and were directed to a small baggage office, where we had to file a report. We were told that our bags and trunk might be on the next bus, arriving that evening, and since we could provide no local forwarding address, we'd have to check back. We decided we might as well look for a place to spend the night, or a number of nights if we could find a place cheap enough. We bought a map, on which nothing was familiar, including the fact that while two-dimensional maps were quite adequate for flat Chicago, they were far from adequate for grasping the ramifications of the steep hills of San Francisco.

So we stood there trying to figure out where we were in relation to where we wanted to go, but since we had no clue about where we wanted to go in this undiscovered country, we just remained wide-eyed for a while. With no bags to encumber us, we began looking around for the non-existent tourist information office, or a tourist counter, or a tourist desk, or a tourist anything. What we did find was a bulletin board. One of the bulletins affixed to it advertised the YMCA

Hotel, the name of which suggested to us (based on zero experience) that it might be cheap, reasonably clean, and hopefully not too seedy. Moreover, it was located only about four blocks away, at 351 Turk Street.

Norm and I headed out to find it, looking at all the new sights and street names, as we sniffed our way across Market Street and into the part of the downtown area we would later learn was locally known as the Tenderloin. That epithet meant nothing to us, carried no values, no associations (other than pork and beef), no implications or insinuations or stigma; it was just a name. We found the Y easily enough, entered, went to the counter to speak to the receptionist, and with minimal delay were assigned room 442, with two single beds. The toilets and showers were located down the corridor. The weekly rate of $14.83 was cheap (compared to typical hotel prices), but even though it was within our budget for the first few weeks, it would never be anything but temporary.

Because we couldn't do any of our own cooking, our total living expenses would probably end up being as much as or more than the rent we might expect to pay for a cheap apartment. But before we could think about apartments or make any calculations about anything, we would need to find jobs.

Suddenly the real world was upon us. There'd be nobody to pick up the tab, nobody who felt obliged to lend us a hand, nobody to watch over us or out for us. It was a little scary, and yet the exciting part was bigger than the scary part, because we felt *free*. The first big wave of such feelings was the freedom to act – to lead what we might have supposed were "normal" lives – without sneaking. So, contradictorily of course, we bought cigarettes, thus potentially putting ourselves on a fast track towards a new kind of bondage. We never made a to-do list comprising everything that had previously been forbidden; that would have been too obvious. But there was an undeniable extra rush every time we did something that had previously been strictly and sternly off-limits for all our young lives.

My old moral compass had been formed by repression, slavery of the mind, and arrogance towards the real world and nearly everyone in it. What new compass would I have to find or create to guide me? When would I even come to realize that I needed one? It would take time to discover how to use my new-found freedom to think, and to see that only by applying the freedom to think wisely would the freedom to act be likely to produce anything reasonably intelligent and sound. My childhood and youth had actively discouraged me from daring to think anything that wasn't certain to be in line with the thoughts of the Lord as laid out by my parents, the Meeting and the Bible, a book that bore witness to a fundamentally grim and highly mercurial supreme being. But now, suddenly – if only I would realize it – I had the freedom to *test* new ideas as well as old ones, bad ones as well as good ones, on their own merits, and not simply accept them without question. I no longer had to face the constant threat of righteous wrath and stern disapproval from those whose approval I was emotionally conditioned to seek and depend on. But I hadn't grasped all of that yet, nor did I realize that I wouldn't be much freer than I was before if I merely did whatever was contrary to what I'd always been commanded to do (or not) and to believe (or not).

After getting settled (without luggage) in our room, Norm and I once again had to do something about our hunger. We went out to find a corner store or market where we could pick up some necessities like rolls, jam, fruit, potato chips and cigarettes – things that might still our hunger without requiring cooking or other preparation, or much money. Then we went back to our room to eat, and to talk about what to do next.

We were feeling pretty damn tired and scruffy after that arduous bus ride; a shower was at the top of our list. The showers – down the corridor, stalls without curtains – were clean enough (not like home, but at least there were no bars of soap to punish the utterance of erroneous and evil combinations of phonemes). We wore our towels and carried our room key down the corridor. We encountered a few other guests there as well, mostly guys in their 20s, some of whom seemed not to be there only to use the shower facilities, but to lurk in them, and to ogle us as if, well, something. We'd never been ogled before. It was a strange experience. I'd done plenty of ogling myself, and I suddenly found myself wondering how that made the girls I'd ogled feel.

We also had to explore our new urban environs further, and I was going to visit Sally later that evening in the delusional hope of losing my virginity on the very first night of freedom in San Francisco. I'd jotted down the name and address of her hotel before she took off from the bus depot, and I said I'd meet her at her hotel at a certain hour that evening. But after our showers, Norm's and my next priority was returning to the bus depot to see if our luggage had arrived. Although it hadn't, we now had an address to give them, to which they said they'd deliver it once it appeared. They certainly didn't seem as concerned about it as we were.

At the appointed hour, I found Sally in her hotel at Union Square, which faced Powell Street where the Cable Cars were straining, creaking and clanging, and the driver was pulling and pushing big strange levers. The receptionist called up to her room for me and when she said I should come straight up to her room, my hopes soared. The room was overtly overly lit. She had some fruit and other edibles, but I wasn't there for my stomach's sake, nor did she expect me to be. We spent half the night lying on her bed kissing. She let me take her blouse off, but her bra was welded on and her lower body remained entirely off limits, its impenetrable defense aided by the protective armor of her cast-iron girdle. She turned out to be a real prick-teaser, at least from my testosterone-loaded, 18-year-old point of view; on the other hand, I was a real chauvinist, a prime example of the classical young, they're-only-interested-in-one-thing male. After a few hours of fumbling and fencing futility, I returned to the Y. Norm had been needlessly jealous of my prospects with Sally, but since he was already convinced I'd lost my virginity, my ego was content to let him think so.

The next morning, with our concern about our missing stuff mounting, the reception called to say that our luggage had finally arrived, and could be picked up in the lobby. With immense relief, we hurried down to retrieve it, and brought our bags (including my guitar and the big black trunk) to our room.

Norm and I spent the first couple of days just exploring the central areas of the city, on foot or riding the fantastic Cable Cars, taking in all the totally new sights, sounds, smells and feelings, trying to learn the names of the streets, various landmarks and where to find things, while keeping an eye open for signs with messages like "Help wanted" or "Now hiring". We did most of our initial exploring together, but sometimes we headed in separate directions. We went to the movies at a theater on Market Street – not in any way a remarkable thing for a normal person to do – but it was in fact the first time either of us had ever been to a movie in the evening without having to sneak away; we were no longer living under the authority of and dependency on parents whose religious beliefs expressly forbade us to be part of or take part in the pleasures of sin in the world around us.

Norm, the more socially interactive of us two, discovered that in addition to a pool and gym to which we had free access, the YMCA hosted one or two sock hops every weekend. I don't remember whether the dances were for the hotel guests only, but there were enough young people (males *and* females) to fill the dance floor. Norm and I were excited about being able to attend a sock hop for the first time ever. And again, we didn't even have to ask anyone for permission! In we went, and before long Norm found a girl in her mid-20s, named Peggy (or she found him), who thought Norm was older than she was.

That very first sock-hop night, Norm lost his virginity back in her room (also at the YMCA Hotel). I was chagrined and never went to another sock hop. I simply felt out of place, but not because my parents had convinced me that it was sinful; on the contrary, the opportunity to be sinful was my primary motivation for going at that point. The main reason was that my parents' long-standing ban on dancing had the adverse side-effect of assuring that I wouldn't ever feel anything but awkward on a dance floor. My athletic ability should have made it easy enough for me to learn quickly, but I think the problem was in my mind; the movements of 1960s sock-hop dancing looked outright silly to me. This was probably a sour-grapes defense mechanism to be able to bear being left out all those years; I had to make fun of it somehow. Moreover, I was uncomfortable with the noise level – the din – which made it all but impossible to converse with a dance partner. The slow, quieter dances were OK; I could fake the steps, although not well, because my mind was elsewhere, related to the definition of dancing as "a vertical expression of a horizontal desire".[1]

On June 15th, a week to the day after our bus pulled into the terminal, I saw the kind of sign we'd been looking for – "HELP WANTED" – in the Market Street window of The Emporium, San Francisco's biggest department store, diagonally across Market Street from Powell, where the Cable Car line came to an end after its descent down Nob Hill. I went in, was directed to the personnel department on the top floor and was hired on the spot to work in the stockroom for $1.89 an hour. I told Norm that I'd heard there might be other openings in the stockroom as well, and by the end of that same week, we suddenly both had jobs – and thus the means to start looking for less temporary accommodations.

During the process of eruption from my cocoon, I never felt the least bit guilty about the smoking, the movies, my lewd thoughts, my lewd longings, my increasingly uninhibited choice of words – all the behavior that until recently had been branded as wicked by nearly everyone in my insular world. It never burdened me with a load of sin; it just felt good. But at the same time I was

---

[1] A metaphor variously attributed to Robert Frost, George Bernard Shaw, Oscar Wilde and others.

inexplicably anxious to demonstrate to my parents that I had not turned my back on everything, and that I was still a True Born-Again Christian despite having turned my back on the Meeting. I was about to develop a double identity.

Throughout my life, I've met numerous, fervently patriotic Americans who have never lived for any extended time in another developed country, never learned the language of that country (or any other language) fluently, and are deeply convinced that America is the only country in the world that is truly free, just, prosperous, or even livable. Yet it's all they've ever known! And while the USA isn't the only country in the world, it's the only country in *their* world, which seems to be plenty big enough for them. (I presume there are similar blinkered views to be found in most other countries as well, but since most of those countries don't rule the world much, it's less scary.) I was like that about my born-again identity. I'd never known anything else, never dared to imagine there *could* be anything else (apart from the road to perdition).

Within a couple of days after starting to work in the Emporium stockroom, while having a chat with one of my new co-workers, Haskle Jones, I realized I'd found somebody my parents might *almost* approve of, even though he wasn't in the Meeting. Haskle was a Baptist, a highly conservative Baptist. After we traded a few biblical clichés, he told me about a fundamentalist Baptist Church within walking distance (about eight blocks) from where Norm and I lived, just off Van Ness and Geary. (Haskle went to one near the southern edge of San Francisco, closer to his home.) I attended the Hamilton Square Baptist Church for the first time that Sunday, June 21st, and insisted that Norm join me, which he did without enthusiasm. Norm was simply no longer the least bit interested in religion once we got to San Francisco. He'd somehow managed to lift off the whole weight of years of indoctrination like a cape of rusty chain mail. But I, for some reason, turned out to have to slough off, scrape off, many, many layers of it, to strip it off like the coatings on an old wobbly chair that has been faithfully slathered with paint every year for nearly two decades.

The Baptists were a big enough first step for me. I felt certain that their basic doctrinal messages were roughly the same as the Meeting's, or at least close enough to satisfy me that it might satisfy my parents. I knew most of their hymns already, from the *Echoes of Grace* (they didn't, of course, use JND's *Little Flock*), but they had an actual pulpit, an altar and an organ, as well as a choir that made noises that resembled singing (all new experiences for me), and the pastor wore some kind of flowing dress-like gown that clearly obviated the need to put on further airs, which is not to say he didn't. There was no baptismal font at the front. Instead there was something that looked more like a tiny elevated pool – bigger than a bathtub and unlike anything I'd seen before. Apparently it wasn't a permanent fixture of the altar area, but was only wheeled out of the wings when it was going to be put to use. I figured it was how Baptists lived up to their name; then I suddenly remembered with some alarm that Baptists didn't acknowledge infant baptism. Grandpa Larson's efforts with me nearly 19 years earlier would mean naught among this crowd.

I was also surprised by how frequently and fervently the pastor talked about *money* and about how generous we should all be by giving more of it to the Baptist Church. Money was seldom mentioned in the Meeting, except pejoratively as "filthy lucre", and how "*the love of money is the root of all evil*". Few Meeting people were poor financially, and seldom made the common mistake of claiming that the Bible says that money (rather than the love of it) is the root of all evil (I Timothy 6:10). The Meeting's Sunday morning collection was never preceded by a sales pitch, unlike the Baptists' verbose pleas to dig deeper into one's pockets; they sometimes even enjoined the congregation to stand up to facilitate the digging. In the Meeting, Sunday morning collections were always conducted in total, pious silence, and there were no collections at all at any of the other Meeting meetings. I was unprepared for the Baptist minister's great emphasis on surrendering one's money and giving to the church till it hurt.

Now gainfully employed (well, at $1.89 an hour maybe not that gainfully), Norm and I got one of the local newspapers – the *Examiner* or the *Chronicle* – and eagerly combed through the apartment rental ads with our map next to us. Our first criterion was low rent, of course, then a convenient location. Our present Tenderloin location (I prudishly informed my parents that our place was in a district called "Lower Nob Hill, downtown side") was most convenient for getting to work at The Emporium, taking the Cable Car, and reaching everywhere else we'd found interesting. It was all just minutes away. We soon spotted an ad for a tiny furnished apartment for $110 a month, which amounted to less than $50 a month more than the Y, or $25 more each, and we were sure we'd quickly recoup that by not having to eat out all the time. Moreover, the apartment was just three blocks from the Y, at 450 Ellis Street (two blocks up the hill from Turk Street), between Leavenworth and Jones; it would be quick and easy for us to move. We phoned about it, walked over to have a look, and met the managers, a friendly couple, rather old (in their 30s).

More than a third of the façade of the off-white five-story building was clad with fire escapes. The entry – in the middle, up half a dozen steps from the sidewalk – was tidy, but somewhat shabby. Straight ahead was an elevator, and to either side was a narrow corridor. The managers, who occupied the first apartment on the left, showed us to apartment 106, the last door along the same ground-floor corridor. We gave it a cursory look, then told the managers we'd take it. We'd seen enough; there was no need to search any further.

The door to our apartment opened into a tiny hall with an adequate bathroom to the right, a tiny kitchen to the left, and a small living room straight ahead. From the kitchen there was also a doorless doorway directly to the living room. Since the back of the building was farther up the fairly steep slope of Nob Hill, the only natural light came through two basement-like transom-like windows (and one more in the bedroom alcove), each about one foot by two, along the top of the wall to the left in the living room, an outer wall with a view underlooking some sort of parking lot at the level of tires, bumpers and California license plates.

The tan-walled living room contained a small Formica table, a couple of unpretentious kitchen chairs, an off-white hide-a-bed sofa, a well-worn, orange-and-brown striped Danish modern easy chair, a desk with an extra chair and a floor lamp. The desk was placed in front of the right-hand wall that comprised storage closets accessed by sliding doors. The wall straight ahead had a wide doorway to a bedroom alcove, also accessed by sliding doors, with just enough wall left on either side to encase them. The alcove was just big enough for two twin beds separated by a shared bedside table with a lamp.[2]

We officially took over the apartment on July 1st, but since we were paid up at the Y until the 6th, we had a few extra days to move our stuff piecemeal, which was good because we worked at The Emporium on Saturdays and had somewhat irregular hours. When we were still in the process of moving in, we received a brief and superficial visit from Norm's sister Margo and her husband. I don't remember whether any of their kids were in tow.

My black trunk served as our coffee table. I stood my guitar in one corner, and placed my typewriter on the desk. Our books by no means filled the bookcase. We each took a section of the closet for our clothes and other belongings, including my guitar case. I bolted the three sections of *Man with Guitar* together and hung

---

2   See drawing of the apartment in Appendix 1.

it on the wall of our living room, between the kitchen doorway and the doorway to the hall. My trunk also contained a number of practical things for the kitchen (including my electric waffle iron for making grilled cheese sandwiches), some towels, and some extra clothing. Once the trunk was empty, we stored our empty suitcases in it. We bought six sets of sheets and pillowcases at The Emporium for just $17, thanks to sale prices and employee discounts. The apartment building managers lent us some pots and pans (the kitchen cupboards already included the basic dishes, glasses and utensils), but there was still so much we needed.

Norm and I were rather proud of ourselves for having found jobs and an affordable apartment so quickly, on our own, and in less than a month. We each opened a bank account into which our wages could be paid, as required by The Emporium. We would no longer have to rely solely on the traveler's checks that constituted our savings from home and my next egg for the prevention of prodigalism. I sent a letter to Mom and Dad, informing them of our new address, telling them about our jobs and that we were fine. It felt like we'd made it!

This called for a celebration. There was, however, one major obstacle: the legal age for buying alcohol in California was 21 (at that time, only New York State, as far as we knew, which wasn't far at all, had an age limit of 18, but what good was that to us?). I was a young-looking 18, while Norm was an equally young-looking 17, unless it was Peggy doing the looking. We would have to use our never-acquired Chicago street smarts.

Just across the corner of Leavenworth and Ellis, half a block west of our new apartment, was a convenience store where we planned to buy some groceries anyway. The proprietor was an elderly lady (probably over 40) with fairly thick glasses. As we were picking out our groceries, we started chatting her up, joking, complimenting her, making her laugh and say "*Oh dear!*"; in short, making sure she would remember us. We quietly noted that all the booze was on the shelves behind the counter, her domain. Then we paid for our groceries and took them home.

Early the next evening we were back. She did indeed recognize us; in fact she was clearly happy to see us again, and our chatting and joking resumed. When we'd picked and placed most of our new round of goods on the counter, and as she started tallying them, we casually asked her for a bottle of this wine and another of that one. "*Oh, then I'll need to see your ID,*" she said. "*But we didn't bring it today – you saw it yesterday!*" we exclaimed in mildly offended protest.

She looked confused for a moment, hesitated, and then mused, "*Yeah, I guess I did...*". And Norm and I were about to have another new experience.

I was so excited, so curious, so impatient and thrilled about the prospect, not just of my first whole glass of wine, but what it would feel like to get *drunk*. I could hardly wait. As soon as Norm and I got home – *home*! – to our new apartment, I poured us each a big glass, took mine over to my bed, did my best to empty the glass in one swig, and then lay down on my back on the bed, with my head hanging down backwards over the edge to enable my freshly alcohol-laden blood to rush to my head faster and still my curiosity at last. I must have looked pretty silly. Norm started laughing at me a little, shaking his head. But I didn't feel drunk. However, since I didn't know what it felt like to be drunk, I couldn't know that it was a different feeling from what I felt, and what I felt – spurred by Norm's chuckling – was an enormous wave of hilarity. I began chuckling, giggling, roaring, guffawing. Everything was suddenly so goddamn funny. "*Hey, Norm,*" I slurred, after refilling my glass and taking another huge swig, "*you think it could be the wine tha'sh making me, thish, all thish, what ish all thish?!, feel sho, sho, shit, man, thish ish FUUUN!*" and I laughed and laughed and laughed.

I realized over the next few weeks that apart from my cameo appearances at the Baptist Church on Sunday mornings, I'd scarcely given more than a fleeting thought to praying or reading the Bible or any of that stuff since leaving Oak Park. I wrote to my parents that Norm went with me "once in a while", just to save him some flak from home, but Norm only remembers joining me that first time, very reluctantly. But I felt I couldn't convince my parents that I hadn't strayed as far as they feared unless I became a *bona fide* Baptist, an official member. Why I felt I had to convince my parents of any such thing after already having completed the Great Escape will always remain a mystery.

One Sunday, I decided to have a word with the pastor after the service. I said I wanted to join. He asked me whether I'd accepted Jesus as my savior and I said yes. He asked me whether I'd been baptized as an adult. Without flinching I said yes; it wasn't as though I was going to let some sanctimonious jerk in a dress dunk me in front of a bunch of strangers (I'd witnessed that indignity already), just to be able to tell my parents that I was a Baptist, which I'd already understood probably wouldn't thrill them all that much anyway. And thus the following Sunday, having used a lie to avoid the need for getting dunked, I was received as a member of their congregation; I was a Baptist. (Norm wasn't having any of this.)

Over the ensuing weeks and months, the pastor tried to get to know me better, to encourage me to come to additional church services, activities, functions, and to contribute more money, but I figured I needed to bring down my lifetime weekly average for attending religious gatherings. I therefore limited myself to arriving for those Sunday morning services at the last minute (sometimes with a hangover), singing along with the hymns, and dashing out as soon as it was over, making excuses about pressing commitments, keeping the Biblical side of my vocabulary active through occasional chats with Haskle and my letters home, spiced with things like *"went to the Baptist Church again last Lord's Day"* – a level of hypocrisy that makes me both cringe and smirk as I write about it today, more than half a century later. And then I began missing a few Sunday services.

My job at The Emporium was the worst job I'd ever had in my short working life, with the exception of the *Oak Leaves*. The work itself and the people I worked *with* were OK, but the people I worked *for* and the store policies made working conditions insufferably despotic for me (I'd always had some problems with authority...) and for many others in my department. Of course, stockboy jobs were easy to fill, and management seemed to devise their policy accordingly, which meant they'd milk all they could get from you and then fire you just as soon as look at you. The turnover rate among stockboys was high, apart from a small core of veterans – middle-age stockboys with nowhere else to go.

On July 20th a phone was installed in our apartment. I informed my parents by letter (long-distance calls were expensive), but they seldom found us at home when they tried to call. Norm and I both worked a couple of evenings every week, and Norm was now spending many of his other evenings and sometimes nights with Peggy, who was now sharing an apartment with another girl a few blocks away.

That summer, Norm and I spent as much of our free time together as work and Peggy would allow, taking the Cable Car to Aquatic Park to sit on the grass and have a picnic, me occasionally bringing my guitar to help arouse the interest of young people of the female persuasion. Norm always seemed to find it much easier than me to make new friends, and unlike me, he tended not to become instantly infatuated with every girl who responded to his lustful attention. (Or was it *their* lustful attention to him?) When we were at Aquatic Park one day he met a couple of older girls, one of whom, Sherry (if that was her real name), fancied herself to be a budding *haute couture* model. The girls found us both charming, or at least interesting enough to invite us back to their place, which turned out to be a kind of women-only, dorm-like apartment building known as a guest house, on Van Ness. They had to sneak us in.

We were only a dalliance, however; no lost virginity for me here, and nothing new for Norm, who still had his Peggy to keep him well supplied in that department. I don't know what brought the other of these two girls, whose name I've forgotten, to San Francisco, but her linebacker body and coarse physiognomy suggested it had little to do with modeling. The girls told us about a cool coffee house straight east from where they lived, and straight up Nob Hill from where we lived, on Bush Street, called *The Precarious Vision*, where a few young people like or unlike us could hang out, play guitars, sing, talk about deep and shallow things, dress like bohemians, or not, and watch foreign, mostly black-and-white "art" movies every Sunday evening: Truffaut, Buñuel, Fellini, Bergman and others, including obscure films like Teshigahara's *Woman in the Dunes*, bringing into my view a plethora of perspectives beyond my usual inbred Oak Park sources, and creating many fronts from which my insular right-wing views were rapidly being laden with questions and beginning to crumble under the load.

About five weeks after we arrived in San Francisco, in mid-July, the Republicans held their National Convention at the Cow Palace on the southern edge of town, and I followed it on the radio (we couldn't afford a TV). The liberal Nelson Rockefeller ("Liberal Republican" was not yet an oxymoron in 1964) was struggling to stave off the fiery rhetoric of Barry Goldwater, who was still my favorite as I hadn't yet gained the ability to overthrow the persuasive powers of Keith Sartorius. Norm had no such sympathies, and couldn't figure out why I did, but then he'd never met Keith.

When Goldwater won the nomination with the promise of bombing and nuking the hell out of the North Vietnamese, thus making Johnson the peace candidate by default, I was impassioned and thrilled, but I couldn't understand why *nobody* in my new circles – not Norm, not my workmates (with the possible exception of Haskle), not anybody at *The Precarious Vision* – showed anything but disdain for Goldwater – and loathing for the War. There were parts of me that hadn't yet left Oak Park (or Santa Monica). I was like the cartoon figure who runs off a cliff into thin air, continues churning his legs, then suddenly realizes there's no longer any ground beneath his feet.

Norm and I also discovered Tad's Steakhouse on Powell Street, where we could get a decent steak, a baked potato, some sourdough bread, and a fresh salad for $1.19. Since that translated to just over 60% of an hour's paltry wage, we indulged ourselves there about once a week that summer. The rest of the time we ate corn flakes and sandwiches, including the grilled cheese sandwiches I made two at a time on the waffle iron I'd brought from home in my black trunk.

We also discovered North Beach, San Francisco's most concentrated nightclub and coffee house district, where I strained to catch some of the jazz and folk songs being played inside, and where the new "go-go" clubs and silicone-enriched Carol Doda were making headlines. But we were too young to get into most places, and they would have been far beyond our budgets anyway. The biggest impact on me came from the new wave of "protest songs" (an outcropping of the "folk song" movement I'd been smitten by), especially those of Bob Dylan, whose *The Times They Are a-Changin'* (look up the lyrics!) spoke straight to another, newer part of me. Despite being totally unaware of the extent of what was happening to me, it turned out that I was a-changin' too.

One day as I was riding along in a Cable Car towards Aquatic Park, something caught my eye about halfway up Nob Hill along Powell Street, just below Bush Street: the San Francisco State College Downtown Extension. I instantly jumped off the Cable Car to find out what I could about their curriculum, entrance requirements, and the cost of enrolling for courses. My academic aims at this point were eventually to major in art and to make painting my life's work. My plan was to work at The Emporium during the summer and fall, augment my small savings, take an evening class in September to get started, and then enroll full-time for the spring term of 1965.

What I found out that day required some rethinking of my plans. First, the Extension offered no painting courses; these were only offered to full-time students at the main campus in the southwestern part of San Francisco, the other end of town; thus there would be no art course for me in the fall. (Imagine my surprise when in 2011, on my first visit to San Francisco in many years, I found that the Extension had moved down to Market Street, and the former premises on Powell Street were occupied by The Academy of Art University!) Then I was informed that while I easily met all the academic requirements to enroll at the main campus full-time in the spring, I wouldn't yet be an official California resident. I naively thought I was, living in San Francisco and all, but was told that I would not be deemed an official resident until I'd lived in California for a full calendar year. And as a non-resident, the tuition fee was beyond my reach financially, which meant I would have to delay the start of my full-time studies until September of '65.

But I also found out that no matter what kind of degree I would eventually be pursuing, there were certain basic courses, such as English, that were required for all degrees in all disciplines, and that the Extension offered such courses, and that the course fee at the Extension was the same for non-residents, and that there were some vacancies left for the fall semester. I decided to go for it. But I didn't know how tough university-level studies would be (despite my default optimism, I've always tended to imagine obstacles to be bigger than they usually turn out to be), nor did I know how difficult it might be to juggle my work schedule if the courses happened to be held on evenings when I had to work. Consequently, I signed up for just the one course. I was eager to get my brain back in gear (with hindsight, I could probably omit "back").

Norm and I worked on different floors at The Emporium – I predominantly in men's clothing on the second floor of the stockroom building, Norm in china and glassware on the fourth floor – and we frequently started at different times, owing to the evening and Saturday opening hours and the possibilities of overtime or different days off. We also found ourselves pursuing after-work social activities in increasingly different directions from each other and with entirely different people. But we still did quite a lot together, including drinking.

Thanks to some older workmates of ours, we managed to extend our alcohol supply sources beyond the near-sighted lady at the corner convenience store. One Friday, one of my co-workers did me the favor of accepting some of my hard-earned cash to purchase a half-gallon bottle of Gilbey's gin on my behalf, which I proudly brought home to our pad. Now Norm and I were going to get serious about Tom Collins. I prepared one each, in tall glasses with ice: nice and refreshing and strong. We quickly polished them off and returned to the kitchen to recharge our glasses. Since we were already feeling the effects of the first, we were both already laughing our heads off.

While I was getting the ice and the mix, Norm picked up the heavy gin bottle to add a generous helping to each glass – and *dropped* the nearly full bottle on the hard floor, where it broke into hundreds of gin-soaked shards. We were both horrified, Norm doubly so, since he was also horrified about how furious he presumed I would be with him. (Many years later, Norm told me that ever since that day he always hated gin; I, in turn, avoided buying huge bottles of anything for many years to come.) My focus was solely on bemoaning the fact that the floor was too dirty and the glass shards too fine to salvage the puddles of gin. What pain! What remorse! What a mess! What a smell that lasted for days! What a good thing we had no straws...!

The main Market Street entrance to The Emporium – aka "the Big E" – opened onto a huge ground floor with towering ceilings all around. In the center, the ceiling was not merely towering; it was a majestic dome, at least six stories high, somewhat reminiscent of those in a few capitol buildings I'd visited, like Des Moines. Along the outer perimeter of the ground floor were different departments, starting with (counter-clockwise from the right-hand corner as seen from the entrance) tobacco, men's dress-wear, men's casual-wear, men's shoes, men's jeans and luggage in the far right-hand corner and over to the back doors leading out to Jesse Street (which was more like an alley), across which was the stockroom building.

In the middle of the ground floor was "Dome Square" – comprising a series of counters shaped like oval rings with sales staff inside, for selling specially featured or marked-down merchandise from a wide variety of the store's departments, placed directly beneath the magical dome. All around the dome above the ground floor were the balconies of the other floors. Just beyond Dome Square on the ground floor was the book department and then the escalators. In the far left corner was the entrance to a small room containing a freight elevator that went to all floors. Along the outer left-hand wall there were departments for towels, bathroom furnishings and accessories, ending up back at the front of the store with a big handbag department. Between the main entrance and Dome Square were the perfume and candy departments.

On the upper four floors were the many departments for women's and children's clothing, carpets, china and glassware, silverware, sporting goods, and probably a few more whose relevance for me was too small to have lodged in my memory. The basement contained a number of departments with cheaper clothing and a variety of other goods. There was a liquor department, as well as a cafeteria in the rear left-hand corner, next to the employees-only entrance to a tunnel under Jesse Street, leading to the stockrooms, which were thus across Jesse street in a separate building. There were also two enclosed, elevated skybridges with direct connections across Jesse Street between the stockroom building and the department store, on the third and fifth floors respectively.

The Market Street entrance was not to be used by employees. We had to enter and leave the building via Jesse Street, past a security guard, past a locker room where we could hang up our outer garments (which in San Francisco usually meant raincoats) if we didn't want to take them with us to the stockroom, then on to the employees' stairs or elevator down to the basement (for those who worked in the stockroom basement or on floors one and two) or to the third floor (for those who worked on stockroom floors three and four).

The first floor of the stockroom building was for the marking department – sorting incoming goods from suppliers, pulling big cartons off conveyors, removing the contents, checking for flaws and defects, attaching price tags to every item, then addressing the goods to be sent either to the stockrooms of the respective departments or directly to the department store floor – as well as for the shipping department with its truck bays for incoming goods and outgoing shipments, mostly to sister stores. The Market Street store was the flagship of The Emporium chain, but there were a number of branch stores all around the Bay Area, most of them at shopping centers, identified as Santa Rosa, Marin, Stevens Creek, Stonestown, Stanford and Hillside.

In the stockroom building, the only workplaces where women were in the majority were the area for sorting and marking conveyors on the first floor, the area for processing women's clothing on the third floor, and the book department's special stockroom in the basement.

On arriving for work each day through the basement tunnel, I first had to punch in at the clock inside the glass-walled office of Joe Elliot, the grumpy boss of the stockroom for the basement and the second floor, as well as for supplying the extra help that might be needed to handle the traffic on the first floor. Mr Elliot's typical attire was a dark-blue pin-striped suit over a starched white shirt, and a tie. He was a squat, ruddy, wizened, bespectacled man in his late 50s, with slicked-back gray-streaked black hair. He kept a sharp eye on the comings and goings of everyone through the tunnel. He would also make frequent rounds of the stockroom areas, and was reputed to fire on the spot anyone he caught goofing off or loafing.

The supervisor for the low-ceilinged basement stockrooms was Jim Gillingham, a congenial guy about two or three years older than me, who quickly took it upon himself to show me the ropes and take me on a round of introductions throughout the building, presumably with Joe Elliot's approval, if not at his behest. One of the stockboys under Jim (and also under his wing) was Tom Brown, a rotund, jovial, late-middle-aged fellow whose ruddy complexion suggested he may once have had problems involving fluids I was eager to learn more about.

We were all called stockboys (there were never any stockgirls) regardless of age, unless one of us got promoted to floor supervisor, like Jim, who was less than half Tom's age. The basement book department stockroom, beyond the freight elevators, was a large separate room with a separate administration. I was never entitled to set foot there during my first year.

Jim, Tom and I occasionally had lunch in a public cafeteria in the store part of The Emporium basement, but usually at a nearby food court across Jesse Street, where food was cheaper. A few times we went across Market Street to a busy, noisy, fascinating deli, where Jim introduced me to the sensory pleasure of a hot pastrami sandwich on a long San Francisco sourdough roll, dipped lightly in the juices of the meat.

The basement crew also included, for a time, a guy in his late 20s who didn't seem to fit in at all. He was tall and elegantly dressed in expensive tailored suits that were highly unsuitable for the work in question. He looked a lot like the actor Troy Donahue. Jim told me that Mr Elegant was the son of one of the top Emporium executives, and that this son had misbehaved in some way and was obliged by his lofty father to work for a time in the stockroom as punishment. (Were *our* jobs a form of punishment?!) Although he was *in* the stockroom, he let it be known that he was not *of* the stockroom. He was never referred to as a stockboy, but he did design to undertake my purchase of that fateful half-gallon bottle of Gilbey's.

The second-floor stockroom could be reached via a stairway adjacent to Joe Elliot's office, along the short corridor to the incinerator room, but access was usually via one of two freight elevators beyond and behind Joe Elliot's office. This was because going up to the second floor was invariably part of the process of pushing and/or pulling of one or more of the many trucks and wheeled garment racks it was part of the jobs of the stockboys to move around.

The second-floor stockroom (which basically served the first floor of the store) was much larger than the basement, as it extended into extra wings on both sides. Immediately facing the elevators was the small shoe stockroom (not a stockroom for small shoes – the room itself was small, since most of the shoes were kept in another stock area behind the shoe department in the store itself). The stockrooms for departments 507, 509 and 515 (all three menswear) were the primary responsibility of Fred Bito, a Filipino nearly 10 years older than me. His English was pretty good, but he didn't seem entirely comfortable with it. He was friendly enough, but kept tight control of his emotions, seldom breaking into a smile, and only rarely into laughter. He was a devout Catholic.

The second-floor supervisor was Bill, a tall, skinny, highly serious black guy whose seriousness occasionally erupted into a huge smile that could light up a room. He always wore a starched white shirt and an impeccably knotted slender tie. To the left of the 507 stockroom section was a large caged-in section for men's dress shirts, department 501, the exclusive domain of one of the veterans, Vince Noli (he liked to be called by his surname only), who with his pencil-line mustache looked like (or at least seemed to be trying to look like) the actor David Niven, albeit a much shorter version. Noli's mincing step, *oh-la-la* laughter, and arching eyebrows stood in sharp contrast to his occasional claims of nightly escapades with people of a different gender from his own. He was congenial enough, in most of the expressions of his mercurial temperament, and he stuck to his turf, except when he was called upon to swish down to the department store with a particular shirt or two of a size or color to match a customer's wishes. He often needed help from me to unpack, sort and stash unusually large incoming shirt shipments.

Immediately to the left of the elevator (as seen from leaving it) was a small cage for watches and clocks, and another for silverware. These cages were normally off-limits to the stockboys. Up the slight ramp to the left was a wing that was largely the domain of ladies' handbags. The stern handbag department head was frequently present to hand-pick handbags for persnickety customers and to make sure that "her" stockboy, Haskle, was not being made to work in anybody else's section when there was work to be done in hers.

It turned out that Haskle was not only an emphatically born-again Baptist (who might have found a comfortable home in the Meeting), he was also planning to study for "the ministry". Having innocently and prematurely informed him that I was Saved, which led to my becoming a Baptist too, I soon found it necessary to steer clear of him or watch my mouth carefully around him and avoid excessive depth in our discussions, which were sometimes (thankfully) curtailed by the sudden arrival of the handbag department manager-lady. Haskle's handbag wing also included luggage and a caged-in candy stockroom where one evening I would discover the insane pleasure of dark-chocolate-covered almond paste, imported from Europe.

Up the ramp towards the wing to the right were a few stock departments that normally had a slower turnover rate and less activity – sheets, linens, napkins and all kinds of home accessories – which, to the extent anyone was needed to be there at all, became my initial assignment, my domain. I usually managed to do whatever work needed to be done there quickly, and ended up spending most of my time helping Fred, Noli or Haskle, or going down to help out the shipping department on the first floor. Later, after my first year, I would also help out in the book department's stockroom in the basement.

The shelves throughout the stockroom building consisted primarily of military-green erector-set-style racks that reminded me of those in the basement storage area of the BTP. The shelves extended from just above the floor (the bottom shelf was about three inches above floor level, just right for stashing books beneath it) up to a height that required standing on a wheeled step-ladder to reach the topmost shelves, but those shelves were seldom needed.

Above Joe Elliot, hierarchically speaking, with responsibility for the entire stockroom building, with particular focus on the logistics of the first floor, were the tall and stern Mr Squires, a cruising great white shark of a middle-aged man; and his sidekick, Mr McNutt, a tiny guy who reminded me of Bob Kettlestrings and who followed Mr Squires everywhere like his personal pilot fish. I was told by some workmates that Mr Squires was "a nice guy, as long as you didn't cross him." I couldn't understand how a guy could truly be nice if he didn't remain nice even after being crossed. My failure to understand this may have been related to the difficulties I was having with the concept of a loving god creating hell, then sending people there.

My working day normally began at 8 AM. The store didn't open until 9. The first duty of the second-floor stockroom boys was to head straight out to the first floor of the department store and start pushing or pulling any trucks or garment racks – as soon as they'd been emptied, loaded with returns to stock, and cleared for removal by the respective department managers – back to the small manually operated freight elevator in the rear corner, from where they would be taken down to the basement for further transfer to the respective stock departments in the basement, second floor or elsewhere.

A "truck" was a kind of highly robust four-wheeled cart, about five feet long and two feet wide, in fairly heavy metal, painted military green. It had a flat metal worktop or shelf surface at a working height of about two-and-a-half feet, caged in on three sides by heavy-duty, diagonally patterned metal mesh about a foot-and-a-half high. A mesh gate could be attached to the open long-side if needed to prevent goods from falling out during transport. Beneath this surface was a sturdy solid metal shelf for stashing full or empty tote boxes.

Entire trucks, tote boxes, and individual goods could be marked with color-coded four-by-eight-inch paper labels indicating to which of the Emporium branches the so-labeled goods should be sent. The absence of such a label meant that the goods were to be sent back to the respective stockroom departments. Some of the heavy-duty cardboard tote boxes were labeled "claims", or "returns", which meant the goods were not to be put back on the normal stockroom shelves but on special shelves in the respective departments.

It was essential that all trucks were off the department store floor before the doors were opened to the public. The sight of any truck on the floor after store opening would engender the fury of top management. That fear sometimes resulted in stressful situations – usually when department managers were insufficiently organized or foresightful – requiring me and the other stockboys to push one heavy truck with one hand while pulling another to the elevator at the greatest possible speed, then run back for more, in the final minutes before the doors on Market Street opened.

One or two of the more experienced guys started early each morning, around six, to get all the trucks that were filled the previous afternoon and evening from the stockrooms out to the right departments in the store. Fred Bito often did this, because he needed the overtime since his wife was pregnant. When I worked in the men's departments, my job was to fold things – shirts, sweaters and pants – and arrange them by style, color and size, and then put them on the appropriate shelves.

The department managers would usually spend some time each day picking out what goods were to go to the department and what was to be shipped to the respective branch stores. When a truck for a branch store was fully loaded, it was to be parked in front of the freight elevators, where one of the operators would pick it up and take it to the shipping department on the first floor, but when the operators were busy with other things, I had to take it down myself, and gradually got to know the guys who worked there too.

Despite the low pay, both Norm and I were making a bit more than we were spending, a principle about which I agreed with Mr Micawber (see Dickens'

David Copperfield) as the recipe for maintaining solvency and sanity. Occasionally I was asked to work up on the third floor, where incoming women's clothing was unpacked, placed on hangers, then moved along overhead rails past a few stations where the wrinkles were steamed out with high-pressure nozzles hanging from the ceiling.

While undertaking this task one day – I was still learning how to do it – and trying to untangle some overlapping hangers, I momentarily forgot where I was pointing the steam nozzle and gave myself a severe second-degree burn on the back of my leg, through my now-unwrinkled pants. I was in great pain and they sent me to the store's nurse who helpfully told me to be more careful. This store had no union representatives or members, and with my right-wing views, I probably would have argued vociferously and valiantly for the right of management not to adopt safer working conditions that would cut into their profits, nor for the right of workers to benefit from such safety measures. There were a few fringe benefits, however, in addition to job-dependent health insurance (that went into effect only after the trial period was over, but which would be lost immediately on termination of employment). One of the more unofficial fringe benefits was that I got to buy a $20 imported sweater for $4, just because it had been returned by a customer due to a nearly invisible snag in the knitting. It was deemed too stretched to resell (and imports couldn't be sent back to the manufacturer); the department manager simply pulled out a pen and marked it down for me.

I didn't pay much attention to the significance of the health insurance at the time; I was, after all, perfectly healthy, young and naïve. There's no need to fix a roof when it's not raining. I didn't understand that healthcare wasn't automatic for anyone and everyone who became ill. It wasn't a lack of empathy; it simply never occurred to me. Decades later and much farther down the bumpy road of my life, I not only see what a horror the lack of universal healthcare can mean to anyone unfortunate enough to be ill *and* out of work. I also see that my homeland is perhaps the only democracy that regards healthcare as the privilege of those who can afford it, rather than as a human right. Perhaps it would take a pandemic to make that clear in America.

Some of the guys at work laughed when they heard that Norm and I were living in the Tenderloin and provided one explanation – presumably the most sordid, squalid one they'd heard of – as to how the neighborhood acquired its name: a place of prostitution and perversion. Despite the district actually having a different (but less interesting) etymology, the neighborhood seemed in practice to be waging a less-than-subtle campaign to live up to the more squalid of the rumors, including that of San Francisco's Skid Row.

Many of my workmates seemed to equate "perversion" with "homosexuality". Before moving to San Francisco, I'd never knowingly heard "gay" used to mean anything but a somewhat archaic word for "happy". I had, however, heard many other terms for homosexuals, all of them pejorative. Literature makes it clear that formerly accepted, innocently used words can quickly come to be viewed as pejoratives, sometimes unfairly causing an entire work of otherwise excellent literature to be withdrawn from general use. "Gay" didn't come to refer to "homosexual" until the 1970s, and seems (so far, 2020) to have escaped pejorative connotations in the more civilized sectors of the population.

Back then, in 1964, I felt that the bigger issue was surely why anybody should be entitled to be bothered, offended or incensed by anybody else's sexual preferences. I still feel that way. One explanation I've heard about why people take offense is that the offended person him- or herself is aggressively repressing his or her own natural inclinations. Another explanation is that most mainstream religions have traditionally driven the persecution of homosexuals, as explicitly commanded by their religious treatises, which many of those followers obey to some degree. A third explanation is that it's easier for ignorant, frustrated and intellectually lazy people to attempt to bring others down rather than lift themselves up, which requires much more work. The latter explanation also says a lot about the origins and persistence of racism, as well as a vast and sickly array of other prejudices.

Sometimes somebody at the PV (our quickly adopted nickname for the *Precarious Vision*) would host a party or get wind of one somewhere in town, preferably nearby, and a bunch of us, perhaps most of us, would head off for it. The only beverages served at the PV were coffee, tea and cocoa; they had no license to sell, serve or allow the presence of alcohol on the premises, which consisted of a long ramp from the street door down to a spacious, dimly lit room with a counter for serving the aforesaid alcohol-free beverages, and a lot of chairs and large cushions scattered informally around the room to sit or lounge on, with or without a guitar. There was a small, low dais to the right where those who were moved or urged could perform on an *ad hoc* basis. The far wall was for a big screen on which the Sunday evening movies were shown from a projector near the coffee machine. The ceiling was mostly covered with old empty dimpled egg cartons, suspended there for the acoustics (good) and for the visual effect (interesting).

Occasionally one of those external parties would be located further afield, like once in Sausalito, a groovy little town across the Golden Gate Bridge and down by the Bay. Norm and I went there one evening with a number of the others from the PV to the Charles Van Damme ferryboat music club bar hangout restaurant to hear the blues of Lightnin' Hopkins. We had some pizza and some people might have bought us beer and drinks – we probably couldn't have afforded any at that kind of place, nor were we old enough to buy – but the music was so cool, and we had a great time.

From there, 20 or 30 of us moved on to someone's house nearby. Whoever gave us a ride from the city (I don't remember who) didn't remember to bring us back. As a result, late that night Norm and I had to find our way on foot out to Highway 101 and try to hitchhike home. We were eventually picked up by a guy in a Rolls-Royce (the only time in my life to date I have even sat in such an auspicious vehicle). Norm and I were laughing merrily (not gaily), and I think we disappointed our driver by not being at all interested in being picked up in any other way than for the ride itself. But he was kind enough to drive us back to the city, in fact all the way to the Tenderloin, although we took the precaution of having him drop us off a few blocks from our apartment. I suppose we were a little paranoid.

The summer of '64 rolled on. I wrote to my parents weekly. Letters from my mom were frequent, but I didn't know how to respond. They were filled with triple-underlined moaning, festooned with multiple exclamation marks, and packed with possibly lugubrious clichés (*"Oh, how I cry unto Him that Knoweth...!!!, Oh, how I have cast my heart upon Him...!!!!"*) that just made me cringe and feel embarrassed on her behalf. Having escaped a world where I'd heard such clichés daily, multiple times, to a world where heart-casting hadn't been practiced for centuries, if ever, Mom's excesses now came across, quite frankly, as pathetic gibberish. Nevertheless, I generally spiced my own letters with a few clichés of her own, trying to please, but I focused on replying to specific questions, relating specific events (some of them) in my new life, and making sure to add some comment about the Baptist Church each time, for whatever that sop might be worth to them.

But it wasn't as though I considered myself to have thrown off all I'd been imbued with throughout my childhood (I was still largely unaware of how much my life was the product of indoctrination), nor that I didn't believe that Mom was truly, genuinely sad. Of course she was. But her grief didn't seem to be about *me*; rather, about the fact that I wasn't turning out to be the person she wanted me to be, which would require me to accept as true *all* the things that she believed, and *all* the things that I was increasingly disinclined to accept as true just because others had for generations and millennia been claiming they were. I was beginning to do something quite radical: to place a few demands on having proof of a thing before I was willing to accept it as true.

The big problem for me, which I was unable to see clearly at the time, was how to convey to my parents that I truly loved them yet wanted nothing to do with their religion, but they seemed unable to conceive that the one could be separated from the other. I cannot know whether their love for me was truly conditional on my sharing their beliefs; but they (especially my mom) usually *expressed* it that way. My love for them had no such caveats, but they often seemed reluctant to accept it unless it were on their terms.

Norm and I were finding our way around the central parts of San Francisco with ease now, and we were adjusting to our jobs – the kind of workplace with a high enough employee turnover rate to deprive us fairly quickly of our rookie status. We'd adjusted to San Francisco's weather as well; we no longer drew hasty conclusions that gray, foggy, rainy-looking skies at seven in the morning meant that we would have to wear a raincoat to work; the sun might well be shining by ten. But I used to wear or bring along my raincoat to work anyway. We also came to realize that few if any of the beautiful girls making eyes or whistling at us along Ellis, Eddy and Turk streets on the alternative walking routes to and from work were, in fact, girls. The drunks lying on the sidewalks were easier to spot.

Norm was making frequent use of Peggy's hospitality, although nothing remotely like romance seemed to be involved, at least from Norm's point of view. I would gladly have settled for such an arrangement, but nothing was happening for me in that department. Norm kept meeting new girls; the only ones I met were through him, and none just wanted to have fun in the way that Norm was having fun with Peggy, the kind of fun I so urgently wanted as well. I was still 18. I wasn't thinking of marriage in order to have sex; I could have stayed in Oak Pak for that. But life was fun and freedom was fabulous, and apart from my sexual frustration, I was downright joyful most of the time.

Norm and I had managed to share an apartment for nearly two months now, with few of the conflicts and sharp edges that often emerge when two otherwise compatible friends or acquaintances begin to share living quarters. And after a couple of disgustingly unpleasant experiences of talking on the Great White Telephone, clinging desperately to it while I retched my guts out, a realization slowly began to dawn on me that the pleasure to be derived from the intake of alcohol was somehow related to a hitherto unknown limit to the quantity imbibed, and that I would be doing myself a great service to learn to recognize where that limit was, that I might thereby henceforth cease to exceed it. It would take me some 18 years to fully master the ability to locate this limit.

Two events in August 1964 would have an important impact on my life. The first took place on August 2nd, when the *USS Maddox*, a US Naval ship patrolling off the coast of North Vietnam in the Gulf of Tonkin, claimed to have been fired upon by the North Vietnamese. (It is not clear why the North Vietnamese would have done such a thing. After all, if a North Vietnamese vessel were patrolling off the California coast, we would certainly have treated it with kindness and brought its crew members cookies.)

Conflicting statements were issued by various US authorities, and the level of murkiness was high, but that didn't stop a drastic decision of a magnitude that one might expect to be based only on confirmed, reconfirmed and validated evidence: Congress passed the Gulf of Tonkin Resolution, providing the "legal justification" for the US to deploy conventional troops to Vietnam. America's role as "advisors" thus escalated into open (albeit undeclared) war. Perhaps this was Johnson's way to prove his "hawk" credentials in the face of the Goldwater challenge. That, at least, was the result, and it would turn out to have life-changing implications for me.

Even in my boyhood, I'd begun to discover that my country could in fact be wrong, first regarding its treatment of the Indians, then the Blacks, then the hypocritical American blockade of Cuba. I realized that it wasn't enough for me to question the Meeting; there was so much more out there to question and doubt. But now, with the approaching huge military buildup in Vietnam, the questioning would be of a kind that was totally new to me, and one that hit me on a most personal level. I might soon be drafted and sent to fight a war that was beginning to look very wrong to me, that it had been wrong right from the start.

Fortunately, Norm and I had unknowingly, serendipitously picked the best place in the country to find the questions that I needed to ask, and to find a lot of answers that made more sense than those provided by the government. The San Francisco Bay Area – including the state university campus in Berkeley – was perhaps the heart of the entire country's rapidly growing tidal wave of protest against the War. And there I was, increasingly likely to become eligible for the draft, quickly. I still retained the illusion that I might be able to qualify for conscientious objector status, even though the Baptist Church (unlike the Meeting that I never joined) had no pacifist credentials (quite the opposite, I would eventually discover). And I allowed myself to admit to myself that my objections were not at all based on any Wilderness Wide arguments, but were increasingly political – and survival-related. To be on the safe side, at least for the time being, I had to set my hopes on enrolling as a full-time student in order to qualify for a student deferment, but full-time studies were more than a year away. My first major anxiety had arrived.

The other august event that occurred that month began innocently enough. One late afternoon when Norm and I came home from work, he told me he was going to shoot some pool at a bowling alley a few blocks away, and wondered whether I wanted to join him. I said sure. He said we'd be meeting the Chinese girl we'd met in Aquatic Park a few days earlier. I didn't remember who she was, but apparently she remembered me and told Norm that she thought it would be fun if we both came along.

Before leaving, Norm and I may have had a drink or two (we sometimes did things like that). The girl, Margaret, was rather pretty and pretty friendly, and seemed to be some years older than us, perhaps in her mid-20s. We played a little pool and laughed a lot. I think we also ate some pizza there, but we all wanted drinks, and since Norm and I had no chance of pulling our *"you saw my ID yesterday"* trick at the bowling alley, we suggested returning to our apartment to play cards. Once back at our place, I set about mixing some Tom Collinses, while Norm broke out the deck of cards and the three of us began playing gin rummy or hearts or something like that. (Our gin supply had been replenished after the Gilbey's tragedy, and my memory is that Norm hadn't yet sworn off gin, so either my memory is correct or Norm had something else.)

The ratio between concentration and inebriation was becoming increasingly inverted as the evening drew on. Norm had to get up early, so he staggered off to bed after an hour or two, closing the sliding doors to the alcove behind him. Margaret didn't want to find her way home alone (she lived out by Twin Peaks), so I pulled out the hide-a-bed for her and she and I continued playing cards. The hide-a-bed made considerable inroads into the limited floor space of the living room and into my concentration on the card game at hand, as did the lingering way she was looking at me. My concentration didn't increase when Margaret and I decided to continue our game while sitting on her bed, but the game didn't last longer than the time it took us to change the venue. We not only quickly abandoned our cards, but our clothes and our inhibitions as well – and I at last abandoned my virginity, reaffirming my reckless abandon over and over, for what seemed like all night long.

We also abandoned caution. I started out with a condom, and the feeling (even with the condom) was vastly better than I'd ever been able to fantasize, and amazingly more exciting. There were only the slightest pauses from full erection to nearly full and back to full again. But the pauses, in combination with the fluids we both contributed, were enough to loosen the condom, and neither of us had the presence of mind – or the sobriety or common sense – to take time out, clean up, and start over with a fresh condom. It eventually just sort of splashed off and we were at it again, feeling even better, with brief pauses of exhaustion before each new round.

In the morning I was blissfully, euphorically dead to the world. Norm told me later that when he got up to go to work, Margaret was obliged to leave for work too; they left together. I finally woke up to an empty apartment, feeling like I could fly to the moon and have dinner there.

Norm also told me later that Margaret had expressed astonishment when he told her it was my first time. A day or two later, I phoned her and went out to her place to test my beginner's luck again. I don't know whether it was the absence of alcohol, or the presence of her toddler son, or the not-too-fragrant spermicide cream she used, but neither the magic nor the thrill was there. The absence of the magic was palpably embarrassing; after a brief and somewhat mechanical encounter, we parted amicably. But we never met again. My thrill at no longer being a virgin, however, was still exhilaratingly present.

I've often wondered why, after all those years of indoctrination, I felt absolutely no remorse, no sense of having "sinned", no guilt feelings of any kind. On the contrary. A young woman and I gave each other a night of great and prolonged pleasure. Nobody exploited anybody, nobody took advantage, nobody lied or deceived, there was no reproach, nobody claimed to be entitled to be hurt. Maybe that was why.

On Tuesday, August 18th, Norm and I experienced some difficulty getting home from work; the Beatles were in town to play at the Cow Palace. The four musical sensations were staying at the new Hilton at Union Square (*not* the hotel where I visited Sally P.), which was only a few blocks from the route Norm and I usually took between work and home. But on that day we encountered hundreds of frantic adolescent girls rushing to join the great flow of thousands upon thousands of their screaming friends heading for the hotel, all vying for a glimpse of the British stars.

In that one magical summer, Norm and I managed to divest ourselves of a tremendous amount of the unwanted flotsam of our Oak Park and Elmwood Pak heritage. That was no small feat. We had, in fact, landed on our feet, but perhaps we weren't yet fully aware of everything the new ground beneath them would entail.

CHAPTER 2

The fall of '64

On September 12th, 1964, Norm and I received notice that our phone service was going to be cut off for non-payment. We'd naively sent payment for the $18.95 monthly bill in cash, which of course never reached its intended recipient. Thus we had to pay the equivalent of ten hours of work – again – and change our bank accounts to checking accounts to handle future transactions. Effective September 14th, the day after my 19th birthday, my 65-day probationary period at The Emporium was over. Both Norm and I got raises (to $2.085 per hour), as well as inclusion in Blue Cross medical coverage and life insurance benefits. I had no clue about the potential importance of this at the time.

In the evening on September 25th, I jumped on the Cable Car at the base of Powell Street, where everybody else got on, and I managed to avoid paying the fare – as Norm and I had often done – until I reached the San Francisco State College Downtown Extension halfway up Nob Hill. I jumped off in mid-block and hurried excitedly up the stairs to find the right classroom for *English 6.1 – Reading & Composition*, to be taught by Dr William E. Walsh, every Friday evening from seven to quarter-to-ten.

In the first 20 minutes of the first lesson, it felt like the mild-mannered, distinguished-looking professor had already taught me more things worth learning than I'd hitherto acquired in my entire life. (He was, in my eyes, nearly the spitting image of William Faulkner: gray hair, mustache and all.) The objective of the course, he said, was to be able to express oneself in one's own way. One of the main tools for that is logic, which is a fine way of breaking down propaganda. He told us, in his sublimely understated way, that we might find it useful to learn to make distinctions, first by looking for differences in things that seem similar, then by looking for similarities in things that seem different.

In writing, he told us, there are lots of rules about punctuation, many of them antiquated, which many creative writers tend to ignore (e e cummings ignored them all). But the only worthwhile purpose of punctuation is to achieve clarity, like the gestures you make with your hand (some make more than others) or the natural pauses in your cadence when speaking (some run out of breath sooner than others).

Two things cannot be argued, he claimed: facts and matters of taste. Argument is to advance a purpose, put on a reasonable basis, and reach a conclusion by means of evidence. *Evidence*! I couldn't remember anyone ever having asserted that claims of truth must be backed by evidence! In fact, everything I'd been taught by my parents suggested that a demand for evidence was the antithesis of faith, and their faith *was* Truth, and faith in the Lord was the only righteous thing to be concerned with.

That was just the first 20 minutes. It went on and on that evening, and one evening a week throughout the term. *"We have to make a living,"* the good professor acknowledged, *"but we also have to make a life."* He kept opening one door after another into new worlds, new perspectives, new premises, holding each one open for us like a gentleman, never pushing us through any of them, but always showing the adventures, perils and delights that might await us. He conducted magical tours of literature from the ancient Greeks to the present day, he spoke of (and with) style and clarity, of politics and philosophy, of the immense joys of learning and questioning, even when one's questions have no answers. He spoke with the greatest – and most genuine – humility I have ever heard, and laid out a platform, not only for knowledge, but for wisdom, unlike anything I'd ever even dreamed of. There was nothing cold and uncaring about his unswerving rationality; precisely the opposite.

And then came what for me would be the bombshell that would blow away some of the biggest and firmest of the recent plans I'd been making for my future, and set me on a course that would significantly define the rest of my life. It began with a quote he attributed to Ernest Hemingway: *"I learned to write by looking at pictures in the Paris museums and by listening to music."* Dr Walsh proceeded to expand on this statement, speaking sincerely and without notes, as if eloquence came as naturally to him as coughing to a heavy smoker, and I scribbled furiously to capture everything.

If you can't turn a piece of writing into some other art form, it probably isn't worth anything, Dr Walsh claimed, because all the arts are related. The arts can be defined as the various forms of creative, tangible expressions of reactions to ideas or feelings. Within the minds of most people, there is an ability to express these things, some by painting, some by music, some by drama, others by writing. Not everybody *develops* this ability because it often proves difficult to *cultivate*.

Dr Walsh also felt that Hemingway may have had no talent whatsoever for painting, music or drama, but he definitely had a great deal of writing ability. Perhaps Hemingway's own writing ability was unaroused by reading the writings of others, because his own style was quite different from the prose with which he came in contact. The paintings in the Paris museums, and music, however, may have drawn out an acute desire to express himself and, not worrying about following the patterns of other writers of his time, he did. "*This principle works in all directions,*" said Dr Walsh. "*Painters can be inspired by music or writing. The same holds true for actors and musicians. The arts are related, and not at all distantly. They all have the same mother, Creativity; and the same father, Expression.*"

By studying literature, I inferred that I was *already* studying art. Instinctively, that made sense to me. A look at the evidence showed me that few of the painters I considered great went to universities to study painting; they just painted. The passion and curiosity that inspired and drove them wasn't taught to them, it was who they were. I felt as if I no longer had a clue where I wanted to go, much less how to get there, or why. But I learned something important about who I was. And to me it was incredibly exciting.

In parallel with all this, the older girls that Norm and I occasionally visited on Van Ness were joined by a new tenant, not in the same apartment, but in the same guest house: a strikingly (to me) sensual girl our age named Leslie, from Redding, in Northern California, who came down to San Francisco for reasons I've forgotten, and with whom I was instantly and madly smitten.

As usual, nothing came of it for me; she had a boyfriend back home, but she didn't mind flirting with me in a way that led to some heavy necking, but second base and dry-humping (me fully clothed) on her bed was as far as I was ever going to get; she soon brushed me aside. Believing I'd fallen in love with her, I fell flat on my face, and agonized over Leslie far longer than I should have, and far more deeply. In reality, I probably *had* fallen – not in love, but in heat – and having all my carnal intentions rebuffed or relegated to that somewhat melancholy dry-humping (Margaret had been the one bright exception) was becoming too painful for me.

As the relative warmth of the San Francisco summer – mercifully with no sweltering Midwestern heat – gave way to the slightly cooler and wetter late September days, I looked forward to continuing my weekly Friday evenings at the Extension, each time wondering what new doors Dr Walsh was going to hold open. Those classes, in combination with Norm's and my different evening shifts at The Emporium, meant that Norm and I were working or entertaining ourselves in increasingly different ways and venues and at different times. Only rarely did our evening plans still coincide at the *Precarious Vision*.

On one such evening we went out on a casual double-date with a couple of girls we met there, but apart from that, Norm was tending to meet his new-found friends more often, while I seemed to be stuck in neutral (or neuter, so to speak), occasionally adding to the summer's long, only-once-broken string of PT (prick-teaser) flirtations. Norm and I were also starting to talk about looking for other jobs, better-paying jobs, and maybe moving out of the downtown area to be able to find a cheaper place. The downtown location of the Tenderloin drove up rental costs, despite the somewhat squalid condition of many of the premises. In late September, I bought a football that we took to Aquatic Park and threw around a few times. Norm mentioned that some day he might like the experience of going to sea, maybe in the merchant marines or something. We even spoke of buying some cheap motorbikes to get around on and broaden our range. In short, we were becoming a bit restless.

Fairly early in Dr Walsh's course, and certainly stimulated by it, a new direction for my life began to crystallize. What I now wanted more than anything was to be able to earn a living through painting. The practical side of me realized, however, that extremely few artists manage to do that, particularly if they are unwilling to sacrifice their deepest and most vital artistic impulses to the shallower dictates of the marketplace. Buoyed by Dr Walsh's lectures on the interrelatedness of all the arts, I started considering the idea of following in his footsteps: teaching literature on the college level. This soon became my new goal: Stan Erisman, Professor of English Literature – and painter of whatever the hell I felt like painting.

In the early days of October, Mom wrote to tell me they'd be going to the LA Bible Conference at Christmas, and would be stopping to see me in San Francisco on their way, and did I want to join them to the Conference? The mere thought of a Bible conference – the Meeting – was already totally preposterous to me, not to mention outright nauseating, and the more I tried to imagine what it would be like, the more I shuddered. I didn't reply immediately, since I knew my reply would come across as far too emotional and aggressive. I decided to wait a while and let the boil slow down to a simmer.

As to where my mom was mentally at this time, I can only surmise from the October 1st entry she made in the special diary she kept for her wedding anniversaries, in which she wrote that she and my dad *"...count on Him to break our beloved Stan down ... and make him a vessel unto honor."* What a tragic, vicious attitude! (Although she frequently conveyed this message indirectly, I didn't actually see the diary containing this chilling desire until I was researching for this book.)

Shortly thereafter, on Saturday evening, October 10th to be exact, I was up at the PV to see if there was anyone to talk to or anything to do; Norm was out with one of his girlfriends. There were around a dozen people at the PV, guys and girls, most of whom I'd come to know in a casual sort of way, a few by name, some by facial recognition only. There was a growing restlessness that evening about being in the alcohol-free environment of the coffee house. Everyone seemed to be just waiting for someone to suggest a different venue where we could spend the remainder of the evening with some wine. I suggested 450 Ellis.

These impromptu parties weren't about freeloading – most people chipped in and brought wine with them, picking up a bottle or two at convenience stores along the way. All we wanted was a place to meet up (the PV) to decide where to go to drink (somebody's apartment). They weren't riotous bashes either; we met to play guitars, sing songs, talk seriously about art and culture and politics and the escalating War, maybe find someone to cuddle up to or with, that kind of thing. A dozen or so of us trooped the five blocks down the steep hill to our apartment, and with a necessary minimum of lighting, distribution of glasses and opening of wine bottles, we had the venue and the ambience we sought for the rest of that evening.

It was low-key – lots of conversation, lots of wine, music and singing, lazily enjoyable and relaxed. It was the first time anyone there had seen our apartment. My painting *Man with Guitar* attracted quite a lot of attention. One artsy guy declared that there was no way I should even think of selling it for less than $300 – close to a month's wages for me at the time – but I hadn't thought of selling it at all.

After a while I noticed one girl I couldn't remember having seen before, sitting on the floor (as a number of us were, there not being as many proper seats as there were posteriors to fill them), and staring with considerable contemplative concentration at *Man with Guitar*. I scooted over to talk to her. Her name was Jeanette. (Norm claims that she was the one he was with when he and I with out with two girls from the PV a week or two before. I have no memory of it, nor of her then, but nor do I have reason to doubt Norm.) She was about my age, excitingly cute, with dark hair and eyes, and a curiously engaging manner that combined earnestness with sarcasm, passion with aloofness, humor with *angst*. I told her that the painting was my work, and we started talking, moving, almost racing, through one topic after another, as though we'd been told that we had only a couple of hours left until we would never be able to converse with anyone, ever again. When we at last came up for breath at some point, we realized that we were now alone in the apartment; when or how all the others had wandered off without our noticing was a total mystery. We laughed, a bit nervously. And then we kissed, and kissed some more. But nothing further than that.

We agreed to meet again the next evening, Sunday, and that day I wrote to my parents, quite dispassionately and truthfully, that *"I won't be able to go with you to LA at Christmas. I'll actually be working every day at that time, except Christmas [Day], and I couldn't take off because I need the bread."*

Jeanette and I agreed to go out for pizza that evening. She had a favorite place on Mission Street. She also had a car, an old Chevy, and she said she'd pick me up. The only codicil was that she usually went to Sunday night mass. Could I go with her and then we could go for pizza afterwards? *She was Catholic!* I might have guessed that from her having told me that her father was from Ireland – the south – and that her mother's parents came from southern Italy.

I was curious; I'd never seen the inside of a Catholic church in my life, and I hardly knew what to expect. While I *didn't* believe I would find the Grand Inquisitor pouring boiling oil over screaming heretics (True Christians), I had no reference points, nothing on which to base the preconceptions I might otherwise have been likely to form. The Meeting didn't have "churches", just those sterile meeting halls, and the only churches I'd ever been to were the one where Al and Nancy got married (if indeed they got married in a church – I have no clear memory of it) and the brightly lit, modestly furnished Baptist church near Van Ness.

Entering St Patrick's Church, also on Mission Street, near 3rd Street, that Sunday evening on October 11th, was a totally new experience for me. Its incredibly high vaulted ceiling, rows of arches and stained-glass windows were unlike anything I'd ever seen. It made my jaw drop. Yet it was surprisingly dark, with at least half of its dim light coming from candles, many of which were placed around the feet of a number of statues (*graven images!*), mostly complete strangers to me, meaning they weren't mentioned in the Bible. And there were crucifixes all over the place (*more graven images!*) and a variety of versions of the Virgin Mary (*more!*). They were following a liturgy – also an entirely new concept for me – most of it in Latin (new for me again; the Catholic Church didn't start adopting the vernacular until 1965), parts of which were read in a kind of monotonal, monotonous chant that only changed at the end of a section, suddenly dropping, or rising and falling, or tailing off in a minor key in what I associated with Gregorian chants.

The priest and his boy helpers were wearing much more decorative dresses than the Baptist minister and seemed to take themselves even more seriously than he did. The congregation was sometimes repeating what the priest said, sometimes saying something different, in response to what he said, sometimes in that new old language. The part where they said, in English, *"speak but the word and my soul shall be healed"* struck me as a beautiful, comforting thought – provided that the referred-to word, whatever it might have been, was actually spoken, but there seemed to be no greater incidence of healed souls in this congregation than in any other, including those who congregated at 49ers' games. I supposed the healing word was being left *un*spoken for some reason.

The people – the congregants – were sometimes kneeling, sometimes sitting, sometimes standing, often crossing themselves. With all this bouncing up and down, genuflecting and gesticulating, I was having a little trouble knowing what to expect next while keeping a straight face. Jeanette was occasionally eyeing me a little nervously, but I didn't want to disturb or offend her. I was totally fascinated by the sheer pageantry of it all. When they arrived with the swinging censer, with smoke pouring out, my jaw dropped again. What a show! And when they rang what sounded to me like a dinner bell, I nearly burst out laughing – *not* in mockery, mind you, but simply because the theatrics were stunning. Yet I couldn't believe that anyone took it *seriously*.

Afterwards, when we went to Little Joe's (Jeanette's favorite pizzeria farther along on Mission Street, near 22nd), she explained to me that this was what she'd been brought up on (the Catholicism, not the pizza), what was done in her family, what was expected of her by practically everyone she knew and cared about and associated with. But she didn't *believe* any of it, she assured me; she just liked the meditative, cavernous, candlelit atmosphere of the church with its mysterious-sounding magical Latin mantras.

Her Irish-born father never went to church himself, but demanded that she did. Her Italian mother, however, went to church every week and sometimes "made a novena", Jeanette said. *Made a novena*? Jeanette might as well have told me that her mom made a *przepaść*.[3] Nor did I understand a great deal more when

---

3   Polish for "precipice" (why not?)

she explained that a novena was a prayer recited on nine successive days (with a mass held for each of those days, and a monetary contribution to the Church each time, of course) in order to get a special favor from God, and that the prayers could be addressed to Jesus, but also to the Virgin Mary or to one of the saints. I wondered how anybody could pray to anyone but Jesus? What was so special about nine? Was there anything that showed results after nine times but not after eight? Wouldn't any possible results be even greater after, say, 13 times or 81 times or 99 times? And was there anything that showed that these novenas gave any results at all? I was incredulous, and Jeanette seemed more amused and intrigued than bothered about being bombarded with questions she may have thought of before, but that nobody had ever asked out loud, including herself.

When we left the pizzeria that Sunday evening, Jeanette offered to drive me back to the Tenderloin, but since she was going home in the opposite direction, down Mission all the way to Geneva Avenue, I told her I could take the bus from the stop close by; she had to work the next day too, and it was getting late. She seemed to appreciate my consideration, and before we parted, we sat kissing in her car for a few minutes.

After she drove off, probably just after 11 PM, I stood there waiting for a bus to come along. I was trying to absorb the next major new round of impressions: of Jeanette, of the Catholic mass, and of the unspectacular but interesting Mission District, a down-to-earth part of San Francisco I'd never seen before. The buses were infrequent on Sunday evenings, which in October were beginning to be a bit chilly. The car traffic was also sparse, though there were many more cars than buses, at least two a minute. I stuck my thumb out for each one.

For what seemed like a long time, nothing happened. Of the few northbound cars that came along, each one passed me by without any signs of slowing down. I scarcely noticed a southbound Volkswagen Beetle slow down slightly as it drove by me heading in the opposite direction, but when it suddenly made a U-turn about 50 yards farther south along Mission Street and started heading back my way, I did notice.

The driver, a man about 30 years old, wearing thick glasses, stopped and leaned over to open the door for me. I got in and commented on the chilly evening. He asked where I was heading. I told him Ellis Street. "*Oh!*" he said, "*I happen to be going there too! Whereabouts on Ellis?*" A little alarm bell went off in my head. He'd been heading *south* on Mission, yet said he happened to be going to Ellis, in the opposite direction. I said, "*Near the corner of Hyde*", which was more than a block away from my actual destination. I was suddenly chillingly alert and a bit nervous. I was making neutral banter, trying to sound casual, but wondering whether I'd just been picked up by a psychopath. He didn't say much the whole way, but when we were a block or two away from Ellis and Hyde, he moved his hand from the gearshift to my thigh. I immediately moved it off, with firmness – and some relief, assuming that his intentions were not psychopathic. (Of course it never occurred to me that someone could be both gay *and* psychopathic....) When he stopped at the next stop sign, I abruptly jumped out, thanked him, and took off down to Eddy, to throw him off the track if needed. But it wasn't.

Jeanette and I continued to meet during most of the ensuing evenings. Our backgrounds were incredibly different; we needed to calibrate each other. Each time we met, we discussed lots of things, and enjoyed our long, earnest, frivolous, sometimes bandying discussions. She was working as a managerial secretary at Pacific Cement & Aggregates, but found it boring and was about to quit. She was still living with her parents near the southern edge of San Francisco, and since she'd lived all her life in San Francisco, she knew where all kinds of places were outside the downtown area, places I'd never been.

We kissed and necked a lot, but never anything beyond that; talking played a much bigger role. I found myself looking forward to meeting her again each time, but from time to time she seemed kind of hesitant. Then she told me she'd had an on-and-off relationship with a guy named Gary, who'd already asked her to marry him, and her family approved of him; he was Catholic. Jeanette was unsure of what she wanted to do and whether there could be anything between us, but I continued to intrigue her.

Then one Saturday or Sunday in late October, Norm casually but proudly informed me that he'd slept with Leslie, and I thought my world would collapse around me. I have no idea why I reacted that way – she brushed me off weeks before, and now I'd met Jeanette – yet I became so sad and so outraged and (more than anything else) irrational. If I'd been rational, my first response might have been somewhere between "*Good for you, Norm!*" and "*So what?*", or I might even have listened to the rest of Norm's story (which I wouldn't hear until half a century later) and found it hilarious: that he and Leslie were awakened afterwards, after the (f)act, by a call from the front desk of the guest house, informing her that she had a visitor: her fiancé from Redding. She and Norm had to scramble to get their clothes on, but before Norm could get out the door, Mr Fiancé was knocking on it, and Leslie concocted a miraculously tall tale that enabled Norm to get out of there alive.

But I'd stopped listening, and stopped thinking. I somehow misconscrewed[4] the situation, concocting a position whereby Leslie was "rightfully mine", despite the fact that I was now going out with Jeanette daily, and despite the fact that I hadn't bothered to ask Leslie whose she was, if indeed anyone can be anyone's, and perhaps even more despite the fact that I'd once gone out with Mary Lou (despite her being "rightfully Norm's"), and despite the fact that she clearly wasn't Norm's either.

It probably had more to do with unbridled envy, the result of my having lusted boundlessly after Leslie to the point where it almost made me sick, and that I didn't get to share her bed, but Norm did. Instead, my first action was to phone Peggy and ask her if I could come over. She said yes, and we went straight to her room and closed the door, to talk. She was sharing an apartment not too far from us with another girl who was entertaining a sailor that evening. He must have arrived just minutes before me, because he still had his clothes on. It didn't take long before Peggy and I had our clothes off, but to no avail; I was too totally turned off by the whole situation, too unattracted to Peggy, too agitated about Norm and Leslie, to be able to do anything with anybody or any body, including my own. I went back home, pulled out my pipe, and fumed.

I'm fairly certain Norm never had a clue about the extent of my stupid passion for Leslie, and certainly not that I retained any feelings for her once I started going out with Jeanette, on whom I was now totally focused. Was he supposed to know (much less "respect") that I'd still feel entitled to a "claim" on Leslie, to whom I didn't matter at all? What was I thinking? That he was clairvoyant?

In the days that followed, I began calming down. I continued seeing Jeanette nearly every day, but remained foolishly sullen towards Norm (when I saw him, which was hardly ever). Was he angry? Sad? Happy? He might have still been in total bliss over Leslie for all I knew, since I hadn't even paid attention to his story. Or perhaps he just felt it best to stay out of my way for a while. At that point I was probably not rational enough to know what he felt, or to care.

On top of that, a few evenings later Jeanette made some reference to my earlier exploits with "Suzy Wong" (the name and title character of a critically

---

4   *sic*

acclaimed movie from 1960). Jeanette said that Norm told her that I'd lost my virginity to a Chinese girl, and Jeanette seemed to have a bit of a problem with it. A total falling-out with Norm had already been in the making, *my* making; now the center wasn't holding; things were falling apart.

Having knocked down the prison door and made our way to San Francisco together, it seemed that bursting into freedom would also mean bursting apart from each other.

On Sunday, October 25th, I went with Jeanette to my first NFL game ever, at Kezar Stadium in Golden Gate Park, to watch the Forty-Niners play the Vikings. During the game, San Francisco fumbled and a Vikings player, Jim Marshall, picked up the loose ball and took off, sprinting 56 yards to the end zone, with the San Francisco crowd cheering like mad – because he ran the wrong way, to the wrong end zone. I didn't realize that I might be doing the same thing. (Not until 2009 would I discover that Norm was also in the crowd that day, with other friends, at the other end of the field, and was so drunk that he missed a step, fell down the stairs and was bleeding, and looked up to see a cop laughing at him.)

Sometime during October, I was helping Fred Bito, who was now my supervisor, in the department 515 stockroom section, folding sport shirts and sweaters that came back from the store, and putting them neatly on the shelves. One tote box was marked "returns" and I asked Fred what we should do with them. He said they were going to be thrown out – destroyed – and should be placed in a special bag. "*Thrown out?!*" I exclaimed, "*But there's nothing wrong with them! Aren't they at least going to charity or something!?*" But Fred was certain they would just go to a dump or a furnace. I was flabbergasted – and disgusted.

Then he said that I could ask the assistant department manager – not the manager, because he was too grumpy – if I could take some returns home. Fred had done so himself, many times, he told me. There were Emporium procedures whereby the manager or his assistant *could* fill out a form that would formally authorize removal of "claims goods" from the store, a form that would then have to be approved higher up and then presented to the security guard upon exiting the building. But usually the assistant manager didn't want the bother and just told Fred to wear garments out of the store. (Did something similar go on at Mandelbaum's in Des Moines in the 1920s?) This was long before merchandise was equipped with concealed magnetic strips and other more sophisticated alarm devices. The detective who usually stood at the employee entrance/exit, a man I knew to be a long-retired police officer, was never interested in more than facial recognition – that the people who passed him were indeed employees. I had a word with the assistant manager, who waved his hand dismissively: "*Of course!*" he said, "*you can wear anything you want out of here. Claims are just a pain in the ass.*" And thus I was able to begin upgrading the limited wardrobe I brought with me from Oak Park.

Fred, 28 years old, now with an infant son, also told me about a project he was undertaking at his new home, just across the city limits to the south, in Daly City. He was converting the back end of his garage into a tiny apartment that he would rent out for $25 a month as soon as he finished (which he expected to do by the end of November) and as soon thereafter as he could find a suitable tenant. This information came back to me now, in late October, when I was in the midst of my moronic rift with Norm.

I realized that the location of Fred's house was within my youthful walking distance from where Jeanette lived, and we were continuing to see each other nearly every day. It was also much closer to the main campus of San Francisco State, where I hoped to start full-time the following September. It would cost me less than half of my share of the rent for the apartment on Ellis. Norm and I had to give one month's notice if and when we wanted to move, which meant that if we gave notice within the next few days, by the last day of October, I could be the tenant that Fred was looking for one month later.

I first had to clear this with Norm in the days that followed, to allow him time to find other accommodations. I told him of my wish to move out. He didn't ask why, but he seemed not to be surprised, although he could have been hiding his feelings well. Or I could have been totally blind to them, or both, or neither. In any case, he said it was no problem, and that he might be going to sea anyway, so I gave notice to the managers. We'd be moving out of the Ellis Street apartment by the end of November: I to Daly City, just across the southern San Francisco city limits. Norm would be moving elsewhere, I knew not where and didn't seem to care.

Norm wasted no time taking action to fulfil a long-cherished wish: to go to sea. The very next week (the first week in November) he began the paperwork for becoming a merchant seaman, but his initial enthusiasm was dampened a bit by bureaucracy.

On November 10th, I wrote my parents: "*Norm will be a seaman on a merchant marine ship, but he will still be a civilian. It might actually be several months before he ships out, since there is so much red tape and all to go thru. I understand his folks aren't too hep on the idea."* I had no idea whether Norm really wanted to pursue his notion of going to sea (of course I didn't ask). Maybe I told myself that was what he wanted so I could absolve myself of any guilt about leaving him in the lurch. I had anesthetized myself. I've never understood why.

Tuesday, November 3rd, was Election Day, and Johnson won by one of the biggest landslides in US history. Since I was still under the waning influence of Keith Sartorius and Oak Park, I was briefly disappointed. But after all, in terms of Vietnam, the election was more a choice between Johnson's big war and Goldwater's huge War.

Throughout November, I continued seeing Jeanette, who was voluntarily unemployed now, and my feelings for her were turning into something I'd never experienced, something that went beyond the incessant flirts, mostly frustrated lusts and indefatigable infatuations that constituted the entire emotional span of my previous encounters with the opposite sex. Yet Jeanette remained coquettish – interested, yet keeping her distance, like the fascination many people (myself included) have for watching snakes, hour after hour, as long as there is thick plate glass in between. Did she find me dangerous in some way? Or was it because she hadn't officially broken up with this Gary guy?

She hadn't introduced me to any of her family members yet, but I met her three closest friends. One was Jackie D, a diminutive girl with a jaundiced complexion and short medium-blonde hair who didn't share Jeanette's after-marriage-only approach to sex; she'd had an illegal abortion and was living with her new boyfriend, a tall skinny guy. We went on a double date with them somewhere. Another friend was Carol G, who looked nothing like Jackie; Carol was much taller, somewhat stocky, with black hair and a dark complexion, reflecting her Hispanic background. The third friend was Elsie G, a small Filipino girl who looked frail and nervous, but was sweet and amiable. All three of her friends, including Jackie, were Catholic. As far as I knew, Jeanette was friends with all three individually – they never met as a group.

Jeanette said she'd felt the very closest to her fourth friend, Marie Gilfeather, who was killed in a car accident when they were in the early years of high school. Jeanette couldn't say her name without her eyes welling up, and she carried Marie's picture around with her in her wallet, always. Marie's untimely death made a significant contribution to Jeanette's abandonment of the faith she'd been obliged to choose.

On November 15th, Fred took me out to his home to have a look at the "apartment" he was building, and into which I was already committed to moving just two weeks later. I must have turned pale. All he'd done so far was frame up two walls in one corner of the garage, a two-by-four stud frame construction with plasterboard on the inside. That was it. There was no kitchen, no toilet, no closet – yet. The room was unpainted and unfurnished, but Fred assured me that it would all go quickly, and he showed me with vague waves of his arms where such amenities would be sprouting out of the damp concrete garage floor in the coming days. He was doing all the work himself, in his spare time. For me, there was no turning back. Notice had already been given. I tried to think of other things, to draw all I could upon my natural optimism.

In late November I got a letter from Mom, asking me what to do about my painting *The City* (painting #2), which I'd left behind in Oak Park. They said they could bring it with them in the car when they came to see me in late December (on their way to the LA Bible Conference). Mom said that they liked that painting very much. So on November 22nd, I replied, offering to make them a deal: since they liked it, they could keep it in return for one year's tuition (a $348-dollar registration fee – there was no tuition at that time for California residents) at San Francisco State. I wrote, "Take it or leave it!" They left it and brought the painting with them.

By the end of November, it was clear to me that I was in love with Jeanette. I couldn't stop thinking about her, I couldn't stand being away from her, not hearing her voice, feeling her hand, seeing her vitality. My feelings for her were far from platonic, and yet sex wasn't the big thing for either of us – which was fortunate, given her immutable and unwavering determination to remain a virgin until her wedding night, like the good Catholic she wasn't.

Her fear of even considering anything else, combined with her strange allegiance to an institution whose doctrines and dogma she rejected, seemed highly paradoxical and contradictory to me. I began to realize that the power of indoctrination and brainwashing was by no means confined to the Meeting, but I still was largely unaware of how many of the fundamental premises of religion and of Oak Park conservatism I retained myself.

Deep in November I do still remember going to a jeweler's just around the corner from The Emporium on 5th, and buying a star sapphire ring for Jeanette for Christmas, which I'd ordered engraved "*JM – love – SE*".

Nearly everything about the final weeks of my relationship with Norm remains enshrouded in a fog. I did learn that he'd be moving to the apartment of a friend of his from work (whom I'd never met), somewhere in the direction of Twin Peaks. I must have been numb throughout the split-up phase. I don't remember what Norm and I said to each other about our imminent move, or whether we talked at all. We saw so little of each other during November anyway.

I suppose we must have spent a little time sorting out who was taking what, but our possessions in that furnished apartment were pretty much limited to what we'd brought with us half a year earlier, plus our respective additions of clothing and a few books. The sorting was so basic it could have taken place in a few minutes, in silence. I don't remember how we said good-bye. It's all a complete, dull, aching blank.

Moving day for me was on Sunday, November 29th. It was the only day that both Fred and I were off, and I was dependent on him and his car (or did he borrow a pick-up or a van?) to get my stuff to his place.

San Francisco turned out to be the fork in the road for Norm and me, and we let each other slip away. As it turned out, we'd already started heading down different roads almost as soon as we arrived at the bus terminal, possibly even earlier, although I don't think either of us saw a split-up coming. It shouldn't have ended that way, or that quickly, after less than six months. It probably shouldn't have ended at all.

CHAPTER 3

A different footing

Like a significant percentage of small, single-family homes in the San Francisco area, 574 Evergreen Avenue in Daly City had the garage and storage area at street level and the living quarters on the floor above it. The narrow, two-part door of the Bito garage was to the right. To the left was an arched entrance to an enclosed porch-alcove where a small ordinary door led to the garage – and to my room – on the right-hand side. To the left were brick-red tile stairs leading up to the front door of the Bito residence.[5]

On arrival on my moving day, I was greatly relieved to find that Fred had at least managed to putty the walls, then paint them a neutral grayish-greenish blue, and put down a cheap moss-green wall-to-wall carpet to hide the concrete garage floor beneath it, and give my feet some insulation from the dampness. He'd also installed a gas heater in the corner to the left, nearest the doorless doorway, and furnished the room with a twin bed; a well-used three-drawer dresser with a mirror above it, hastily repainted a slightly lurid shade of yellow; and a table lamp on the dresser to complement the harsh ceiling light.

For the first few months I could only use my kitchen for having breakfast cereal, for boiling water, and for plugging in my waffle iron to make my increasingly repetitious grilled cheese sandwiches. Even worse was that I had to go upstairs to use the toilet and shower, which seemed to inconvenience Mrs Bito even more than me, understandably enough. She spoke little English and eyed me with great suspicion, bordering on hostility, whenever I showed my face. I had some difficulty comprehending Fred's attraction to her, but surmised that the lack of attraction was mutual, or at least balanced; yet they did have an infant son to contradict my incomprehension. In a way, I didn't mind Mrs Bito's glares; I was certain they meant that she was nagging at Fred daily to finish my apartment and thus obviate the need for my further intrusions upstairs.

The boundary of my room, my box, my hovel at the back of Fred's garage ran about seven feet in from the outer wall at the back, and about eleven feet out to the left from the far right-hand wall of the garage, thus creating a seven-by-eleven-foot room. The back wall had a large single-glazed window permanently

---

5   See drawing of the apartment in Appendix 1.

dripping with condensation that helped to feed or drown the earwigs on the narrow ledge inside. The window overlooked a tiny patch of weeds with dubious potential for ever becoming a garden. Fred was planning to build another wall to separate the part of the garage that was for his car from the part that would become a small corridor leading to my room. The short wall of my room had a doorway opening – the entrance to the room – but no door.

Although Fred and I had only been standing in my room-to-be for a few minutes when he took me to look at it, our body heat doubled the quantity of condensation on the windows, causing it to run down the pane, over the peeling paint of the window frame, and start forming small puddles on the ledge, reviving a couple of the earwigs I'd thought were dead. I had to keep reminding myself that the rent was just $25 a month – which I naively assumed would be the rent for the *completed* apartment.

There were just two rules: no loud music or noise (and hardly any noise at all after 10 PM); and no overnight visitors, especially not girlfriends (the Bitos were also Catholics) – not that I thought it would ever be possible to impress anyone's pants off in the back of Fred Bito's garage. On moving day, after Fred brought me and my stuff to my room, my new home, he left me on my own to unpack what I could. In addition to the trunk and other baggage I had with me on the bus from Chicago, I'd acquired a few paper shopping bags of stuff, mostly my additional customer-return clothing. There was room for my socks, underwear and a few other items of clothing in the dresser in my room; the rest I had to stash in the trunk until the corridor was finished and I could begin using the shelf and hanger space that Fred promised to install there. I soon put up a small bookshelf in the corner behind the heater, and I could also use the kitchen table outside my room as a desk (with my blue Royal portable typewriter for the essays). The kitchen/study was lit by a bare bulb.

I made my twin bed with sheets from my share of the ones Norm and I bought, and I purchased a bedspread with green, yellow, blue, and black stripes. There was room on the walls for my two paintings (*Man with Guitar* and *Bottle*), which immediately gave the tiny room its only identifier that this was now my home. There was a wall phone next to the doorway, above the edge of the bed, which eventually turned out to be convenient for late-evening calls with Jeanette. She liked me to "talk her to sleep", or at least until she was so drowsy that hanging up after a mumbled "*g'nite*" was all she could muster before drifting off. She said she loved the sound of my voice. She also claimed, to my dumbfoundedness, that I had "sexy ears".

I had few dishes – nearly all the ones Norm and I had been using belonged to our apartment landlords – but neither did I yet have much need for any. I did have the waffle iron for grilled cheese sandwiches, still my only culinary skill – and the tiny fridge Fred placed in what was to be the tiny kitchen enabled me to keep the cheese and butter on hand, as well as my breakfast milk supply. I also had a towel to bring with me upstairs to the bathroom. On the wall above my bed I put up a small reading lamp that could be turned and swiveled and extended for reading while I lay there. (I doubted I would be doing much *laying* there.) I also bought a lamp with three swivel fixtures mounted on a pole that could be adjusted to hold it in place using tension between the floor and the ceiling. The fixtures could be swiveled in any direction for general lighting, or to make something cozier (my mom would have called it "a den of iniquity") out of my cubicle. I would also have to get something for the open doorway to my room, a drapery perhaps. None of this was going to be easy.

My urgent need to save as much money as possible to be able to afford going back to school full-time the following September was the principal reason for saying *yes* to Fred about the "apartment". And it would be closer to the main San Francisco State campus, as well as a walkable distance to Jeanette's home. But what had formerly been a simple matter of going half a block to pick up groceries, or just a few blocks to buy pretty much whatever else was needed, I was now living out in the sticks, relatively speaking. The nearest main street was Mission Street, six blocks down a hill, then a few more blocks right or left to the nearest store of any kind. And then back again, heavily laden, and all uphill. I was in pretty good shape; the weight wouldn't be a big deal, but bulky, awkward things were trickier and every errand took much more time. The steepness of the hill fluctuated with my energy level at any given time. I had no car and couldn't afford one; it would therefore be necessary to plan better, and to make lists. There could be no more "just popping back to the store again" to get the one little item I'd forgotten.

I'd experienced zero separation anxiety after leaving Oak Park, but after splitting up from Norm, I did. Apart from my still-uncertain relationship with Jeanette (the uncertainty was almost entirely hers), things occasionally looked pretty bleak.

Considering how euphoric my first sexual experience had been, it might seem strange that I didn't actively pursue as much sexual experience as possible with as many girls as possible. Perhaps it was my fear of undesired fatherhood.

But I think it was that my feelings for Jeanette, which willy-nilly turned into love, managed to wrestle my libido to the ground. If Jeanette had been willing, however, life would have been a walk in the park.

Moving from the vibrant, cosmopolitan downtown area out to sleepy Daly City added a lot of stress to my days. In addition to the physical inconvenience of procuring necessities, I no longer had a brisk five-minute walk to work either. Instead, there was that six-block walk down the hill to Mission Street, then a further block to the nearest bus stop. And although the bus took me all the way to 5th Street (a block from work) without transfers, it stopped at almost every other corner and took forever. I had to allow at least an extra hour each way, and on Fridays I now had to remember to bring my books with me to work; I could no longer make a short detour back home to pick them up before class.

After work, unless I was working in the evening, starting the bus ride from the downtown area in the rush hour generally meant no seat, sometimes even no room to board. But Fred tipped me off about the Mission Street jitneys, a kind of oversized taxi that went all the way out to Daly City in about a quarter of the time it took for the buses. The vehicles themselves were mostly large old cars (some of them similar to London taxis) that were licensed to cruise along Mission Street picking up passengers who hailed them. Some of them vaguely resembled mini-buses, with room for 5-6 passengers, or even more in the slightly larger models. They cost a bit more than the city buses, but the time savings sometimes made it worthwhile.

After class or when I was working late, Jeanette occasionally picked me up in her old Chevy so we could go out. She came to see my apartment and, after turning slightly pale, helped me pick out some things to improve the feel of it, like strings of bamboo rods and beads for the doorway (instead of a drapery) that we found at Cost Plus in Fisherman's Wharf. Sometimes when she came to visit, we had to sneak in and out, in case Fred or his wife were on the alert for possible rule-breaking; and we had to keep tip-toe quiet.

I did manage to eliminate one of those extra trips downtown each week by immediately transferring my church membership (and again lying about my adult baptism) to the Calvary Baptist Church just 10 blocks away on Mission Street, where Haskle, as it turned out, was still attending before he left San Francisco for the East Bay. My attendance at the new church was as perfunctory as it had been at the old one, and was increasingly sporadic. The new pastor seemed like a kindly, avuncular fellow of advancing years, but I remained as elusive to him as to the other one. To my parents, however, I simply wrote that the new church was much closer, equally conservative, and the two pastors were close friends, representing *"the same sound truth"*. I knew the jargon; it made me nauseous to use it. (And it makes me gag to relate it here!) The frequent and direct appeals to all members of the congregation for money, money, more money, were the same at Calvary, but by now they no longer surprised me.

I was aware that I was falling deeper and deeper in love with Jeanette, that this was the real thing for me, even though she displayed few signs of being much more than amused, charmed and intrigued by me. But what was I going to tell my parents when they came to visit me for the first time, just before Christmas? Should I even tell them I had a girlfriend? That she's a *Catholic*!?

It would be possible to wonder why on earth I should have given a thought about what my parents would think, in view of the fact that just about every single thing I'd done and striven for over the past three or four years was done with as much *dis*regard for their wishes as I could muster. But for some reason, it *did* matter to me. There were still many layers of my force-fed "learning" to be doubted, questioned, challenged and peeled away. The force of habit – the inertia of rest – served well as an explanation.

Jeanette was nearly 14 months older than me, born on July 22nd, 1944. Her long dark-brown Italian hair and flashing dark-brown Italian eyes offset her fair Irish skin. Her smile revealed a slight gap between her upper two front teeth, a feature she was at once sensitive about and proud of, the latter because someone told her that it meant she was going to travel a lot, and she said she liked to travel, even though she hadn't done much of it yet.

She could be moody, ranging from distant and melancholy, fast and furious, serious and deep, to lighthearted and silly, but the sequence of these moods was sometimes sudden and seldom predictable – at least not by me. She frequently seemed uncomfortable and awkward about showing affection, particularly within view of anyone else ("PDA" she called it disparagingly – public display of affection). She was far more intelligent than she ever gave herself credit for (or would allow me to give her credit for). She was never boring and seldom bored.

When we were alone, standing facing each other, me holding her close to me, she would sometimes look up at me, then press her chin hard against my breastbone (she was that short, 5'3"). While still looking up at me, she would open and close her jaw rapidly against my breastbone, making it impossible for me not to laugh.

Jeanette's parents, as well as countless generations preceding them, were Roman Catholics. Her mother was a practicing Catholic and her father practiced the belief that his children should be practicing Catholics even though he was neither a practicing nor a believing Catholic himself. Jeanette's education was exclusively at Catholic parochial schools, both elementary school and high school. She knew her Rosary. Most of her friends were Catholic, also more by default than by choice. She'd been christened and confirmed, and was imbued with confessions and Catholic guilt. It had become part of who she was; the ultimate purpose of all that force-feeding appeared to have been served – except for the fact that she didn't exactly believe it.

One big difference between her indoctrination and mine was that she didn't have it shoved in her face multiple times every single day, almost every waking hour. Another difference was that apart from the sex taboo, she was allowed to do just about anything she felt she might enjoy and that I'd always wanted to do, all of which the Meeting prohibited. Perhaps this only served to make the version of the mendacity she was being fed more palatable; she had much less to rebel against. As long as a person can avoid asking too many of the wrong questions, life can go on, lies and myths become habits, habits become traditions, and traditions become necessities for warding off anxiety and anesthetizing doubt.

Mom and Dad would soon be visiting me for just a day on their way to the LA Bible Conference, our first meeting since I left Oak Park. I was not eager to have them see my far-from-finished living quarters, knowing how horrible everything would look to them, but I doubted I could prevent it from happening.

They were coming by car, staying at a hotel near downtown (I've forgotten which) and arrived as scheduled in the middle of the day in the latter half of December. I'd taken the afternoon off work. There were lots of hugs, of course, but there were also loads of tears, mostly from Mom; avalanches of clichés, only from Mom; and guardedness in every direction. Mom felt obliged to put on the saddest possible face for the entire time. For them the guardedness seemed to be due to fear of what they might discover about me, fear of how far I'd fallen, fear of what I might or might not say, fear of my having no interest in their hoops, let alone jumping through them, fear that I might be coping all too well.

For me, it was fear of hurting them, fear of that they would entitle themselves to be hurt just because I was being me, fear of all kinds of slips of the tongue, fear of not finding anything to say to each other, fear of how they might react if I told them about Jeanette. We got off to a good start: they wanted us all to get down on our knees right there in the hotel room and thank the Lord volubly and verbosely for bringing us together once more. I struggled through my bit, until I felt I'd spewed forth a minimal, barely acceptable quota of clichés. Just as our routine of each family member praying aloud gave my parents a reading on the state of our faith when we were kids, I'm sure my struggling performance spoke volumes to them in that hotel room, especially since it was the first time I'd prayed about anything since leaving Oak Park.

It felt very odd, kneeling there, talking out loud so my parents could hear and judge, talking as though some other invisible entity could hear, and could or would give a damn what I said, talking to a room. I began to ask myself whether I'd ever felt those kneeling exercises in Elizabethan English meant anything at all, but I pulled back sharply from my own question; I wasn't yet ready for *that* much freedom.

Apart from the mere physical proximity, I was uncertain about how "together" *He* had managed to bring us, although I'm sure my parents didn't see my shortcomings as *His* fault, however much they would have given *Him* credit had I performed well. Dad took a photo of Mom and me sitting on the bed in their hotel room, me smiling and Mom suitably ashen.

At their insistence, we then drove out Mission Street to Evergreen and up the hill to 574. My vast new home took about 20 seconds to view, and probably to confirm their worst fears about the low life into which I'd fallen. But my hovel didn't look that horrible to me, especially since I kept it tidy. Jeanette helped me pick out, bring home and decorate my first Christmas tree since Glendale, which immediately dominated the room. Dad took another photo, which included the tree. (When I discovered this photo years later in a box Mom had, it had been cut in half. The half with the Christmas tree lay by itself at the bottom of the box; I had to tape the two halves together.)

Then we went back downtown to do a little sightseeing, and ended up having an early dinner together at Alioto's in Fisherman's Wharf. Towards the end of our meal that evening I told them that I had a girlfriend, someone I was in love with. I could almost see them jump, like firemen awakened by a fire alarm, ready in seconds to start battling the flames.

It began with a studiously cautious (in the way that a lion might size up a young and isolated impala before pouncing) and probing, but entirely predictable interrogation. *Was she saved?* I told them I was working on it. *Did she go to church?* I said sometimes. *What church?* I said she was raised a Catholic. Mom gasped, but remained seated. Both of them lost some color from their faces, then seemed to decide not to ask any more questions for fear of not being able to handle my answers. This was the kind of situation that would call for even more prayer than their usual overdose. I was relieved when they departed for LA the next morning. Perhaps they were too.

Jeanette was probably also relieved that I hadn't arranged for her to meet them, but not nearly as relieved as she would have been if she had known what a grilling she would almost certainly have been subjected to (remember Nancy?). I was also greatly relieved. She hadn't yet introduced me to her family either; I was ready to meet them, but Jeanette wasn't there yet. The meet-the-parents step was traditionally associated with a fairly official courtship, if not a serious relationship. And while I already felt ready – just two months after our first meeting – for all the seriousness, commitment, marriage, the whole deal, just not the meet-the-parents part, it would take her a much longer time, *except* for the part about meeting *her* parents.

With Christmas rapidly approaching, and buoyed by its genuine and/or artificial spirit of goodwill, community and familial harmony, it would soon be time to make that step. Jeanette seemed no longer to have anything to do with Gary, as far as I could read between the lines. She indicated that she'd mentioned me a few times to her parents in the early weeks, then more and more frequently, although probably not much more about me than bare facts, including the fact that I was not Catholic, which elicited some wariness. I got the impression that she conveyed no further details about me to anyone in her family except for her elder sister Marilyn, who'd married less than a year before and had a baby nine months later (but not too soon!), and lived on Amazon, just a block off Mission and a block north of Geneva.

Marilyn and her husband Vic were the first members of Jeanette's family I met. The size and configuration of their home on Amazon Street was similar to the Bitos', but was in impeccable shape. They both seemed nice enough, though a bit skeptical towards me as they sized me up. There was a close family resemblance between Jeanette and the two-year-older Marilyn, but their personalities were different. Marilyn seemed to have already acquired the well-defined, well-defended, fortress-like comfort zone of middle age, whereas Jeanette was a seeker, vulnerable, almost as though comfort made her uncomfortable. Vic, a year younger than Marilyn, was an electrician who worked for a construction company. He was pleasant and oozed self-confidence bordering on but without being excessively macho. The two of them seemed happy, both individually and together, but reacted with spontaneous discomfort and distrust to most things and people they perceived to be academic or intellectual. They already knew how they wanted life to be. And yet they seemed to accept me well enough, at least for Jeanette's sake.

Having apparently passed that first test, I was now "ready" to meet Jeanette's parents, twin brother, and younger sister, all residing at 145 Seville Street, a few blocks south of Geneva and a few blocks east of Mission. The first presentation was kept as casual as possible – I wasn't going to be introduced in a formal way, at a fancy family dinner or anything like that.

Rose (Jeanette's mom) came to the door when we arrived. Jeanette was nervously acting as casual as possible. Rose appeared to be looking for something to say once she'd said it was nice to meet the boy Jeanette was now spending so much time with. Jeanette's home-dwelling siblings – 12-year-old Rosanne (the late arrival, about eight years younger than Jeanette) and Jeanette's twin brother Michael (five minutes older) – were lounging about in the living room, watching TV. They eventually hauled themselves to their feet to greet me. Rosanne made little effort to hide the fact that she was sizing me up. Neither she nor Michael said much, but quickly and smirkingly resumed their seats and their sprawling positions on them. Rose returned to the kitchen, Jeanette followed her, and I followed Jeanette.

The bright-yellow kitchen was at least four times the size of my current apartment, but a bit messy due to a lengthy and ongoing refurbishing project being conducted by Jeanette's dad, Mike. Rose asked whether I wanted coffee or tea. I said I'd prefer coffee, which Jeanette and Rose also did. The three of us sat at the kitchen table.

Jeanette's family resemblance to Rosanne was obvious, but little resemblance to their mother was apparent to me, at least not until Mike emerged from the ground floor garage, where he'd been retrieving some tools. Then it was immediately clear that all the children took more after their mother than after him. Rose was short,

Age made her a bit stocky and gave her somewhat coarse facial features. There was no reason to doubt her Italian ancestry (her maiden name was Natole, three syllables). Her grandparents on one side came from the area around Naples, and on the other side from a tiny island called Isola di Salina, just off the northeastern coast of Sicily. They all wound up in Wappingers Falls, New York, before most of them moved on to California. Rose "learned" Italian in much the same way that my mom "learned" Swedish, except that Rose learned a few of the expletives.

When Mike Minihane swaggered into the kitchen, it instantly became *his* kitchen, his space. He was a big, gruff-looking man, for whom smiling didn't come easily, if at all. In social contexts, he always looked as if he'd rather be somewhere else. Mike was born in Baltimore, a tiny village in southwesternmost Ireland. (The "a" in the last syllable of Minihane is like in "hand", not "brain", something Mom could never learn. It wasn't until researching this book that I discovered that in Jeanette's birth certificate, as well as her baptismal certificate, Minihane is spelled "Minihan", but I have no record of an official change.) He emigrated with his family from County Cork when he was 14.

Mike still carried traces of a brogue, particularly noticeable when he was angry. But there seemed to be no Irish cheerfulness or jocularity, and nothing of the troubadour or poet. The body language between him and Rose was mute, as far as I could tell. I never saw any physical contact between them, never heard any pleasantries or kind words, nothing discernibly like affection, not even much of anything resembling politeness or respect. There seemed to me to be a lot of lines drawn that Rose would never dare to cross. I commented on it to Jeanette, and she just shrugged, as if resigned to it.

Mike's main job was as a California State Highway Patrolman, but he also had a side job with a small haulage company downtown, driving a small truck and making various kinds of local deliveries. He seemed to disdain the world and what it had done to him. It was never clear what that might be, beyond having moved him across the Atlantic and the breadth of North America, if that could be where the problem lay. He treated Jeanette and her brother with an off-handedness that in my experience always indicated scorn, but Jeanette dismissed that too, claiming it was "just how he is". The only visible traces of affection were reserved for his "baby", Rosanne, which frequently made Jeanette and Michael roll their eyes.

Mike – nearly always the moniker he used to distinguish himself from his son Michael – gruffly acknowledged my presence and shook my hand with no smile or attempt at making conversation. Then he went about his business, while Jeanette, Rose and I went back to our cups of coffee. After a while Mike rejoined us for a cup of tea, but the conversation was minimal. At least they didn't grill me about the Lord or anything else, as my parents would have done with Jeanette, which was a nice change. I tried to engage in pleasantries, and while I didn't get a much of a response from Mike, I seemed to make a good impression on Rose, which was important to Jeanette, and thus to me.

Just a day or two later I was invited to join the family's highly informal Sunday dinner at the Minihanes' large kitchen table. (The dining room was also in the process of being renovated, but even after completion, it was used only rarely in my experience.) Although Rose hadn't picked up much of the Italian language, cooking was another matter entirely. I know I was probably ravenous, in addition to having an opportunity to break my boring homemade grilled-cheese sandwich and pizzeria diet, but these factors couldn't account for more than a small part of my astounding first encounter with Italian home cooking, the first of many it would be my privilege to enjoy. The flavors and smells were indescribable. The lasagne! The ravioli, home-made with fresh pasta! The sausages from the small local Italian butcher! The veal scaloppine! If I'd been a dog, I'd have been wagging half my body. I ate like a horse, and probably could have gone on and on until I made myself sick, when I realized that the others were used to this kind of food, and that there was a risk that I'd make a spectacle of myself.

My gushing praise didn't harm my efforts to be seen favorably by Rose. I would have a much harder time proving myself to Mike, who preferred bland Irish stew with the potatoes boiled, my least favorite form. Nobody said any prayers at the Minihanes' table, and wine was generally served with dinner, matter-of-factly, a custom I found highly civilized. This was my first meal in a family-type environment since Oak Park. The meal and the family were different to me in countless ways. There was constant banter around the table among Jeanette and her siblings and mom. Mike only occasionally interjected a grunt; if he offered a comment, it usually had the effect of stopping the conversation or emphatically closing the topic without starting a new one, a task he left to others. There seemed to be a certain fear of Mike. The tone of the banter was also different: lots of sarcasm and scorn, not necessarily always playful. I loved the food.

Jeanette and I continued seeing each other every day, and we mutually agreed to meet at her place on weekday evenings instead of going out. I found a shortcut between Seville Street and Evergreen, which served me well, since I had to get up fairly early every weekday morning. Jeanette was still without a job, but was now looking for a new secretarial position. Due to my night school on Fridays until almost 10, we usually only went to Little Joe's to talk and have pizza afterwards, before going back to Seville Street. Saturdays were our night out – I only worked until around four – and we began trying new restaurants (Jeanette picked them; they were all new to me, at least), going to movies or meeting some of Jeanette's friends. Once or twice we went bowling (without my aunt Maxine's permission!)[6] near the Cow Palace with Jim Gillingham and his girlfriend Judy.

On Sunday evenings we still often went to the PV to see foreign movies, but Jeanette also knew another movie theater where they also showed a lot of foreign movies, way out on Balboa Street, not far from the ocean, in a part of town I'd never yet seen.

When Jeanette went to mass it was usually on Sunday evenings (never in her local parish), and I went with her to learn more about what Catholics believed. I was still fascinated by the pageantry. I was also beginning to discover how little what Catholics believed and what Jeanette believed had in common, apart from the strong emotional bonds that traditions and shared beliefs (however fallacious they might be) tend to create. At the same time, Jeanette was beginning to discover that what I was saying I said I believed wasn't making a lot of sense to her either.

I was a frequent supper guest at the Minihanes' on weekday evenings, although the depth of our conversations was limited. We watched TV for an hour or two with the family (but seldom Mike, who usually went to work, or back to work, after dinner), but Jeanette and I spent more and more time saying goodnight on the Minihanes' enclosed front porch, usually more than an hour to say those two syllables. That porch was where we had the privacy to talk and kiss, standing up (there was no furniture), while keeping our (my) hands strictly above the (her) belt at all times. The frustration caused by Jeanette's Catholic sex taboo was partially circumvented, or at least vented, by grinding our fully clothed pelvises against each other, eagerly bumping our bodies in direct contravention of my mom's only words of sexual advice to me, when I was nearing puberty.

Grandma Minihane, Jeanette's Irish grandmother – her dad's mother – lived in the house directly opposite, and was usually in bed by the time Jeanette and

---

6   cf. *Natural Shocks*, chapter 4

I entered the porch for our goodnight sessions. There were big windows all around the porch, but little risk of being seen; the windows were not only fitted with venetian blinds, they also steamed up quickly once we got going, giving us sufficient privacy to cavort within our frustrating limitations.

Since Jeanette was obviously going to be spending Christmas Day with her family, she suggested that we could meet at my place in the early evening on Christmas Eve to exchange presents, then go to her aunt's place "up the hill", Minihane parlance for where her mom's elder sister and cousin lived, in adjacent houses on Joost Avenue, where there was a gathering of Jeanette's somewhat more extended family. I wore a sport jacket for that occasion.

Jeanette arrived at my place with a whole shopping bag full of presents for me. It flummoxed, astonished and delighted me. I was also a bit apprehensive, yet at this point I had no choice but to stick to my plan. My only visible gift for Jeanette under the tree was a small wrapped tubular present. I boldly suggested that I open all my presents first.

She looked a little alarmed at the sight of all the presents she'd brought, compared to a single small tube from me – a significant imbalance. Anyway, I started opening mine. There was a beautiful blue-green glazed pottery box. There was another pottery vessel – a round green dish with a lid – and a brownish green coffee mug. There were a couple of other small items, and a card she'd found. The printed text read: "*In this extra-civilized and over-sophisticated world we live in...* [and on the inside of the card] ...*you're basic!*" To this, Jeanette had added: "*Fun-loving, Generous, Intelligent, Honest, Considerate – But!!! Difficult to under<u>stan</u>.*"

I was much moved and thanked her profusely, in spite of not understanding why she found me hard to understand. At that point in my life, I probably thought I understood myself pretty well (I might even have *known* that I understood myself), so why should it be difficult for anyone else?

Now it was her turn to open that one little gift, although it felt more like my turn again – I was rippling with excitement to see her reactions. I handed her the small tube from under the tree, and she began unwrapping it slowly, cautiously, as if afraid of what she might find. What she found was a package of Life Savers, spearmint, and she looked almost like she was going to faint; the imbalance was far worse than she could have imagined. But before that reaction was more than a couple of seconds old, I pulled from my sport jacket pocket her *real* present: the small box whose size and shape is customarily identified with rings. The sight of it instantly blew away her spearmint reaction, but she looked even more alarmed. "*Wha...?!*" she gasped suspiciously as she started opening it, slowly, smiling nervously. I think she was immensely relieved to discover that it was *not* a *diamond* ring, which could only have meant one thing, a thing that would have horrified her. The star sapphire ring, however, was beautiful, but was it *just* beautiful? "*This doesn't mean...? We're not...? You're not asking me...?*" she pleaded agitatedly.

Even *I* got that message. I reassured her that, no, it was not an engagement ring, it was not to be seen as such, it was just such a beautiful ring that seemed just right for someone so beautiful whom I cared for so much. I had the presence of mind to avoid saying the three little words I wanted to tell her but knew she wasn't ready to hear from me. I hinted as obliquely as I could that there might come a day when we might want to consider another ring. She sat there on the floor of my room, admiring and puzzling over the ring and her own reactions to it, and to what may or may not have motivated me to give it to her. The thousand thoughts racing through her mind were subtly animating her face with rapidly changing expressions, like the aurora borealis. She put the ring on, and was trying to figure out what to think, and what to say to the gossipy aunts and other relatives we would be meeting in an hour or two.

When we got to Auntie Anna's house, nearly 20 people, all relatives by blood or marriage, were eagerly creating a din of conversation. Our arrival caused an immediate (and fortunately temporary) lull, as everybody took on board the appearance of an outsider, a total stranger: me. But our arrival was in no way unexpected, and after a quick perusal, the buzzing resumed in full force, and the main characters quickly began moving in our direction. I think Rose noticed the ring first; her reaction was similar to Jeanette's, but once Jeanette answered her principal question in a quick aside, Rose smiled broadly and stood prepared to inform anyone else who might ask such questions, or stared at Jeanette as if they might. And I had a houseful of new people to meet.

Compared to her sisters, Rose looked young and well-preserved. Auntie Anna was considerably older, portly and with once-white curled hair (reminiscent of Matilda Johnson's, except that the tint was pink, not blue) in a sort of puffy helmet around her round head that made her head look bigger. She was "married" to Al Rybicki, a friendly looking elderly man of Polish extraction who, as Jeanette explained to me, could sometimes be a little too friendly. His excessive friendliness wasn't limited to his earnest conversation, but led to flashes, or flashings, of considerable family embarrassment on several occasions. They tended to keep a watchful, protective eye on whoever might wind up alone in a room with him. Over the coming months and years, I would pick up occasional expressions of anxiety over Auntie Anna's being barred from Holy Communion, as they called it, due to her divorce and shacking up with Al. There were also indications of endless and futile attempts to obtain an annulment from the Church, without which she was deemed to be living in mortal sin.

Auntie Jo, also older than Rose, was gaunt, with a somewhat sardonic smile. Her heavily wrinkled skin had a dark, almost greyish-brown complexion like that of an aging iguana. One of Jeanette's older cousins, Marie, a widow, was there with her two daughters, Pauline and Maureen. The youngest, Maureen, was Rosanne's age. Another elder cousin was Louie, a salesman for Levi Strauss, whose look and style bore a striking resemblance to Gene Kelly. Jeanette told me that the family had vague suspicions that he might have Mafia ties.

There might have been other relatives present. All the faces were new for me, and all the names, mostly Italian, were swirling around in my increasingly confused head. After all, people kept handing me drinks (mostly whiskey sours) that went down like soda pop, and I was getting happier and happier, and might have started seeing two relatives for each one who was actually present. Jeanette had already learned to recognize the early signs, and found a way to whisk me away before the whiskey did, both of us laughing and giggling at having survived the gantlet run.

Jeanette's family used the English language in a few ways that I'd only heard in movies before – things like *"Wudgiz gonna do?"*, *"Youze goin out?"* and *"Takin'it widgiz?"* – that I found strange, charming and crude all at once. In fact, nearly everything about life in the Minihane family was new for me; it was my first real in-depth experience of life in any family that was not a Meeting family, and of course I was tempted to draw the hasty and erroneous conclusion that the Minihane family was the typical non-Meeting family, which of course it wasn't. Perhaps the only way to meet any "typical" family is to be unobservant of any differences.

But I was unaccustomed to and unprepared for the atmosphere of sarcasm and mild ridicule among all the family members, what seemed to me to be a constant and destructive hacking away at each other's self-esteem. Even if there would be a small degree of audible praise of someone's accomplishments, a sarcastic comment would soon follow, as though the praise of someone else was too difficult to go unavenged. Sarcasm became a weapon, both offensive and defensive. Marilyn was the least involved in this, but she was married, had moved out – to escape it? – and often winced when she and Vic came to the house for dinner. Sarcasm didn't seem to have played as big a role in Vic's childhood.

The tone between Rose and Mike often seemed to me to be one of veiled hostility, a sullen recognition that this was it, this was as good as it was going to get, and it wasn't much good at all. Most of this hostility expressed itself in deafening silence: sullen or defiant looks of irritation and rage, grunts of disgust, sneers. The only thing that seemed to prevent immediate divorce was the powerful Catholic taboo against it, resulting in their children growing up not knowing much of what harmony and love sounded, felt or looked like. These, at least, were my impressions.

For the Christmas break in my English course, Dr Walsh gave us an assignment to write a story in the style of one of the authors we'd just read, but on a contemporary topic. I chose the style of the medieval classic *Le Morte d'Artur* (1485) by Thomas Mallory, and for my topic the NFL championship game (now a joust), wherein the Cleveland Browns and their great knight Jimmy Brown did upset the Baltimore Colts. I called the Associated Press and talked someone into providing me with the play-by-play transcript of the game, on which I based my medieval version. It was a particular advantage for me to have been immersed in pre-Elizabethan English my entire life to that point.

Dr Walsh was impressed with my work, and informed me that he would be giving me an A for the course as well. I found the whole course highly stimulating, which made it easy – I seemed to remember everything once I'd taken the notes in class, and despite Dr Walsh's frequent admonitions to all his students to write drafts, then revise, then revise again, my final draft was nearly always my first one.[7] Since I was no good at typing, I did my best to avoid the extra work: typing slowly, thinking it through as I went along, doing everything I could to get it right the first time.

The weather before, during and after the Christmas holidays was rainy, day after day, week after week, and I was despairing that Fred would never get the rest of my apartment into shape. I'd never acquired any skills in the area of

---

7   Utterly unlike this book! But then Word makes revisions easy....

construction or I might have volunteered to do some of the jobs myself. But at work I was finding new diversions. For the past couple of months, I was spending an increasing number of breaks with a guy who worked on the shipping platform, a slender Hispanic guy named Rodrigo whose spare-time studies comprised an unusual combination of karate and philosophy.

At first we argued about politics – friendly arguments, but from nearly opposite initial standpoints. He challenged me constantly, gainsaying almost everything that came from Keith Sartorius via my mouth, and disallowing the validity of my naiveté. By forcing me to think about things for myself, rather than simply belching back what once upon a time I'd swallowed or had shoved down my throat, I found that my right-wing views had nothing at all to do with the actual values I'd begun to identify as my own: compassion towards the disadvantaged, equality before the law, education and healthcare as universal rights rather than privileges, the priority of the intrinsic value of life over the extrinsic value of wealth – things that clearly placed my values in an entirely different sector of the political spectrum. On being relieved of the burden of past values I could not defend, I started reexamining my whole parrot-like, kill-the-commies views. They didn't stand up to examination any more than an over-inflated balloon stands up to poking with a sharp pin.

I realized that in fact I didn't want to kill *anyone*. But what if someone were viciously attacking me or Jeanette? Would I be capable of killing in self-defense? Recognizing what the influence of adrenalin can do, I had to admit I probably would. And yet I was unconvinced by the notion of government by adrenalin; surely the law and the actions of governments should be better than that?

Two incidents in my recent past showed me how little free will I had once the adrenalin started pumping. The first was when I was walking through the handbag section of the stockroom to find and pick up any merchandise marked for shipment to other branches. Haskle was nowhere in sight or sound, and I assumed he'd gone to the toilet or was on a break. Suddenly he leaped out from behind a row of shelves just a foot away from me, roaring like the bear he vaguely resembled. Before I had a clue what I was doing, I found myself raining a torrent of blows on his substantial torso, and his roars turned to whimpers of protest. He'd only been horsing around, of course.

The second incident was when I was working alone (I thought) on the second floor one evening, standing at one of the trucks, opening and sorting by color and size the contents of cartons of newly arrived 511 dress shirts. I suddenly sensed somebody stealthily coming up behind me. As I slowly turned my head slightly, I caught a glimpse of someone sneaking up behind me with a box-cutting knife. My blood froze. A split-second later my left leg lashed out in a powerful karate kick straight behind me. My foot hit the knife-bearing hand, sent the knife flying down the corridor, and caused my colleague – as it turned out – to grab his hand in pain and ask me with great astonishment *how the hell* I learned to do that?! I had no idea; it just happened. I'd never trained karate, just mimicked a few moves I'd seen Rodrigo do, as well as some from movies.

Those two incidents made me willing to go to great lengths to avoid getting into situations where adrenalin might take command of my actions before my brain could intervene. What about World War II – was stopping Hitler justified? It seemed clear to me that it was, even after thinking about it dispassionately. Yet I now felt certain that the Vietnam War was dead wrong. Was I entitled to decide which wars were justified and which were not? I concluded that such a right must be implicit in a society that claims to be free and democratic. Was I being a "selective pacifist"? Is it necessary to put a label on it?

One day Rodrigo asked me, intending to stay within the boundaries of politics, "*Do you believe in original sin – that man is born with a sinful nature?*" I told him yes, because the Bible said so, and I believed the Bible. He said he wasn't aware that the Bible said that. I started quoting him a bunch of things from the Bible, largely irrelevant to his objection, and informed him of the only way to be saved. As it turned out, he then related our conversation to a couple of other guys at work, and they came to me eager to join the discussion. They apparently considered themselves atheists. I'd never met such people before, people who I'd been taught were worse than devils, on the basis of James 2:19 ("Thou believest that there is one God; thou doest well: the devils also believe, and tremble"), but whom I found to be nice guys.

Mom wrote to ask me how I'd spent New Year's Eve. I replied that *"I guess they had a New Year's watch at Calvary Baptist, but I didn't go. I went out with Jeanette."*

In January 1965, Jeanette started a new job as a secretary and receptionist at Marvin C. Frank Ltd, a small brokerage firm in San Francisco. By the end of that month, Fred finally installed my toilet, which sharply reduced my need to go upstairs. He also started putting up a wall to separate the corridor part of my quarters from the garage.

My last class was on January 29th, and Dr Walsh did indeed give me an 'A'. Now that I'd experienced my first university-level course and found it both stimulating and easy, I decided to increase my load to two evening courses when the spring term started on February 18th, in order to get a bigger head start when I finally began studying full-time in the fall. On the basis of that first English course alone, I naively drew the conclusion that all my future professors and instructors would be equal sources of inspiration to me, of the same stratospheric caliber as William Walsh. It took me a while to realize how extraordinary he was. I wish I'd thanked him more profusely for the positive impact he made on my young life.

On around January 25th, I ran into Norm at the Emporium – our first encounter of any kind since the split-up. I almost didn't recognize him. He didn't have much to say; nor, presumably, did I. But about a week later, I got a letter from Mom, saying that Norm was back in Elmwood Park, so on February 3rd I replied: *"So Norm is home?! What are his plans? Is he home permanently or just for a week or two?"* My curiosity was far from idle; the strong emotional bonds remained, no matter how much I buried them.

On Sunday morning, February 7th, my karate-philosopher-co-worker comrade stopped by my apartment for a chat. Fred was finishing my hall walls, including my closet space, and I was getting ready to leave for church. I asked Rodrigo if he would give me a ride there, since it was on his way, and we could chat in the car. He said OK, and when we got out to the car, it suddenly occurred to me to ask him if he wanted to come along to church with me. He said that he wasn't dressed for it, and before he could say anything else, I was back inside getting him a sport coat and tie (he was roughly my size). Thus he joined me, apparently out of the same curiosity that led me to the Catholic Church with Jeanette. The pastor's subject was about God's rage as shown in the minor prophesies. My friend's only reaction was, *"He sure talked a lot about the wrath of God!"* I said that there was a lot of it in the Bible, so it was understandable, wasn't it? He just said, *"Well, yeah...."*

Having a wall to separate my quarters from the garage was a major improvement, of course, but it still wasn't entirely private; when the Bitos needed to get in and out of the garage, they accessed it from a door in "my" corridor. Usually it was only Fred who did this; his wife and baby would wait outside for him while he pulled in or backed out the car. I still didn't have a shower or fully functional kitchen facilities. And although the toilet was installed on an elevated section of the floor to allow for drains, the bathroom walls were not yet built, creating an effect that for several weeks could most forgivingly be described as a true throne.

Fred also put in some storage shelves and a pole for hangers along the corridor wall, hidden by a drapery.

The next letter I got from Mom contained further news of Norm, which I eagerly devoured (with some skepticism about my mom's skills as a reporter) – and immediately asked for more, even though she and Norm never met and all her information was second- or third-hand. She must have mentioned in her previous letter that someone had said that someone said that Norm now had a beard, because on February 10th I wrote: "*So Norm has come back for good! Did he shave off his beard? And he's going out with Mary Lou again?!*"

I also heard from Mom that Norm's dad was ill, but no details. Then in late February we ran into each other again at The Emporium, a very impersonal and superficial moment. I would hear nothing further from or about him until the end of March, when someone told me that Norm was bed-ridden with mononucleosis.

One evening in early or mid-February, when Jeanette and I were at my apartment, I turned the subject of our conversation to the Lord. Under constant pressure from my parents, I naively figured that the only way to get them off my back and improve our relations was for me to get Jeanette saved, in their definition and to their satisfaction. I thus appointed myself to perform this high-minded service not so much for the benefit of her soul, but simply to win points from and reduce friction with my parents – the same parents I'd been successfully rebelling against for several years. Why didn't I see that?

Perhaps because I'd never thought to question any of the fundamental premises (axioms to my parents) of their beliefs or my own – like whether there is such a thing as a soul, let alone an immortal one or one exclusive to the human race; or a god, and if so, which one. I'd never considered the complete lack of evidence for a soul – mine or Jeanette's or anybody's – and whether she had one that might be lost and in need of saving. Winning parental points was my only focus. I didn't stop to consider that winning points with them might lose me much more important ones with Jeanette.

Although my mind had been racing around in circles for some time, chasing its own tale, so to speak, trying to find the right way to bring up such a topic, work it into the conversation, and pave the way, nothing of what was going on in my mind was going on in hers or ever had in her entire life. When I began to spout clichés about His blood being shed for us, that He was the only door to salvation, that she had to take Him into her heart, that she was a lost sinner, that she had to, she must, ranting on and on, my language was probably becoming more and more pre-Elizabethan and shrill all the time.

Since I was speaking of a subject I'd only ever heard discussed in terminology heavily spiced with such anachronisms, she stared at me, first wide-eyed as if I was suffering from indigestion, then with mild irritation at my insults in suggesting or insisting that Catholics were unlikely to be True Christians, then turning darker with anger as I persisted, and finally paling with fear that I'd gone stark-raving mad.

I was totally unprepared for her reactions, perhaps as unprepared as she was for my diatribe. Reacting slowly to her unfavorable facial response, I started becoming defensive and tried to "back-peddle". But now *she* was on the warpath. *How dare I say such things to her? Didn't I realize how offensive I was being? What on earth had gotten into me?* She was ready to storm out and I was ready to cry. She let me have it, and I had it coming.

During one of the uncomfortable days that followed, when we were on our way somewhere in her car, a song I'd never heard came on the radio: "*My breaking heart and I agree / That you and I could never be / So, with my best, my very best / I set you free.*" The old classic song was "*I Wish You Love.*" Jeanette, with tears in her eyes, told me it was what she wished for me. With blood draining from my head, for the first time in my life I began contemplating my own non-existence as a way to escape the intense pain I was now feeling.

And I suddenly realized how incredibly, stupifyingly, terrifyingly lonely I felt. This was another huge step beyond that awful feeling I got in my gut that time Al threatened that he'd never speak to me again. After Norm and I split up, I had no real friends, not "back home", not here, not anywhere. My parents continued to rant at me with their contingency plans, my brothers had lives of their own and took ages to answer my letters. My workmates were mere acquaintances. Something about the intensity of my nature seemed to put a lot of people off, if not scare them off completely. And now, when I'd at last met someone I truly loved, I found myself on the verge of screwing it up.

I was distraught and ashamed of myself for having tried to foist on Jeanette something I'd long had serious doubts about myself, just to be able to tell my parents (whose 18 years of preaching at me failed to quell those doubts) that the girl I loved was "saved" or "born again". I knew, when I stopped to think about it, that a "victory" would only meet the first of a nearly endless sequence of barraisings, a chain of increasingly stringent criteria she would have to fulfill before my parents would consider her a True Christian – criteria I'd already largely rejected myself! It was baffling. It was ludicrous. (Then there was the matter of Jeanette's own sub-conscious subservience to doctrines she hadn't yet thought to question.)

Fortunately, Jeanette apparently found there to be enough substance in me and in our sprouting relationship to survive my outburst. I was prepared to drop the subject of religion like a blob of molten lava (or steaming turds), but whenever doubts about her feelings towards me arose in her mind over the next year and a half, she would bring up that awful song again, dredging up my suicidal thoughts along with it.

I must have had a hell of a problem with rejection, a problem that exacerbated all my other internal conflicts. My shame over browbeating Jeanette about religion wasn't great enough to prevent me from writing to my parents that I'd talked with her about the Lord several times, describing my role in the most mealy mouthed evangelical guise I could muster.

Remarkably, I was still convinced that it was the Catholics who were the ones who were extremely indoctrinated. I told Jeanette that I found her religion depressing. On the whole I was feeling more and more torn apart by my inability to reconcile my persistent need to please my parents with my growing love for Jeanette – and my own discoveries of entirely new ways of looking at the world. I was still hopeful that my parents would express their unconditional love for me some day, even if I failed to fulfill their conditions. At one point, I even asked them to pray for Jeanette. How was it *possible* for me to have had the courage and strength to resist all the pressure that engulfed me when I was living at home, to the point where Norm and I actually broke free, only to be still carrying on like this?! I couldn't understand it myself; or to put a finer point on it, I couldn't understand myself, didn't understand myself, at all.

I failed to consider the kind of reaction my account of my talk with Jeanette would produce. Mom reacted like a shark to blood in the water, and not the Lamb's blood either. They were going to send me a Catholic Bible, which they did, with all kinds of verses marked for Jeanette to read. They were starting to ask a lot of probing questions, looking for the jugular. I felt I had to do something to get them to back off a little. I told them that I had another long talk with Jeanette about the Lord. I told them that traditions such as her Catholic ones were hard for her to leave (no insight into my own here!), and that it upset her to think that I'd even want her to.

So I said I felt I should just *"leave it with the Lord"*, a Meeting-approved cliché generally used when even the most fervent prayers didn't seem to be working, giving God the benefit of doubts they never dared to express – or even to have. Prayers didn't work most of the time anyway, as just about any person who has ever prayed could attest to if they allowed themselves to keep tabs. But I couldn't say *that* to them. I couldn't express what I was beginning to suspect: that prayers were nothing but anxious thoughts, wishful thinking in window dressing, words aimed upwards while the thoughts remain below. Instead, I went on to say that Jeanette didn't like to talk about such matters, that she felt afraid that in any discussion with someone of a different faith, they might try to change her beliefs. I would therefore abstain. *"I guess she thinks you might hate her for not changing. She is almost sure you won't understand. I hope you can try."*

While Dad was on a trip to Louisiana to a sugar mill, sometime in late February 1965, he was overseeing the installation of a conveyor system he'd designed, and was caught in a huge dust explosion in an adjacent part of the plant. Dad was apparently uninjured, praise the Lord. However, he turned out not to be unscathed after all – he developed diabetes, but what the hell, praise the Lord anyway. And the others who were killed or injured? Well, praise the Lord, of course, again and again. He controls everything, even numbers the hairs of your head and all that, so it must all be for the best, right?

CHAPTER 4

Off the deep end

During the spring term, starting in mid-February, I took two night-school courses at the Extension on Powell. One was English 6.2, the continuation of Dr Walsh's Reading and Composition course, this time taught by an instructor named Mr Zingales. The other course was in Human Biology, with Dr Araki. The combination, each in its own way, would plunge me deeper into unexplored waters than I'd ever experienced, and make everything else, apart from Dr Walsh's course, seem pretty much like a wading pool.

The primary focus of the English course was on just two works of literature: Shakespeare's *Hamlet* and Camus' *The Stranger*. I'd read *Hamlet* before, in high school, or I should say I plowed through the words, in much the same way (as I was beginning to discover) that I'd "read" everything else, including the Bible. Now we were required to think about the meaning – not just the meaning of the words, but to consider the message, to compare and analyze, to *feel* what lay behind the agonizing of "*to be or not to be*", to postulate that the famous soliloquy might be the very essence of the relatively new philosophy of existentialism as further developed by Sartre and Camus. The latter's claim – that the only truly philosophical question was whether or not to commit suicide – seemed to be a close paraphrase of the core of Hamlet's dilemma.

We were also encouraged to read Sartre's *Nausea*, wherein nausea is portrayed as the feeling we get when we realize that reality is absurd, and that reality is absurd because it can't be explained. Camus described the existential crisis arising from wanting to love life but being destined to die, from seeking some logical meaning in life but never finding it, from hungering for justice yet partaking of injustice. What was I to think of all this? "*Thinking is like living and dying. Each of us must do it for himself,*" our teacher quoted to us (the quote is attributed to Josiah Royce).

And I *was* thinking. I was thinking that the Meeting people held the view that nearly all others, including Catholics, were on their way to hell. I'd also quite recently discovered that the Catholic Church held the view that nearly everyone else, including all Meeting people, were on their way to hell. (Much later I would discover than Islam held this view of everyone else, and then that Sunni Muslims held that view of Shi'ites – and vice-versa, of course, not to mention all the sub-divisions: Sufism, Wahhabi, Wannabe, Wasabi, Wallaby or whatever.) Although I didn't expect anyone to strive to be wrong, I began to see something strange: that in striving to be right, most people apparently found it necessary to proclaim that everyone else was wrong, and also to make pretty nasty predictions or curses about what would happen to them for being wrong, particularly in the alleged hereafter, the existence of which, conveniently, nobody could prove one way or the other. And none of these claims of exclusive truth or righteousness or justice had to be (or could be, or even *should* be) proven with evidence or facts. It was all based on faith. It reminded me of one of Harry (*"Hhhhhh!"*) Hayhoe's hobbyhorses: *"Reason isn't faith and faith isn't reason."* I could certainly perceive the unreasonable, inhumane, barbaric and narrow-minded aspects of everybody wanting to send everybody else to hell.

Biology, the subject I hated in high school under Mr Storey, was an absolute joy under Dr Akari. We started from scratch, the level of sub-atomic particles, the unique ability of carbon to form covalent bonds with itself endlessly, making it the basis for all organic material. Then we moved on to the characteristics of life – reproduction, metabolism, irritability and movement – all carried out at the cellular level. We examined charged particles, ionization processes, and the main groups of organic compounds: carbohydrates, lipids, proteins, nucleic acids, vitamins.

We studied cell structure in much greater detail than I would have imagined possible within the limited scope of such a night-school course. That was just the beginning. Dr Akari carefully outlined and elucidated the principles and mechanisms of genetics and evolution, glandular functions, hormones and hormonal balance, the skeletal system, the central nervous system, the digestive system, the ear, the eye, all in wave after wave of new and fascinating information, presented lucidly by a professor who discouraged neither questions nor being questioned.

He didn't present evolution as a theory. Even by the 1960s, without the additional powerful evidence of DNA and genomes, the body of fossil evidence alone was overwhelming. I remembered the Brethren and their tracts mocking the notion of apes turning into humans, or even apes giving birth to humans, as utter nonsense. And of course it was, if one imagined – as they did – a living individual ape transmogrifying itself into a living individual human being. From their perspective, with a universe less than 6,000 years old, there would never have been sufficient time for all the incremental mutations, permutations, and natural selection processes that evolution requires. What *they* required was to *ignore* – actively, vociferously, categorically and mindlessly – any evidence that contradicted an ancient book written by poorly educated people who had little respect for evidence of any kind: the very definition of ignorance.

But just because those ancient people were uneducated didn't mean they were stupid or ignorant. They were perhaps trying their best to understand the world and the universe they found themselves in with the tools available to them for understanding them. But there were hardly any such tools then. With no telescopes, no microscopes, none of the vast array of instruments through which modern sciences obtains its data, they nevertheless had to come up with something. They were not ignorant – they were ignoring nothing available – but they had no means of understanding. So they made up stories. Today, when people have the means to understand, yet choose to ignore facts and stick with the ancient stories as facts and not myths, that's ignorance in a nutshell with a cherry on top.

Many people say that studying science takes away the mystery and the joy of experiencing life. Back then, I naively tended to agree, never having studied much science before myself. Now that I was learning about it, I found facts infinitely more thrilling and amazing than myths, superstitions and willful ignorance. There are thousands upon thousands of questions that can only be asked if one has learned enough to ask them. And questions – even if they have no answers, or the answers take centuries to find – generate much more excitement than "*Hush!*" (or "*Hhhhhh*").

I had escaped Oak Park. Yet I continued writing my parents groveling, carefully edited and censored tales of my activities and thoughts, to placate their demands by regurgitating their clichés, to appease their insatiable yearnings for me to return to the Fold, the One True Path – the path I never fully entered in the first place, thus making it quite difficult to return. But I was slowly learning that every such comment I made only led them to raise the bar, the stakes, like when they sent me a Douay (Catholic) Bible they'd annotated for Jeanette, like the pathetic, ignorant anti-evolution book they sent me as soon as I told them I'd be taking a course in biology, like the admonitions and endless entreaties to turn back to the world of their clichés that I'd joyfully left. I knew deep down that they would never be satisfied until I belonged to the Meeting and was married to someone who was also in the Meeting – just like Al. They wanted me to stop asking my infernal questions. But that was never going to happen.

In mid-March, during the spring break from school, which coincided with when The Emporium wanted me to take my week of vacation (so they could keep me available throughout the summer), I found there were some cheap commuter flights to LA, and I decided to visit John and Marj. It was the first time I'd ever flown on a commercial airliner. (When I was 11 and we were visiting LA, my pilot cousin Sterling took me and my brothers up in a Cessna – the only time I'd ever been airborne – and after checking out the raging Malibu fire from a distance, Sterling wanted to do some stunt flying – rolling, looping the loop etc – to the delight of my brothers, until I became the killjoy and screamed for Sterling to stop.)

I had a good time with them – no desire on my part to visit Hollywood (or Keith Sartorius!). They didn't drink wine yet (because it was still a principally northern California phenomenon at this time, or was it that they hid it from me, my being underage and all, or maybe John was terrified that I'd let the information slip to our parents?), but we had some good talks and did some fun things. I felt I had John in my corner, and wrote in a slightly less groveling manner to tell Mom and Dad that I wasn't going to take up their favorite topic with Jeanette anymore. *"John agreed with me that the best thing to do would be to just wait patiently on the Lord* [first-rate cliché!!]. *I won't force her into anything. It's too important not to drive her away."*

I can't say *why* I came to love Jeanette so much. Perhaps if one could say *why* about such a thing, it wouldn't be love at all, but some sort of logical decision, which is probably at most only coincidentally related to what love is. She was attractive, but not overtly sexy. She was pretty, but not drop-dead gorgeous. She was smart, but her anti-intellectual upbringing made her do her best to hide or suppress it. She was funny, but occasionally displayed a pretty volcanic temper. She was alert, but not to how her own brain had been molded before she was old enough or aware enough to think for herself (neither was I – we would have to help each other with that). She was, however, increasingly alert to the questionable wheelings and dealings at Marvin C. Frank, and thus increasingly dissatisfied with her new job there.

The more time we spent together – and we seldom missed a day – the deeper I continued to fall, while she seemed determined to maintain a cautious distance, out on the edge. This caused me a great deal of anxiety. On a bad day, depression was quick to park itself on my shoulders and whisper nasty things about my own demise that I was simultaneously drawn to emotionally and repulsed by intellectually.

By mid-April it was confirmed that Dad had developed diabetes, presumably triggered by the shock of the explosion at that sugar plant (praise the Lord, and again I say rejoice!). It was also confirmed that I would be able to work 16 hours a week at The Emporium while studying full-time in the fall, and that I'd been accepted at the College of San Mateo (CSM) – my back-up choice in case I couldn't get through the more extensive admissions procedures for San Francisco State in time for the start of the fall semester.

With the war in Vietnam escalating rapidly, and my wish to kill Commies entirely gone, it was now imperative for me to register as a full-time student in order to qualify for the 2-S student deferment from the draft. It also became apparent that I would need a car – CSM was practically inaccessible by public transportation.

Also in mid-April, Fred was promoted to work in department 515 out in the store, and I was promoted to replace him as the supervisor on the 2nd floor of the stockroom, thereby increasing my hourly wage to $2.27, which meant I would no longer be a stockboy, and would gross about $20 more per month. But now that Fred had finished my bathroom and most of my kitchen, he raised my rent from $25 a month to $50, which consumed the entire raise I'd just received, and a bit more. Thus I would now be paying as much as my share of the rent for the apartment Norm and I shared on Ellis Street, yet I would have a much lower standard as well as a far less convenient location for the San Francisco State Extension and The Emporium. I consoled myself with how close I was to Jeanette's place, and that I would eventually have an easier commute both to CSM and to the Lake Merced campus of San Francisco State.

At that time, student loans were not available in the US to people in my circumstances (they didn't start to become available until the 1990s). I started taking on extra overtime and was working six days a week, including a couple of evenings, going to night school two evenings a week, which also meant some studying and writing papers, and seeing Jeanette as much I could, all of which devoured just about every hour of every day and contributed to quashing any interest I might otherwise have had in the hippie movement that was blooming profusely all around me. During my entire time in San Francisco, through the heyday of Flower Power and Free Love, I never once tried any drugs, never once visited the Haight-Ashbury District nor the Fillmore Auditorium. As for Free Love, my singular experience in August 1964 wasn't a result of any other movement than the pelvic movement of myself and one girl. The Catholic Church's influence on Jeanette quashed the rest.

On April 22nd, I happened to see Norm for the first time in about two months. He didn't go into any of the details of his illness, and I was too inwardly agitated to inquire. I did notice that he seemed pretty pale and weak, but I think he was about to come back to work. This turned out to be our last contact for nearly a year.

In June, I learned through my mom that Norm's father died, and that Norm had come back to Elmwood Park in connection with that, to be with his mother. In the summer, I also heard that he was again with Mary Lou and that marriage might be forthcoming – according to my mom and/or her sources; and then, strangely, that Norm was back in the Bay Area alone later that summer. (It wasn't until more than four decades later, when Norm read the draft text of this book, that I learned that a month or so after he'd recovered from his severe mononucleosis, he'd had shipped out with the Merchant Navy in early June; and that his dad died while Norm was on his maiden voyage, and that he'd had to make his own way home from Japan.)

To a small extent, some of my financial woes were offset by the generosity of a couple of the assistant managers of the men's clothing departments, who were happy to get quite a few customer returns off their hands by allowing me to wear them out of the store, sometimes three shirts at a time. I usually left the building wearing my raincoat – nothing unusual for San Franciscans, no matter what the weather was – and the old detective posted at the employees' entrance/exit never batted an eye at my increasingly padded girth.

Without doing so intentionally, I began boosting my studying efficiency by training myself *not* to study (or not to need to), but to listen well and take notes more efficiently and effectively, making sure I understood what I was taking notes about at the time I took them. The act of writing them down seemed to imprint in my memory what was being said or shown. This enabled me to get my work done *and* keep my grades at the top.

A major student protest against political interference in universities, called the Free Speech Movement, had been launched at the big university in Berkeley (UCB) the previous fall, with students occupying the dean's office, engaging in sit-ins, and listing demands, but I was too busy to notice (and had no access to TV except at the Minihanes, where getting to the front porch with Jeanette was of greater interest to us than watching TV). This movement would turn out to be the precursor to the huge anti-Vietnam War movement for the entire US, and the Bay Area became the center of many of the country's most active debates and protests. Draft-card burnings were becoming more and more frequent and were gaining national attention – including all the way into the Bay Area's university classrooms. I was, at least, not too busy to notice this.

Although Jeanette's hesitation about her relationship with me persisted, I felt I might be gradually winning her over, and at last one evening she told me she loved me. Perhaps this was in response to the fact that I was now telling her that I loved her, daily and in the most entreating way. Without even thinking about becoming engaged, we decided we would marry just after the end of the following school year, on June 11, 1966.

As was my habit when I had big news, I was eager to inform my parents of our plans, foolishly thinking they'd be as thrilled as I was. They were not. They were openly and explicitly opposed to the whole idea – until such time as Jeanette passed the unwritten spiritual exam they were determined to require of her. I was disappointed, saddened, outraged, livid. On May 12th I wrote to them:

> *I'm sorry that you feel the way you do about my forthcoming marriage. You might even expect me to say that I wish it weren't so, but I can't. I love Jeanette, regardless of circumstances. I wish that we agreed on spiritual matters, and perhaps some day we will, but I'm only a human being. I cannot say, 'I'll love you when we are agreed.' You must realize that she could say the same thing also. But the fact remains that I love her now, and love her so much. She is the most important thing to me in this life. I would not and could not go on without her. When this issue came between us several months ago, she was on the verge of calling it off. And I, in turn, was on the verge of calling life off.*
>
> *I never told you anything whereby you could have said I was going to wait until we were agreed before considering marriage. I told you long ago not to expect her to change, but to be happier if she did. I never gave you any indication that she would. Where you got that idea is unknown to me. You mentioned that*

Al waited. You should know that although Al and I get along famously, we are completely different types of persons. I'm not saying that Al didn't love Nancy, but I am saying that if he made it conditional on her agreement with him, it was not nearly so great and complete as my love for Jeanette.

I hope you'll come to the wedding. Knowing how you feel, I wouldn't try to force you, but I'd love you to be there. Since I won't be quite 21 at the time of our wedding, I'll need you to sign the marriage license. You will, won't you?

No reply. They simply ignored my repeated requests for their signature. I got so frustrated and furious that I wrote, with unabashed paraleipsis, on June 2nd: "Think you'd be making a tremendous mistake if you didn't sign our license, but won't talk about it now." I now believe, writing about it decades later, that their refusal to accept Jeanette made me so furious and disappointed that it became *the* major factor in the cessation of my groveling attempts to placate them.

But as it turned out, I'd made a false assumption that led to a great deal of stress and conflict that could have been avoided. I'd incorrectly presumed (perhaps on the basis of California's legal drinking age) that California law also required me to be 21 years of age in order to get married without parental consent. I didn't discover my error until 2017, while researching a new draft of this book! Jeanette and I could have gotten married in June after all. And we probably would have selected another honeymoon destination. All kinds of things might have been different. But they weren't. Isn't life crazy?

Nevertheless, over the ensuing months I continued to ask for their consent, and they remained totally evasive. But as we entered the month of June, I had plenty of other things to think of.

Jeanette quit her job at Marvin C. Frank, partly because she'd grown to dislike it, but primarily because on June 24th, she would be leaving for Europe with her brother, to visit unknown relatives of her father's in Ireland, then tour London, Paris, Florence and Rome. They were planning to be gone for nearly two months, and my heart was aching, but Jeanette assured me she'd be thinking of me and missing me every day, and writing me often.

She even signed her big old Chevy over to me to use as I pleased, and to trade it in for another car if and when I could find one. She also told me that when we got married less than a year later (I hadn't yet told her about my parents' refusal to grant their approval – I was still hoping I could talk them into it), she would work to support us both till I finished school, however long it took.

For the sake of my own mental health in her absence, and to improve my head start in completing my degree, I signed up for a summer night school course in Ethics, and another in General Semantics, running from June 28th to August 6th, two evenings a week for each course. I would have classes a total of four evenings each week. Since I got A's in both of my spring courses without having to devote much time to studying outside the classroom, I felt I could handle the load, even though it would be tough while working full-time as well. I'd already requested permission from San Mateo to carry 21 units (the normal full-time course load was 15-16), since I'd now figured out that with my night school units and heavier course loads, I could make it through the four-year Bachelor of Arts program in three years of full-time study, by then with the support of my loving wife.

The General Semantics course would give me further credits towards the English major I'd now decided upon. The Ethics course was part of the Philosophy program, despite my having no particular interest in philosophy. In fact, my upbringing gave me a latent aversion to that field. The name itself – *philosophy*, literally love of knowledge – referred to *man's* knowledge, and the word was thus spoken with the utmost scorn and disdain by my parents and the Meeting, despite their acceptance of man's knowledge as required for engineering and mathematics, and their turning to doctors when they got sick, or pilots when they wanted to fly, or brokers when they wanted to invest.

My interest in the Ethics course was to expose myself to the possibility that there could be significantly different ways of looking at ethical questions. Other approaches than the One I was used to might not give final, definitive answers, but at least they didn't claim to offer irrefutable "Answers" that were merely blatant errors enshrouded in clichés attempting to hide all the fallacies. I came from an environment where practically everything was deemed sinful – including looking for other ways of seeing things or, for that matter, being born – a view I already strongly questioned. But I only knew where I wasn't, not where I was: off the deep end.

The day of Jeanette's departure had come. At the airport, I was trying not to show her how sad I was, since I honestly did want her to have a great time. But she seemed alarmingly and perplexingly chilly and remote towards me. She looked pale and almost didn't want to look me in the eye, which I put down to travel jitters. I tried not to dwell on it, nor did I demand or ask for any explanation from her.

Then she was off, and I went home to write the first of my almost daily letters to her; I'd bought a supply of aerograms for the purpose, and had the names, addresses and dates for their various accommodations (Jeanette gave me the details a week or two before she left) so they would reach her at their hotels along the way. Rose kindly told me I was welcome to come by as usual in the evenings or weekends while Jeanette was away, but I explained that it might not be terribly often, due to my night school load with four evenings a week plus one evening at The Emporium, but that I certainly would come by, not least to hear what they'd heard from Jeanette (and Michael), in case they got a letter and I hadn't. The prospect of an occasional home-cooked Italian meal wasn't exactly a deterrent either.

I kept sending my love letters and waiting, waiting, waiting for replies. There were only a very few, and they upset me greatly: she wrote that she thought I maybe should find someone else, maybe she wasn't right for me after all! That made me completely distraught, and I wrote back every day to assure her of my complete and total love for her, and that there *couldn't* be anyone else for me. (I didn't write about the girls at my night-school classes who invited me to their apartments to help them "study", all of whom I flatly turned down.) I simply couldn't figure out what provoked Jeanette's sudden change of heart that was breaking mine.

Not until decades later, during my research for this book, would I discover the horrifying reason. On June 21st, 1965, my mom wrote the following letter to Jeanette, which must have arrived (by design?) the day before she left for Europe:

> *Our most beloved Stan has written us about his love for you and I feel I can refrain no longer from letting you know how much we wish to love you too. Perhaps we have appeared cold-hearted and neglectful when quite the opposite is true. We long to be warm-hearted and receptive and pray that God will make it so. He is able!*
>
> *I do not care to speak or write of religion-so called* [an interesting paraleipsis]*, but wish I knew how to begin to express the heights and depths of the love of God! I know in His mercy and grace He has filled the need in my heart that nothing in this world can fill. My heart shall ever praise Him and I long that your desire is to love and praise Him too.*
>
> *When Adam & Eve first sinned in the garden of Eden their aprons of fig leaves*

could not make them comfortable in the presence of the holy God. Blood must be shed to atone for sin and God showed them this when He clothed them with coats of skin. God accepted Abel's offering because he approached Him on the ground of shed blood, whereas Cain came with the fruit of a sin-cursed earth. On into the old testament the priests must offer for the people pointing forward to that day when God would send the Lord Jesus Christ into this world to become the One Offering forever. His precious blood was shed for you – for me! He rose triumphant from the grave for you – for me! He was forsaken of God when He cried out upon the cross for your sins – for mine! We need never be forsaken of God because of this for we stand accepted in the Beloved if we have accepted this Beloved One!! Oh what liberty and freedom and joy overflows the heart of one who knows ALL is well and who is clothed in His righteousness. (Please read Romans 3, verses 22-26 and Hebrews 9, especially verses 9-14.)

The WORD OF GOD has been hammered and abused through all the ages, and still stands as the most modern book of all time. It tells the past, the future, and tho' 'tis true as it says, "there are some things hard to understand" yet the simplest child who feels a need can be led on into all truth through simple faith. Read Ephesians 1, verses 17-23, and Colossians 1, verses 10 to the end of the chapter.

Are you, dear Jeanette, one who has accepted this love and hence become a living stone in the temple of God? (This is beautifully explained by Peter in his letters – I Peter 2, verses 1-12.)

Oh, dear Jeanette, if we only knew that you loved and would confess Jesus as Lord, I believe we would fly to meet you. His love, His claims, His glory are ahead of all things to us, and this is what has cast us before the Lord regarding you and Stan. We pray His will to be done, and shall continue to pray. We most earnestly desire your welfare for time and eternity.

*Most sincerely,
Stan's Dad & Mom*

This letter was among the many saved by my mom in a fruit box for decades (including nearly all of mine to my parents), which she eventually turned over to me. Mom never told me she'd sent it and Jeanette never said a word about it to anyone. I didn't discover it (I didn't give the fruit box more than a casual glance on receiving it) and never looked carefully at its contents until researching this book in 2014. I quote this particular letter in its entirety because my mother's own words best convey what I grew up with and was still trying to escape from.

Had I known what Mom wrote to Jeanette, or even *that* she'd written to her at all, I might have understood Jeanette's sudden doubts about and withdrawal from a future relationship with me. But I knew nothing of it at the time. Nor could I have known that Mom would have made an identical, hand-written copy of the letter to keep for her own reference.

During Jeanette's absence that summer, I continued to argue with Mom and Dad over their latest objections – that "early" marriage would disrupt my school plans – pointing out that Jeanette helped me study, encouraged me in ways that no one else could, and made me study when I otherwise wouldn't. When I wrote them that "*Haskle is back from his honeymoon, grinning from ear to ear,*" they asked me for his address for the stated purpose of sending a small wedding gift, and I provided it. What didn't occur to me was that they would begin corresponding with him (without telling me), and that Haskle would write to them (without telling me) on July 24th, that "*it disturbs me to see Stan push Christ aside and put Jeanette in the center of his life.*" Well fuck you, Haskle!!

My summer course in Ethics, taught by Dr Henry T. Gardner, a portly gentleman with a huge mustache, and a gruff but kindly voice, turned out to be another real eye-opener for me. His first few minutes of introduction told me I'd come to the right place, a William Walsh sort of place. "*A preacher dispenses thoughts that are already concluded, giving the listener a completed argument and requiring acceptance,*" Dr Gardner said. "*A philosopher is not so much involved in a situation as he is involved in thinking about it – not to say 'This is right or wrong', but to find out what makes right or wrong.*"

He explained that ethics deals with choices, without which there *is* no right or wrong, no good or evil. A choice is an action upon a situation in which one could have acted otherwise. A number of questions immediately flashed into my mind: *Did I choose to be born in America, into a Meeting family, as a human being, to be born without wings, to carry genes that predisposed me to diabetes and other ailments?* But these questions were far too frightening for me to look into deeply at that stage in my life; it was a kind of abyss or void from which I'd fled in panic: *discredophobia* – the pathological fear of ceasing to believe.

Dr Gardner went on probing, relentlessly, with questions about the criteria for choice. He pointed out that the different schools of philosophy are recognized by their adherence to different criteria. He then led us through a careful outline of a wide variety of such schools and philosophers: hedonists, deontologists, empiricists, rationalists, Aristotle, Socrates, Kant, Epicurus, Descartes, Spinoza, Hume, Locke, Hobbes, Dewey, Ayer, and many Moore. Their criteria were different, and they all seemed to have different answers. But more importantly, they all had questions – searching, probing questions that were more important to ask than insisting on "final" answers.

The process of searching and analyzing, rather than preaching, was incredibly fascinating for me, a fascination that was gradually making inroads on my fear. Dr Gardner pointed out that nearly all philosophers used logic to "prove" their theories, their bases for defining good and bad. Then he offered a simple, clearly formulated insight – along the line of something Dr Walsh said – and it hit me like a bus all over again:

Logic is a tool that shows what conclusions can validly be drawn from a given premise or premises. But always remember that logic cannot tell you whether there is sufficient evidence to support the premise itself.

Now it occurred to me that this could be the key to resolving a tremendous conundrum: how it was possible for intelligent people like Dad or Al to present impeccably logical arguments that led to conclusions I could no longer accept. It was the same with right-wing politicians and defenders of the Vietnam War. The problem lay not in their stars but in their premises, their unquestioned premises.

Starting from a first premise that there is an all-wise, all-good and all-powerful God, then another premise that every word of the Bible is the Word of that God, Dad could then build a fairly logical case for what he believed (although the logic was inevitably plagued, marred and flawed by the Bible's own myriad self-contradictions). He never questioned those first premises. At the same time, less fundamentalist Christian apologists, backed into corners of their own making by the embarrassing barbarity of the Bible, were struggling to exclude most of the Old Testament from their premises. The frequently used last resort of my dad or brothers might be: "*We cannot understand these things, but He will explain them to us one day;*" or "*It's a matter of interpretation;*" or the ultimate cop-out from reason: "*God moves in mysterious ways.*"

In the political sphere, the first, unchallengeable premises usually involve some sort of party platform of "core values". If you adopt a core value that certain people are entitled to stupendous wealth despite others suffering great deprivation, and refuse to challenge that premise, then you can logically build a strong argument that mirrors the actions of the right wing. If your starting point is the Manifest Destiny of the white man, you can logically pursue a policy of subjugation and extermination of the Indians and others of excessively pigmented skin. If your starting point is that not all human beings have value, you can logically draw all kinds of horrific conclusions, a view that Johnathan Swift so surgically satirized in *A Modest Proposal*. And if your view is *"my country, right or wrong"* – a ludicrous forfeit of reason, common sense, evaluation of decency, abdication of responsibility to anything resembling a moral standard – then you can swallow all the lies, all the hypocrisy that nationalistic fervor can concoct, such as what the American Establishment was doing in 1965.

What a lot of work I now had ahead of me to revisit the premises of the indoctrination of my youth on multiple levels – on every level I could think of! The ethics course, in combination with my course in general semantics under Dr Eugene Rebstock, would turn out to undermine many more of my assumptions and values by delving beyond those starting premises and finding information that, once I had it, made the fallaciousness of the premises perfectly obvious.

That patriotic hymn, *My country 'tis of thee, Sweet land of liberty* was written in 1831 – when most black people were slaves, when Indians were being herded like cattle and massacred, when women couldn't vote, when it was open season on any person displaying deviations from the sexual norms of the majority. "Liberty" indeed! My country never intervened against Batista's brutal dictatorship in Cuba, but put a chokehold on that island nation after Castro's takeover because it wasn't "democratic"! My country's cloak-and-dagger operations were instrumental in the overthrow of democratic governments in favor of harsh dictatorial and military rule worldwide, from Iran (1953) to Greece (1961) to Brazil (1964).

And now there was Vietnam, an ancient civilization with a long history of being overrun, occupied and ruled by the Chinese. After a period of Vietnamese independence in the late 1800s, the French decided they were (for some reason) more deserving to rule Vietnam than the Vietnamese themselves. The French continued to do so for most of the first half of the 20th century, apart from the Japanese occupation during World War II. After that war, the country was split into Communist North Vietnam and Capitalist South Vietnam, and the French began making war on the Communist North, who finally threw the French out of the country following the Battle of Điện Biên Phủ in 1954. But there would be little rest for the war-weary Vietnamese people; civil war between North and South followed, as well as war within the South. Then Eisenhower began sending "military advisors" to South Vietnam in the late 1950s to help fight the Red Menace within and from the North. In order to be "allowed" to send more of these advisors to save the world from Communism (despite North Vietnam's traditional animosity towards China), my country had to assassinate (sorry, actively condone the assassination of) one South Vietnamese leader in order to get a new one who would then turn around and "invite" the US to intervene in Vietnam's civil war. I hadn't understood any of this. Keith Sartorius led me to believe that I wanted to kill Commies. What, was I also supposed to know *why*? Was I also supposed to have *evidence* for why? My upbringing was a form of the Dark Ages; it was high time for some personal Enlightenment.

I knew that semantics involved the structure, internal logic and the history of language. Thus, when I signed up for the course, I presumed that "general" semantics was simply a mildly boring general overview of semantics. It wasn't. It turned out to be an illuminating study of the impact of language on a person – sociologically, psychologically, anthropologically and philosophically. We looked at communication and what factors lead to breakdowns: prejudice, predisposition, close-mindedness, emotional vocabulary, lack of information, false information and others, all of which I'd been actively carpet-bombed with throughout my childhood. And we looked at the roles of such factors in steering our perceptions of the world, of ourselves, of everything.

"We all make maps that take on a life of their own," Dr Rebstock showed us, "and those maps eventually merge with the territory, which then becomes indistinguishable from the map, making the map a substitute territory." There are normally many causes to any one event, but we impose a cause-effect system on the world and tend to look for only one cause, one explanation. Language is a simple way of presenting complex problems, but events change and language doesn't fully grasp it, doesn't keep pace. And since language doesn't just *refer* to experience, but *defines* it, our ability to experience can be enhanced by increasing the breadth and depth of our language. Moreover, learning another language isn't just learning another set of words; it means learning *another way of thinking*, perceiving, experiencing.

Dr Rebstock also outlined the conditions for creativity, starting with openness to experience and achieving efficient perception of the external world. Another point – in line with what Dr Walsh said in my first course – was to develop the ability to see relationships between unique and distinct events, and to learn to tolerate ambiguity. The final condition was to work towards being inner-directed, as opposed to tradition-directed, to be willing to act on one's own perceptions. *This was such music to my ears!!*

That summer of 1965 turned out (as I understand with the aid of hindsight) to have been one of the most chaotic in my life. On one hand I was agonizing about Jeanette's apparent rejection of me, on the other I was euphoric about the profound insights I was gaining in my two profoundly fascinating summer courses. When they ended in early August (I got A's in both), I decided to switch to an English major and a philosophy minor, and develop my painting from all the perceptions that these courses were opening up for me.

Back in the more practical world, I had to replace my Illinois driver's license with the California version. And I had to find myself a car to replace Jeanette's wheezy old Chevy. I ended up with a used, rear-engine Corvair. It seemed to me to be a step up. (I can honestly say as I write this, however, that throughout my life I've never known *shit* about cars.) My only concern was to acquire a car reliable enough to pick *her* up in and drive *her* around for a change.

Then I received a letter one day that chilled me to my marrow and brought instant focus to the fuzziness of my worldview. It was an order to report to an Army facility in Oakland the following week for my *physical* – the physical examination that was the final step before being drafted into the Army and probably being sent to Vietnam. With Jeanette still in Europe, I didn't know whom to talk to.

I stopped going to the PV, where there might have been plenty of anti-war people, but the PV was becoming a watering hole for hippies, who were claiming to be doing their own thing, outside the Establishment, and not following its norms. What I couldn't understand was why it almost immediately became possible to spot hippies a block away by the clothes they were wearing, a dress code every bit as rigid as the Establishment's. Anyone showing up at a hippie party wearing a suit or even a sport jacket would be jeered out of there in no time (not that I ever went around in suits!). How was anyone freeing him- or herself from convention merely by adhering just as strictly to a new one? Whose "own thing" were they doing?

I didn't feel I knew anyone whom I could trust to discuss such controversial issues as opposition to the War. Or maybe I was just relying on my years of experience of turning inwards to resolve problems. In either case, it had been years since I felt I could or should confide in my parents about *anything*.

I arrived for my Army physical determined to fail it, but I couldn't make my feet flat. I pretended not to hear the beeps in the hearing test, and pressed the button randomly, not in response to any sound. I tried to look unbalanced or deranged (or how I imagined an unbalanced and deranged person might look). I claimed I couldn't see more than the top row of letters in the eye test, but they inspected my glasses too. Nothing helped. A week later, I got my 1-A classification: ready for immediate recruitment. I wrote the first of my letters of appeal, on the grounds that I was a conscientious objector to bearing arms (classification 1-0), and besides, I was just about to begin my full-time studies (worth a 2-S deferment). After that? There had to be another way.

During that summer at The Emporium, I met Dave, a guy a little younger than me working under me on the second floor stockroom. We used to tell jokes and laugh a lot, but we both worked hard. One day I got a call from Joe Elliot, my boss, telling me that I was to go with Dave in his car to help him pick up something important somewhere up in Marin County. I said sure, but found it strange that Dave was given the assignment and I was to accompany him, rather than vice-versa. After all, I was his supervisor.

Nevertheless, Dave and I left the building on that bright, warm August afternoon and went to get his car – his Porsche! I gasped. It turned out that Dave was the son of one of the top Emporium executives. It turned out that we were heading to his parental home, one of the more exclusive mansions in Mill Valley. (Dave's palatial home instantly reminded me of Tony Accardo's in River Forest, with its servants' quarters atop the multi-car garage and all.) I was to wait in the car while Dave went to the door and let himself in. It turned out that the something we had to pick up for Daddy was nothing more than an envelope. I presumed, without airing my presumptions to Dave, that Daddy didn't trust him to take that ride all the way home to Mill Valley and back on his own without side trips. I, being his supervisor, was presumably being sent along to make sure that Dave ran no other "errands" or steamed open the envelope, although I doubt I'd have had a problem with that if he'd wished to. I did, however, have a problem with the extravagance, the waste, the flaunting of wealth that the mansion constituted, in the face of the miserable wages and non-existent job security of the stockboys. But Dave was a nice guy; a son of a bitch isn't necessarily a bitch. And I got to ride across the Golden Gate Bridge on a beautiful summer day in a Porsche with the top down – both ways.

I'd been to quite a few American cities before, all of them ethnically mixed to some extent, but none were quite so delightfully diverse as San Francisco. In addition to the various European and Black ethnicities of Chicago, San Francisco had significant Hispanic, Filipino, Chinese, Japanese and even Samoan populations. This polyculture was reflected in the backgrounds of Emporium stockboys.

One was a shy young Japanese stockboy, an exchange student named Kenny Kano who was working at The Emporium during his summer vacation that year. He was always asking me questions about the English language, and he learned quickly. At the end of his stint, he came up to me and ceremoniously handed me a book of Japanese Haiku (in English translation), with an inscription in Japanese and another in English that said "To Professor Erisman". I was touched.

Another of "my" stockboys was a huge mountain of a man – about the same size and build as Muhammed Ali. He was a Samoan about my age, and he gave a gentle impression, a gentle giant. I asked him endless questions about what life was like on Samoa. He told me there was a lot of fighting, especially among young men who'd had too much to drink. In fact, street fights there frequently had fatal or nearly fatal outcomes. But, he assured me, "If I beat you within an inch of your life, you will then be my best friend forever!" I endeavored to keep our relationship on a level somewhat below that of best friends – and never went drinking with him.

Among the Black guys I worked with, one I'll call Gus (only because I unfortunately can't remember his real name) was becoming more and more militant about civil rights, verbally at least, and I wanted to try to understand his thinking. I had no trouble at all understanding the *fact* of the anger and frustration of Black people in America at the sluggish pace of achieving the civil rights that never should have been denied them in the first place. But Gus didn't like it that I said I understood the fact; he wanted me to know that I didn't understand the *feeling*. He pointed to the top of his head and told me to feel his stubby, burr-like hair. "You haven't got this!" he hissed. "And if you haven't got this, you can't *ever* understand!" For him, it was not the smooth milk chocolate of his skin that made "white" people with blotchy pinkish-beige skin regard *him* as inferior; it was the hair that could never be straight. I was astounded that he was spelling out the external differences for me; I knew about them all right. What I didn't understand was why *anyone* should perceive hair *or* skin as having anything to do with inferiority or superiority. Then he relented a bit. "OK," Gus said. "*You're* all right. But you still can't understand it all the way, because for too many people with too much power it *is* a matter of superiority and inferiority, and you can never know how that feels." I had to admit that he was right.

Jeanette came home, full of enthusiasm for Europe but not for me. I was nearly overwhelmed with anxiety about how and where we stood. We went out and spent time together daily, but she kept trying to find arguments for me not to love her. And I kept telling her how much I did. It felt as if we'd stepped backwards six months, maybe more, and I didn't know the cause, nor how to deal with it. She had the advantage, of course; she'd been away, she'd absorbed loads of exciting new sights, sounds, smells and tastes, and she was absolutely overwhelmed by it all. She *loved* Europe! In terms of our hopes and plans, I'd pretty much been standing still, or trying to, treading water, trying not to get swept backwards in strong currents I knew nothing about.

I thought it was perhaps a good thing that I'd soon be going away for about a week myself. My parents sent me a ticket, or the money for one, to fly back and see them for five days at the end of August, before my full-time studies began. I hoped it would give Jeanette a chance to feel that she missed me.

It felt more than peculiar to be back "home". I suddenly felt, more clearly than ever, that I was *not* at home, that I was not the same person who left less than 15 months earlier. I think my parents knew it too. I'd bought a 12-string guitar in San Francisco and brought it along to be able to escape what I correctly expected would be numerous uncomfortable silences – entire herds of elephants in the room – as we discovered how little we could communicate. They were understandably surprised when I told them I wished to accompany them to Reading Meeting on Tuesday evening, the day after my arrival. I doubt whether they let their hopes run away with them to the extent that they truly believed I might be "turning back to the Lord", but could they have guessed my real intention: to show all those Meeting schmucks who'd smugly and sanctimoniously said I'd come crawling back destitute within a few months that they were utterly wrong?

The sheepish expressions on the faces of that Little Flock made it pretty clear that they knew, and that they knew that I knew that they knew. When

I confidently went up to Grandpa Erisman to shake his hand, he stood there looking sternly at me, his hands firmly clasped behind his back, refusing to take my extended one. I shrugged, smiled, and walked away. *What a bastard!*, I thought. I think he realized that I no longer recognized his authority over me.

On the Saturday, Dad, Mom and I drove west to the Mississippi River to meet up for a picnic for a couple of hours with Al, Nancy and their year-old boy Michael. Al was now a graduate mathematics student at Iowa State University in Ames. He and I played some catch with a football he brought along, which was fortunate, since it spared all of us a lot more of those embarrassingly silent moments. There were few "safe" topics. But there was still not a word from my parents about granting approval for our marriage license.

Jeanette was a hot but largely unspoken topic – one of the larger elephants in the room – throughout my visit. My parents could see I was ready for a fight (but that I wasn't going to pick one), ready to defend my love. As a result, little was said, and not much even hinted at. Mom was wearing the heavy cloak of martyrdom most of the time, particularly whenever Dad got his camera out. I couldn't wait to get back *home* to San Francisco, home to Jeanette, back to college, back to sanity.

The day I returned, I got a call from John saying that Grandpa Erisman had just died of a heart attack. When I phoned Mom, she asked whether I intended to come back for the funeral, but seemed to know my negative answer before she asked the question. Instead, on September 2nd, I wrote with thinly veiled sarcasm, *"Please convey my sympathy to Grandma, tho' I'm sure she can find her comfort in the Lord who does everything for a reason which we will understand in His time."*

Jeanette was happy to see me back, to my immeasurable relief, perhaps happy to observe that my trip to Oak Park hadn't rekindled any zealous fires that might cause me to start harassing her again about getting "saved". Although we hadn't yet made it back to where we'd left off before her European trip, I felt that we were on the road to recovery. And I was about to start at San Mateo.

As soon as I got my certificate of registration, I had two photocopies made. I sent one to Carroll Anderson, my Oak Park High homeroom teacher, and within a week the $25 check for my first painting duly arrived in the mail. I sent the other copy to the draft board, by registered mail, citing the relevant articles that entailed my entitlement to a 2-S student deferment.

The anti-war protests were growing stronger, keeping pace with the escalation of the War. More and more draft cards were being burned. On August 31st, a new law went into effect calling for up to five years in prison and a $1,000 fine for card-burning, but the card-burnings continued. The whole War and anti-war climate was heating up; society was becoming polarized. Vietnam was looming closer and closer to me, and touching everyone's lives.

Malcolm X had been assassinated in Harlem in February, but the following month, the protest marches from Selma to Montgomery (Alabama) finally succeeded after having been turned back several times. In early August, Johnson signed the Voting Rights Act into law, banning the discriminatory voter registration requirements that white Southerners employed to prevent Blacks from voting. Unfortunately, these were only tiny steps towards racial equality and they were by no means enough. Then on August 11th, a fight broke out in Watts (Los Angeles) between a white cop and a Black motorist accused of drunk driving, leading to arrests of the driver's family members. There were rumors of police brutality, and six days of rioting ensued, with 34 dead, most of them Blacks – of course.

The situation was highly paradoxical. Lyndon Johnson, who was now the villain of the anti-war movement, at the same time appeared to be an unusually fervent supporter and champion of Civil Rights legislation, as well as environmental protection. He reminded me of those fatally flawed heroes of ancient Greek tragedies. Vietnam would prove to be his fatal flaw.

Jeanette wasn't in a hurry to find a new job after getting back from Europe. After two unsatisfying jobs in a row, she said she preferred to hold out for one she might enjoy for a change. One day just before the start of the term, she and I drove down to San Mateo to find me a good commuting route there and to inspect the campus and parking facilities. The modern school buildings were perched up on a hill, away from everything else. To me, it looked more like a park than a center of learning. A day or two before the term started, I received notice that I'd been accepted at San Francisco State as well, but I'd already paid the registration fees at San Mateo and bought the books for my courses. I'd have to wait until the spring to transfer to San Francisco State. Shortly after the start of school, I was tremendously relieved to receive my 2-S student deferment from the draft. For my birthday, Jeanette gave me a beautiful leather attaché case for carrying my papers and books.

On starting school full-time, my work at The Emporium switched to part-time, which meant I worked in the stockroom on the two evenings a week that the store was now open, Mondays and Thursdays. I also worked on Saturdays, and took over Fred's early-morning role in getting the trucks out in the near darkness onto the shop floors for the basement and ground floor, and sometimes the second floor. I was willing to start at five every Saturday morning and haul out all the trucks for those floors, doing the work of two while only getting paid time-and-a-half. I was on my own most of the time, which was fine with me. And I began to notice that The Emporium's book department carried a pretty good selection of books by a lot of the authors I was studying....

Most of my courses at San Mateo were quite good, particularly one surveying contemporary novels, and another on early English literature from Chaucer to Milton. In the former, five books stand out as having a profound impact on me, the full extent of which I was most probably unaware at the time. Saul Bellow's *Henderson the Rain King* filled me with enthusiasm and daring to pursue a completely different path in life. Albert Camus' *The Plague* deepened my understanding of and fascination with Existentialism. Kingsley Amis' *Lucky Jim* awoke my first notions of skepticism about pursuing a career in academe. Ralph Ellis' *The Invisible Man* gave me my first deep and disturbing view of life as a Black – something I would have wanted to discuss with Gus if he hadn't left the store. And Joseph Heller's *Catch-22* painted a deadly serious and absurdly farcical picture of war and how vastly different personalities react to it, reconcile themselves to it, succumb to it – or row away from it.

I had good use for my King James Bible background when studying Chaucer, of course, but I derived even greater benefit from the persistent hard work it took to grasp Middle English. The big payoff came when I got to *The Miller's Tale*, a true gem among pieces of farcical literature. My background was even more useful, almost essential, when studying Milton's poetic genius in *Paradise Lost*.

But I was generally not enthused about the atmosphere at San Mateo. Night school had been an *adult* school (my age was below the class average), in stimulating surroundings, whereas at San Mateo I almost felt like I was back in high school, a feeling reinforced by the somewhat lordly tone of voice some of the instructors tended to use. Most of my classmates were slightly younger than me, fresh out of high school (I'd been out two years already), and came from affluent, conservative homes like me. But most of them seemed immature and seldom showed any intellectual curiosity or wish to challenge anything.

My San Francisco State Extension courses had given me some insights into the nature of learning. There are basic skills, like multiplication tables, spelling, names of the elements, conjugations of verbs etc that are necessary *tools* for thinking. But learning to *use* those tools, learning to reason, was all about *challenging* – not necessarily challenging the professors (although most of them didn't actively discourage it), but primarily challenging my own preconceptions about anything and everything.

The political science course I took at SMS emboldened me to challenge many of my preconceptions about the US, its origins, and political development. America was indeed a groundbreaking experiment in democracy, in the practical application of the Enlightenment philosophy of Spinoza, Locke, Paine, Jefferson and others. The so-called Founding Fathers were true pioneers compared to anything else anywhere else *at that time*. They challenged the prevailing views of how a society should be structured, and came up with something better, which rightfully placed them in the role of heroes.

But that didn't mean the challenges had to stop there; those times were flawed. Slavery was written into the Constitution. Women were second-class citizens, with few rights. Indians were nobody. You were only a full-fledged, free, first-class citizen if you were an adult white male who owned property. Since then, it was the challenges – the Supreme Court cases and the constitutional amendments – that enabled whatever progress had been made since then. What the Founding Fathers got right was realizing that they couldn't possibly get it *all* right and thus they made those provisions for change, something Conservatives seem unable to grasp.

I was excited about everything I was learning, and in Jeanette I now had a true friend with whom I could discuss it all. She must have been amused, bewitched, and bewildered (but not bothered) by my effusiveness and enthusiasm, and by the new perspectives my learning was giving me – and giving her vicariously. My gloomy brooding about getting her "saved" was simply gone; instead *we* were heading into an entirely new world of our own and on our own.

One Sunday morning in late September, I routinely got up and went to the Baptist Church on Mission Street. The old pastor was pleased to introduce a guest speaker for the day's sermon: a Taiwanese Baptist who worked as a missionary in his own country. He started by telling us that he'd be talking about Taiwan and its customs (moderately interesting), and about the status of Christianity there (even less interesting). Then he moved into politics. "*In Taiwan*," he said, "*anybody even <u>suspected</u> of being a Communist is simply taken out and shot!*" My jaw dropped at what he'd just said. Then, as I saw that the people around me, as well as our own pastor, were nodding and smiling in approval, my jaw dropped even further. "*Sometimes it means that the wrong people might be executed, but the important thing is that we have no Communists!!*" he proclaimed, then grinned, and basked in the approving chuckles of the pastor and most of the congregation.

Wave after wave of horror and disgust swept over me. Where was "turn the other cheek"? What happened to "love thine enemy"? These ignorant, self-righteous hypocrites sitting there nodding and grinning made me wonder why they didn't keep a supply of barf bags in the pews. I felt profoundly nauseous. The moment the service was over, I slipped out of the pew, headed for the exit and never looked back. I was done with the Baptists, and done with much more than I yet realized.

I told Jeanette of my decision, and of how disgusted I was with the whole thing. She was relieved, because it meant that the principal source of our former friction seemed not only to have abated, but had vanished. She reiterated her own inability to believe in Catholicism, particularly because of hell, and admitted experiencing increasing discontent with going to church, and with what it stood for, but she still felt bound to keep up the façade for her mother's sake – *ah, the things parents do to their children!*

After abandoning the Baptists, I read a lot about the beliefs and practices of a few other churches, free from the prejudices of the Meeting, but I couldn't reconcile myself to taking seriously or sincerely the institutional aspects of any organized religion, the pomp and ceremony, the traditions and trappings, the thinly disguised sanctimoniousness. And the obsession with money. I still told myself that I basically considered myself a Christian, however, and I still felt that Jesus was a Good Guy who cared about the poor and sick and downtrodden, and championed forgiveness. I hadn't read my Bible at all since coming to San Francisco, and certainly not with the new eyes my doubting and questioning gave me, or it might have occurred to me that there were a lot of rotten cherries in the bowl from which I'd been picking. But for now, it was all these organizations – businesses – built up in His name that were making me gag.

Over the next month or two, nearly all the remaining tension between me and Jeanette melted away. We spent more and more time together, and although her Catholic taboo about premarital sex unfortunately remained intact, our conversations were deep and harmonious. We decided to get officially engaged, diamond ring and all, at Christmas.

During the autumn, my letters to my parents were less frequent, and I toned down the pretense of a fundamentalist Christian position I no longer held. Nor did I tell them I'd left the Baptist Church. Whether Haskle found out and informed them, I'll never know. Nearly all my attempts to confide in them, whether about my actions or my thoughts, only elicited more preaching of the same type I'd worked so hard to emancipate myself from in my late teens. I didn't tell them of our engagement plans either.

Mom wrote to tell me that she and Dad were again planning to visit me for a day or two before Christmas, in connection with their annual pilgrimage to the LA Bible Conference. This time they would stay at the Mission Inn, a budget hotel/motel on Mission Street they'd located, a brisk 10-minute walk from where I lived. And this time they expressly wanted (demanded?) to meet Jeanette, who wasn't exactly enthusiastic about the prospect, which I could easily understand (and I didn't even know about that letter Mom sent her in July!). We clearly felt it would be wise to avoid introducing Jeanette's parents to mine, and it was agreed that Jeanette and I would have dinner with my parents only, at Alioto's in Fisherman's Wharf.

My "apartment" was now as done as it was ever going to be, and looked quite nice, at least compared to what my parents saw the year before. Although my bathroom and kitchen were tiny, they were functional and reasonably clean, my corridor was now separated from the garage, and I had a few more furnishings. Among them was a small pipe rack on the heater in the corner. It held the three or four pipes I'd acquired so far. (I probably thought that a pipe looked more "professorial" than cigarettes, but I also preferred the fuller taste of pipe tobacco.)

I could easily have hidden that pipe rack from my parents' view for the duration of their brief visit. I debated with myself, long and hard, about whether to do that or to leave it where it was. I decided to be brave. I'd left home, after all. It wasn't as though I took my room from the house on Euclid and plunked it down in the back of Fred Bito's garage on Evergreen. I was making my own decisions, wasn't I? And if people entitle themselves to be offended when other people are simply trying to live their own lives, whose fault is that – the offender's or the offendee's? I had to take a stand, in this case a pipe-stand.

When the day came, when my parents came to my apartment (at their insistence) at lunchtime to pick me up, they showed some signs of relief on seeing that I now at least had quarters that were separated from the garage, as well as a bathroom of sorts (with walls and a door!) and a makeshift kitchen, despite the still-appalling standard. The grand tour ended once we'd passed through the beads and stood there, the three of us occupying most of the floor space of my bedroom-living room. They looked around, less shocked by the Christmas tree this time, perhaps trying to think of something nice to say, or at least polite to say, or at least not *im*polite to say, or at least to break the silence.

Then my pipe rack caught Mom's eye. She gasped audibly, grabbed Dad's arm, nodded towards the heater, then charged back through the beads to the bathroom, making theatrically loud choking noises. The script she'd probably been rehearsing was lost and her prompter was missing. She had to *ad lib* it and didn't know quite how. Dad's anxious look made it obvious that he was perplexed about what to do, but his chief concern seemed to me to be what to do about Mom, not what to do about my pipes.

I turned to him and asked if he'd like me to make him a grilled cheese sandwich. He accepted my offer without hesitation, perhaps with relief, and I immediately set about making some. He didn't make a move to go and console Mom; in fact, neither of us spoke about what she might be up to in the bathroom. I wondered to myself how many times he'd been in similar situations with her.

As the noises and smells of the sandwich preparation were beginning to fill my little apartment, Dad and I began to converse. He asked me about school and work, and how I was getting along (but nothing about Jeanette). He treated me with some respect, but the tension level was still high due to Mom's histrionic absence. The neutral conversation topics served as a blanket to fight the chill and shock. After a few brief minutes that seemed to last for ages, Mom emerged from the bathroom, apparently having realized that not even Dad was going to respond to her overreaction to a pipe rack. I asked her if she'd also like a grilled cheese sandwich, but she declined, and after Dad and I finished ours, he took a couple of photos and then we left to go back to their Mission Street motel and spend some time together until it was time to meet Jeanette for dinner at Fisherman's Wharf. (Many years later, those photos/slides from my apartment were among the ones Mom offered me to take from her collection. They'd been taped over to hide my Christmas tree *and* my pipe rack.) We were all on edge in different ways and for different reasons. At least they didn't stage an impromptu motel-room prayer meeting this time.

Jeanette and I agreed to refrain from smoking in my parents' presence, and they presumably agreed to abstain from overt preaching. There were lots of religious hints, clichés, and probing innuendos that were most likely too subtle for Jeanette to recognize, but which I picked up all too easily. I sat there hoping the tension wouldn't suddenly ignite and erupt into an all-consuming blaze of evangelism. I was extremely taut; I don't remember what we ate or drank (it wasn't alcohol).

Towards the end of the meal, we told them that we would be getting engaged at Christmas. In a "normal" family, such an announcement might be met with the heartiest of congratulations (*"This calls for champagne!!"*), warm embraces and tears of joy. But Mom's theatrically distraught look (and Dad's anxious look at her) was all we got. Hallelujah.

In retrospect, it seems to me that my meeting with Mom and Dad that December may have heralded a major acceleration in the rift in our relationship, and my first cautious steps towards complete independence as an adult. The years of my rebellion as a teenager had given me greater freedom than I'd been ready to accept. I continued to defer to their wishes and demands – from which I'd rebelled mightily to break free. Perhaps it was because those years were so focused on what I was *against*. Now I was just beginning to learn about what I was *for* – to understand what made sense to me instead of someone else's dogma, to be compassionate to others regardless of what they believed, to discover the joy of true love with the otherness of a wonderful human being. But I had an awfully long way to go.

My parents (or perhaps only my mom) were still playing the game I'd grown up with: while doubtlessly loving me, they were making the *expressions* of their love contingent on my adherence to their beliefs. And since hardly anything remained of such adherence, where did that leave us? Should I play their game – make the expressions of my love for them contingent on their *not* adhering to beliefs I no longer held? I'd have settled for them simply getting off my back. But since they, or Mom at least, showed no signs of willingness to do so, I had to accept that we'd have to play it by ear for a while, until some new ground rules for our relationship could be established out of the rubble of those that had been my life until then.

Jeanette and I picked out her ring together. It was beautiful, quite a bit over the top of my budget, but we were both filled with joy. Getting engaged was all we were going to think about for now. After the Christmas holidays, we could start to think about the future.

CHAPTER 5

Weddings and other problems

Getting engaged turned out to be the easy part. When we got engaged at Christmas, we did it our way, consulted only each other, and gave no thought (at least I certainly didn't) to the wedding itself, except that since my parents continued to ignore my requests to sign any consent forms I mistakenly thought I needed to allow marriage before my 21st birthday, Jeanette and I decided to postpone our original plans to marry on June 11th and wait until after September 13th instead.

For some reason, I started calling myself "Stanley" instead of "Stan" at this point. Maybe it was just a way of marking my territory as an adult – emancipated from my parents – or maybe I saw some movie with a Stanley character I liked. Or maybe I was just restless and wanted a change. I've never felt terribly pleased with the name I was given.

In January 1966, Jeanette applied for and got a new and better-paying job as an executive secretary (a role that would come to be called a personal assistant, PA) to Ralph Pifari, one of the myriad vice-presidents at the Bank of America, in the relatively new B of A tower at Market and Van Ness. One evening when she picked me up after work, she noticed I was wearing three shirts. I told her about my special "bargains". She laughed, and said that her father sometimes came home with a few things that "fell off the back of a truck". I thought she meant it literally – the quotation marks were inaudible and I was unfamiliar with the expression. She laughed again.

I developed a particular fondness for Pendleton shirts, rugged and colorful woolen shirts from the eponymous town in Oregon, often worn loose, even unbuttoned, on top of a tee shirt or other cotton shirt. Department 515 carried them, and when there was a customer return on one, I snapped it up immediately. Once or twice a year we'd get in a shipment of Pendleton's new color and pattern samples, most of which I found to be far more stunning than any of the shirts in their standard range, but for some reason, even if they sold immediately, few of those brilliant colors and patterns ever appeared in the standard range. They were never seen again. The samples were all in medium, my size. They were supposed to be sent directly from the stockroom to Dome Square, but not all of them made it that far. Using my five-finger discount, I added as many of the samples as I could to my own growing collection.

The comfortable and rugged ankle-high work-boots I always wore didn't last forever. But since such boots were also among the items stocked on the 2nd floor of the stockroom, I didn't have to worry about them wearing out; I simply wore a new pair out – of the store. And if I had a pair of pants that got ripped, they would make a final, one-way trip to the returns shelf in the 507 section of the stockroom, where they would be instantly replaced by new ones at full discount.

I got good grades in all my courses at San Mateo, but was glad to begin at San Francisco State in late January 1966, where I again took a dauntingly heavy course load. I was helped financially by my ability to acquire some of the books on my required reading lists from The Emporium at the remarkable discounts that only I knew about. I was now attending – very temporarily, as it turned out – the same college as Jeanette's brother, but Michael was a third-year student majoring in biology, while I was a second-year English major in the liberal arts program. As a result, our courses were different, held in different buildings and at different times, and our paths never crossed on campus.

One of the side-effects of switching schools for the spring term was that within days my draft board sent me a new 1-A (ready for Vietnam) reclassification notice, causing a week or two of high anxiety, until I proved to their satisfaction that I'd merely switched schools, not quit school, and I got my 2-S classification back. But with the ever-escalating War now making the headlines on an almost daily basis, alertness and cautiousness regarding the draft were being added to my array of permanent mental fixtures.

The atmosphere at San Francisco State was a vast improvement over San Mateo – much greater diversity among the students (in terms of age, race, social standing, etc), and a feeling that this was a place of learning, not of showing off designer clothes or fancy cars in the parking lot. I remained pretty much an outsider – an affable loner – and had no intercourse (social or otherwise) outside the classroom with any of my classmates. With my heavy course load, part-time job, and "courtship" of Jeanette, I had little extra time to spend with anybody else, even if I'd wanted to. And I had a long-standing habit of fending for myself, not suffering from an emotional need for a great deal of companionship, particularly on a superficial or posturing level.

The courses themselves were good, although few teachers would ever match the impact that Dr Walsh, Dr Gardner, and Mr Rebstock had on me, with their exceptional focus on teaching their students *how to think for themselves*, not merely to memorize bits of information. Reflecting back on elementary school and high school, I realized that the thing in common with the all courses I liked best was the ability of the teacher to inspire, not the subject matter itself. Could I ever become a teacher like that?

One of my two English courses during the spring term was an introduction to the study of language, which looked at how languages work, how they are learned, what they consist of and how they evolve over time. "*Language should not be reduced to a moral issue of right and wrong by arbitrary standards that allow no degree,*" our professor told us, once again deviating sharply from the black-and-white binary world of my childhood and the Bible. We also looked at similarities within language groups (like the huge Indo-European group) and major differences in the grammatical structures of unrelated languages. I found it immensely interesting, but at the same time I wished I could put all I was learning in this course "on hold" until such time as I might learn a foreign language well – if that day ever came.

The other English course that semester was a survey of the "middle period" of English literature, from Dryden and Pope through the Romantic poets. For this course I bought – paid for! – the two thick (1700 pages each, on average) volumes of *The Norton Anthology of English Literature*, which quickly came to serve me as well as the Compton's Encyclopedia had served me as a child – an endless source of pleasure. I was totally unprepared for and swept away by the elegant and razor-sharp satire of Jonathan Swift's *A Modest Proposal*. I was bewitched by Alexander Pope's logomagic in *Essay on Criticism* and *Essay on Man*. Just about every author whose works we touched on in that course or most other English courses, or via *Norton*, was added to my private shopping list for new book acquisitions, either for cheap purchases at San Francisco's numerous used book stores or for unbeatable discounts if they turned up in The Emporium's book department. My universe was expanding.

In harmony with those feelings was my introductory course in the physical sciences. Back in those days, having an English major was considered part of the Liberal Arts program, a wonderful concept based on the benefits of acquiring at least rudimentary knowledge in a broad variety of fields. First in the physical science course was astronomy and the changes in mankind's view of the world implicit in the findings of Copernicus, Kepler and Galileo. It wasn't so much that the knowledge itself was new to me; it was more the *connections* I'd never made before but was now making. With a flat earth and a geocentric universe, "up" to heaven and "down" to hell made sense. But a spherical earth off in some corner of a seemingly endless universe of unknown shape? "Up" and "down" were now in every direction simultaneously (and at the same time), and in opposite directions from themselves! The Bible was wrong and the goalposts would have to be moved again, as new knowledge continued to erode authority of the Word. No wonder the Catholics tortured and imprisoned Galileo! Suddenly two of life's great lessons became clear to me:

- *An idea isn't true just because most people believe it;*
- *Nor is it true just because it's been held to be true for centuries or millennia.*

We looked at the scientific, verifiable explanations for eclipses, tides and other natural phenomena that once terrified the masses into submission to those who claimed to have answers that required no verification, and about which demands for proof could be called heretical or blasphemous and lead to severe punishment, horrendous torture and brutal death. The scientific explanations were much more exciting than the superstitions – and they could and should be tested and challenged as much as anyone wanted!

We got an introduction to chemistry that went quite a lot deeper than Miss Tredenick's, including how atoms worked, the electromagnetic spectrum (and my first introduction to a Swedish diacritical mark: Å for Ångström, the unit of measure for wavelengths) with its tiny windows of human sensory perception, and on into radioactivity and the process of half-lives and degradation. I was extremely fascinated, but probably my unwillingness to change horses in mid-stream prevented any thought of again changing my major at that point, along with my abiding aversion to getting involved in higher mathematics, which would have been necessary for more advanced science studies, particularly physics.

Another course I was taking that term – economics – did that, and I hated it. I think it was one of only two university courses I would ever really loathe. My Humanities 30 course, however, was thoroughly enjoyable. Starting with the Ancient Greeks (as well as a look at some earlier cultures), we studied everything from their political roles and mythologies to Homer and architecture. (The aptly named Dr Colonna went into considerable detail on the differences between

Doric and Ionic columns.)

Of particular interest to me was the ancients' views of morality. The Greek gods gave no real help to humans, despite all the temples built to them, sacrifices offered, and prayers prayed. The Greeks didn't exactly *expect* the gods' help either; everything in human lives was ultimately decided by Fate. The gods were anthropomorphic in that they were capricious, sometimes treacherous, totally unreliable, often schizophrenic and psychopathic. *That* rang some bells I wasn't yet ready to hear!

When we got to the Romans and their gods, there were more similarities than differences. We ended with one more "development": the torturous fantasy world of Dante's *Inferno*, which received the full blessing and approval of the Catholic Church.

Contrasted against all this bloodlust, Dr Colonna shared with us her own remarkably simple and sensible philosophy of life: "*Try never to hurt anyone; try to be humble, because you only have what birth gave you; and realize that you know nothing compared to what can be known, which is why you should always struggle to know as much as you can.*"

The last of the courses I had in the spring of 1966, part of my philosophy minor program, was in symbolic logic. Both Dr Walsh and Dr Gardner had pointed out the great value of logic as a tool (albeit with its codicil regarding unchallenged premises). Moreover, in literature we often looked for symbolism in the writings of the poets and others. Thus I was looking forward to this course with great interest. The day before the first classroom session, I bought (paid for) the only required book and, opening it to a random page, began glancing through it. I thought I would throw up. It was nothing but mathematics on a level I'd been going to great and almost panic-driven lengths to avoid! I miserably saw myself failing the course. I saw myself being forced to drop out of school, getting drafted, being sent to Vietnam, killing and being killed.

The next day – the first dreaded day of class – all of us students were sitting at our desks, awaiting the arrival of Dr Hackstaff, a professor nobody knew anything about, because he'd just come to San Francisco State to do a stint as a guest professor from some university in Indiana. We were all waiting, wondering whether he was having trouble finding the right room, when the door burst open and this 50-ish, balding, near-sighted bundle of tweed strode swiftly to the desk on which he dumped some books and papers and a few pipes, all the while puffing furiously on the unlit pipe in his mouth and exclaiming as he turned to the blackboard while seizing a piece of chalk: "*You gotta see this!!*" And he started writing, scribbling, furiously, accompanied by his own sprinting commentary. When he came to the right-hand edge of the blackboard without having finished what he wanted to write on that line, he continued writing – on the wall.

I don't know whether anyone in the class knew exactly what he was talking about at that point (I certainly didn't), but I was keenly aware that this course was never going to be boring. His insane energy was contagious, and his will for us to understand and learn was overwhelming. It turned out to be one of the best and certainly most exciting courses I would ever take. Our final exam consisted of ten complex logical (mathematical!) problems to solve. In case anyone got stuck on a particular question, he threw in two extra-credit problems that we could try instead. He was the embodiment of that marvelous, all-too-rare breed of teacher whose passion is to convey enthusiasm, knowledge and skills, rather than to see how he can trip his students up in order to spotlight and mock their inadequacies.

I solved all 12 problems. For my final grade, he gave me an A and told me it would have been an A++ if the system had allowed it. In view of his dedication to pipe-smoking, I encouraged The Emporium to enable me to award him a beautifully carved meerschaum pipe, available to me in the store's tobacco department at a large discount at around five-thirty one Saturday morning.

Since my parents' underwhelming response to the Christmas meeting with Jeanette, my motivation to write them was continuing to wane, and they seemed to be finding my letters increasingly terse and unresponsive to the tiresome and repetitive messages they kept regurgitating in my general direction. At one point I felt obliged to assure them: "*Yes, Mom, I read your letters.*"

In mid-February, Jeanette received a four-page epistle from my Mom, with this heart-warming opening sentence: "*It was with mixed feelings that we, Stan's parents, met you in December.*" In the second paragraph, my mom informed my fiancée that "*By natural tendency we are warm-hearted and loving, but since by God's wonderful grace we have learned to know the Lord Jesus as Saviour, His Holy Word stands between us and all our thoughts!*" This was the frankest admission I'd ever seen that the Bible (and their faith) stood between my parents and their natural tendency to be loving, but probably they were never conscious of what a disgusting admission it was; nor was I at the time.

Then the third paragraph began with the claim that "*It is not <u>religion</u> I wish to discuss, dear Jeanette!*", followed by three and a half pages of religion! In closing, Mom penned the prerequisite: "*We <u>long</u> to do things for you and to make you welcome here, but <u>first</u> – what about the Lord?!*" And in case Jeanette failed to grasp the full force of this arrogance, the closing read: "*Most Sincerely, and with restrained Love*".

Jeanette showed me this letter; she was both saddened and outraged. I sighed heavily, with deepest disappointment, yet I was all too familiar with the kind of spiritual blackmail involved. Even my earliest childhood memories involved the fear of my parent's withholding or withdrawing their love from me if I failed to toe the line, to confess my sins, to bow my little will to His omniscient one. Although I eventually came to feel that, deep down, my parents would love me no matter what, Jeanette had no basis for having such feelings regarding herself, nor anything to suggest she could ever expect their unconditional love. She sighed too – in great relief that I was totally disappointed in my parents and disgusted by the contents of Mom's letter. She now knew for sure that I'd never be badgering her again.

But she did feel awkward. A long letter like that begged a response, and Jeanette had no idea how to go about it, having felt almost violated by the arrogance of what Mom wrote. Why arrogant? My parents would have been shocked to have their zeal described with that word. But it *was* arrogant because my parents were totally convinced that their views were unassailable *and* because those same views were unsupported by evidence *and* because they would not permit any challenges to them *and* because they were demeaning towards Jeanette.

Since the letter was only about The Lord (whose first name is "The"), nothing else, there were no small islands or stepping stones of normal conversation on which to find a footing or base a response. I told Jeanette I could reply on her behalf, and she immediately and gratefully accepted my offer. I wrote my parents on March 7th that Jeanette wished to thank them for their letter and good intentions, but that it had seemed to her that they found it difficult to take her as she was. I then told them, from me, to back off and "*leave it with the Lord*". My tone was harsher than before, but it seemed necessary if they were ever going to get the message and stop their arrogant abuse of the girl I loved.

That same day, March 7th, out of the blue, I was blown away by a Category IV storm – a phone call from Norm. That he called me was the first surprise. The second was that the call came from Hayward in the East Bay, where Norm told me he was living with his now-widowed mother – in a trailer park. The third was that he was getting married the next month. And the fourth was that he wanted me to be his best man.

Naturally, I agreed without hesitation, despite not having been able to take in all the news at once. Just the fact of being in touch with Norm again after nearly a year was surreal enough for me, but that he was living with his *mother!* – she who I always thought had been furious (with me too) when we left, and with whom Norm and I had almost no contact (that I'd heard about) during the period of less than six months that we lived together – was almost beyond my comprehension.

But we agreed that I would come out to their trailer a few evenings later to catch up and to go through the wedding plans. Norm hadn't asked Jeanette to come along. And since she didn't feel it would be necessary or appropriate, I drove alone down to the San Mateo Bridge and across to Hayward, and eventually found the right trailer park and the right trailer.

Seeing Norm there with his mother felt almost like I'd stepped right into a scene from (or a set for) a film by Buñuel or Fellini, or a painting by Dalí. It wasn't that any individual thing was out of the ordinary, but the combinations were weird, and so contrary to my expectations, the mental extrapolations I'd unconsciously been making regarding the developments in Norm's life. But that was *my* problem.

I didn't get any explanations at that time as to how Norm and his mom came to be living in a trailer park in Hayward. (Well, maybe I did, but I would probably have been too dazed and overwhelmed by the whole situation to be able to take much in.) I did find out that Norm had *not* returned to the Fold, to the Meeting, and that he was going to be getting married a few weeks later, not to Mary Lou, but to a girl named Barbara, in a small local Lutheran church where we were soon going to have a rehearsal, with me in the role of best man. During the course of our conversation, it became evident that Norm hadn't known Barbara for more than a couple of months.

As of early March 1966, the US had only about 200,000 troops in Vietnam, but the build-up – the "escalation" – was beginning to accelerate rapidly, and 200,000 didn't feel "only". Then Michael received his draft notice; he was to report for military service on March 23rd. I don't know whether he forgot or simply didn't bother to apply for a student deferment, but suddenly Vietnam was staring him – and the whole family – in the face. Jeanette seemed much more nervous about it than the rest of her family, perhaps because her opposition to the War was much more developed. (The elder Mike didn't seem to be opposed at all.) Televised demonstrations were getting bigger, more frequent and more vehement. But Michael just shrugged and said he "might as well get it over with." After just two months of being my unseen fellow student at San Francisco State, he was off to basic training.

Also at around this time, the Beatles created a huge uproar in America when John Lennon stated a simple fact: that the media and the public were giving much more attention to his group than to Jesus, i.e. that the Beatles were currently more popular than Jesus. Instead of counting the number of articles in nearly every newspaper in the country, or on whom the greater number of TV programs were focused, many Americans chose to demonstrate their intellectual prowess by claiming that Lennon claimed the Beatles were *better* than Jesus, and began calling the group "anti-Jesus". Albums were burned; rotten fruit was thrown; rationality was handed another defeat.

When I accepted Norm's request, I knew nothing at all about what being a best man might entail. Norm didn't appear to be terribly well-versed in the traditions surrounding the role either. I served as best man at Al's wedding, but the only function I could remember having was to stand up there with Al and hand him the ring at the appropriate time – presumably because he would be too nervous and fumbly to handle it himself – and when it was all over to walk back down the aisle after Al and Nancy, with the maid of honor on my arm. (I'd never met her before the rehearsal nor would ever meet her again after the wedding.) It's not as though there was any dancing at Al and Nancy's wedding, and thus the maid of honor would not appear on my dance card.

The question of organizing a stag night obviously never arose with Al, and Norm never mentioned one either (at that point in my life, I'd only heard that a "stag night" was an all-guys night on the town, possible watching "stag films", i.e. porn). I had no clue that a stag night in a wedding context is traditionally arranged by the best man. But I didn't know any of Norm's friends, nor did he speak of any who might be involved in the wedding, nor was I much for following traditions anyway. I only knew that I would need to wear a dark suit and tie. As a result, I acquired a dark, handsome three-piece suit at a most affordable full discount from The Emporium.

Weddings and other problems

At the wedding, on April 2nd, I think I was the only one in attendance that Norm knew prior to having met Barbara just three months earlier, and Norm was the only one I knew – his mom was already back in Illinois (presumably she was about to leave when I saw her, although not a word of that was mentioned). Nothing made much sense to me, but Norm showed no outward signs of nervousness, at least none that I could discern, nor of the confusion that I felt.

In retrospect, it is conceivable to me that the wedding guests (possibly even Norm and Barbara) might have been expecting the best man to make a speech at the wedding dinner, but the thought never occurred to me. Nothing occurred to me at all, except to ask Norm to be my best man when Jeanette and I got married, probably in late September or early October – we hadn't started figuring out any details yet. Norm said he would be happy to oblige.

With Norm's wedding having raised the subject, and with spring and summer approaching, Jeanette and I began taking a closer look at setting the date for our own wedding. Since we felt obliged to obviate any need for my parents' approval by waiting until after my 21st birthday (they *still* hadn't responded to a multitude of requests from me for their formal consent – *and* their attendance), and since Jeanette and I met on October 10th two years before, we decided aim for the closest Saturday to that: October 8th. That way we would also avoid the start of the fall term in September, which might cause me to miss important course introductions.

What we didn't yet realize was that beyond setting the date, Jeanette and I would end up having almost no say in anything to do with our own wedding. Perhaps Jeanette was somewhat prepared to be set aside by her mom and other relatives, as well as by family traditions, Catholic traditions and sacraments, all of which would hijack every possibility of planning anything ourselves. But I wasn't prepared for anything like that. I naively thought that since this was *our* wedding, we'd be doing it *our* way, keeping it simple, making it fun, and inviting only the people we liked and felt close to. Fat chance.

The first rude awakening was when we were told (not asked!) that our wedding was going to take the form of a nuptial mass, to be held at the Church of the Epiphany (the Catholic Church nearest to where Jeanette lived, although she always went to other parishes when she attended at all, so I'd never even been inside this one). I was given to understand quite clearly that this was *not* a suggestion, *not* one of several options we could choose from; it was a non-negotiable *fait accompli*, served up to us on a leaden platter. Jeanette's sister Marilyn was married in that selfsame church. Jeanette knew the drill, but didn't seem to mind terribly. She seemed resigned to that being the way things were done in her family, in Catholic families. What I didn't understand at the time was that in the Catholic view Rose embraced, a marriage outside the Catholic Church would never be considered a "true" marriage. But Jeanette knew it, and she and I just had to go along with it. I, however, didn't want to "just go along" with anything; I wanted this to be *our* wedding. But nobody asked me. And I came to hate the concept of "non-negotiable".

The second, even bigger and ruder awakening, was that the priest Jeanette's mom met to book the wedding date we selected (at least we got to choose that!) at the church, and who would be officiating, told Rose that since I wasn't a Catholic, in order for me to be allowed to marry in the Church I would have to fill out forms, submit references, attend lessons and undergo private assessment sessions with said priest, and – as the ultimate, sickening insult to my integrity – *sign a pledge* that any children Jeanette and I might have would be raised in the Catholic faith!

Rose passed the information along to Jeanette, and Jeanette told me, sheepishly, and trying hard to downplay the seriousness of it – "*It's just a formality, no big deal.*" But I felt trapped, mauled, keelhauled, sickened, nauseous, outraged.

Again, none of these things were suggestions, but non-negotiable prerequisites. I had no say in it at all, and felt totally miserable about it. Suddenly I just wanted to have it all over and done with. (Couldn't we just elope?!) This was *not* the way I imagined looking forward to *our* wedding. There was no joy.

I called Norm and asked if I could use him as a reference for the Catholic business, and in the late spring he had to come over to San Francisco, to the rectory of the Epiphany Church, to vouch for me to the priest that I was an upright person who held basic Christian beliefs, and who could be trusted to honor the disgusting pledge they were demanding me to sign – a pledge to submit children I didn't even have to an entire childhood and young adulthood of indoctrination, something I was still struggling to free myself from. The works of Camus and Kafka came to mind.

I don't remember much about my "lessons". The priest certainly couldn't teach me anything I didn't already know about the Bible, if indeed that was on the agenda. I just remember wanting to get the hell out of there. I think Jeanette may have accompanied me to one or more sessions. She certainly had to help talk me down from my agitation afterwards.

This was, as I saw it, every bit as bad as my parents (and me!) having tried to foist their religion on her, except that I sincerely hoped that my parents at least loved me when push came to shove, but the priest clearly didn't love me *or* Jeanette. It wasn't so much the mumbo-jumbo this guy in a dress was saying that upset me – it was his power over us to tell us how to bring up children we didn't have, it was his power to terrify Jeanette if she were to wish to lose her virginity before he has his say of magic words, it was my being in a position of not being allowed to refute any of it – and there was a *lot* I would have wanted to challenge. What did any of this crap have to do with Jeanette's and my love for each other?! I hated every minute of that fucking priest's overbearing power trip, and I doubt that my extreme frustration and irritation benefitted my relationship with Jeanette in any way. Feelings of being trapped were appearing out of nowhere, climbing in and out of my sub-conscious like panic-stricken chipmunks.

Perhaps Jeanette felt guilty about what I was being put through; the similarities between this and the efforts of my parents to "save" her were becoming nauseatingly plain to her, too. Even though it wasn't her idea to put me through it all, she may have felt the need to "compensate" (having the wedding day in sight may also have unleashed some of her own hormones), and her parents' front porch was no longer the venue of choice for our good-nightly necking sessions. We went to my place, on tip-toe. Full nudity was now OK, although the only nudity was hers; I had to keep my pants on – literally and figuratively.

My first confrontation with girdles was in the hotel room with Sally P. Several subsequent encounters (with the exception of Margaret) led me to believe that this business of tightly encasing the lower female torso in impenetrable elastic or Lycra sheathing was the way things were, just like the discomfort I experienced in putting on a tie for any formal or semi-formal occasion, and wondering why the hell any guy ever got it into his head (or around his neck) to come up with such an uncomfortable idea. Getting Jeanette's girdle off was not the most romantic procedure ever concocted, but it had to be done if I was to get a foretaste of conjugal bliss.

The talk that went on between us during our more intimate sessions revealed another somewhat disappointing obstacle we would be facing. Jeanette was not going to hear of taking the Pill, not because of what the Church said, but because of her not-unfounded fears of medical side-effects. And Vatican Roulette would be far too dangerous, as Marilyn found out when she got pregnant on a "safe" night within days of getting married. This would mean condoms on our wedding night and forever after. We even spoke of our mutual disinclination to have children, largely due to how messed-up we (especially Jeanette) felt the world was – not a nice place to bring up children. I had the added motivation of neither wanting to break a pledge nor raise a child to be a Catholic or anything else that child him- or herself didn't choose to be.

On Monday, May 2nd, I had a full day at San Francisco State, and hurried home because I had to get to work at The Emporium in the evening. I was pressed for time. After a quick sandwich, I jumped into my Corvair and headed down Evergreen towards Mission. At each intersection down the hill, I braked, looked both ways and proceeded. At the corner of Irving, the last block before I would turn right onto Mission Street, all was clear, but as I started into the intersection, a teenage driver on Irving roared out from the left at full speed, without slowing down at the corner, much less looking. I slammed on my brakes, but the speed of the young driver's car carried it to the middle of the intersection before I could bring my car to a complete stop. I hit it broadside with my left front fender.

The police arrived on the scene and the officer seemed to be a good friend of the teenager's family. A citation was given – to me only – for which I would have to appear in court. The damage to the front of my car was considerable. The hood had buckled, partially blocking the view out the windshield, and the left front fender was reminiscent of an accordion, but it was still possible to drive; the engine was in the rear. I could only afford the minimum insurance, but nothing that would cover repair of the damage to my own car, and my already slightly rusty Corvair wasn't worth what it would cost to fix.

Jeanette and I decided we'd try to get another car after the wedding, and I would continue driving the wreck. On my day in court, Friday the 13th of May, the police officer who ticketed me failed to show up. The judge simply tossed out the citation, mumbling under his breath about the officer's absence.

In late May, following his basic training, Michael returned home for a few days' leave before being shipped out to Vietnam. He looked like a different person with his shorn head, uniform, missing flab – and fear in his eyes. Despite the increasing coverage of the fighting appearing daily on multiple TV channels, and despite the rising intensity of US bombing, the reality of Vietnam still didn't seem to have sunk in, except to some of those fervently protesting against what the US was doing. Nobody in the family seemed to know what to say to Michael, apart from the obvious *"Be careful!"* Michael himself was never an orator, debater or conversationalist by nature. He was off again without much comment.

I found that with my heavy course loads during the first two semesters of that first academic year, in addition to a whole semester's worth of credits from my night school courses, I was still on track for getting my degree in June '68 even if I didn't take any courses during the summer before our wedding. We would need all the cash we could scrape together, particularly since we now also needed to replace the Corvair.

One evening in the beginning of June, Jeanette and I were having a pizza at the nearby Sal's Pizzeria, close to the corner of Mission and Geneva, when I got an idea. I asked Sal whether he might need any extra help around the place, part-time, evenings, starting as soon as school let out. He said that in fact he would need someone who had a car (bashed up or not) and could deliver pizzas, mostly nearby but sometimes a bit further afield. The job might also include some dishwashing between runs.

This meant that during the summer I could work full-time at The Emporium six days a week, till around five, have a few hours off, then work at the pizzeria from eight to ten on weekdays and till midnight on Fridays and Saturdays, and get free pizza for my evening meals, plus tips. I was also promised an occasional evening off, so Jeanette wouldn't forget who she was about to marry.

A guy at The Emporium told me about a moonlighting job he had, selling sets of the *Encyclopedia Americana* for a couple of hours every evening and making some good money – commission only. I figured I would have a couple of hours between The Emporium and Sal's, into which I might be able to fit a third job that summer. I got the address and went to see about it. I was taken to a clean, well-lit room containing around a dozen small cubicles divided by soundproofing material about two feet high on three sides. Each cubicle had a desk, a notebook, a phone, and a phonebook.

My training for this job took five minutes. I was given a card on which a pitch was printed: *"Hi, my name is [name of salesperson], and I just flew in from LA. I was given your name by someone I met on the plane who knows you and said you place a high value on education, because I told them that was my line of business. I have a fantastic special offer for you, blah, blah, blah...."* We were then given a list of people to call; that list had a name – it was the phonebook – and we were to select names from it, totally randomly, dial up our intended victims and hope our mendacious pitch would get us invited to visit them, to show them the amazing volumes, and to make a lucrative sale.

That pitch not only sounded incredibly silly to me, but I also reacted to the blatant lies. Instead I used my own pitch: "*Hi, my name is Stanley Erisman and I'd like to offer you a fantastic treasure of knowledge – the Encyclopedia Americana!*" And then, if they hadn't already hung up, I would add, "*May I come out and show you, so you can see for yourself?*" In four days, I got two house calls; they were both to lonely people who simply wanted some company. I got no sales, no commission, no money. Thus I gave up my budding career as a powerhouse salesman.

One day during the early part of the summer I received a long, chatty letter from Linda, my high school heartthrob. I gasped when I saw who it was from, and again when I discerned that she was now interested in having contact with me. And then came waves of road-not-taken feelings – the resurrection of feelings never developed, never requited, the pain of rejection, the loss of nothing I'd ever had, the realization that I had in fact moved on, or at least most of me. I wrote her a lengthy reply, basically summing up what I once felt, and the fact that her feelings were now one year late, two years later, three years too late.

I had little vacation time during the summer, and it wasn't as though Jeanette and I could go on a trip anywhere together and share a room – and *a bed*. A couple of times we went with Jeanette's family for the day to Guerneville, in the Russian River Valley in Sonoma County, a couple of hours' drive north of San Francisco. One of Jeanette's aunts had a country cottage there, a short walk from the river at Johnson's Beach. The cottage was apparently available to the family whenever anyone felt like going "up the River", as they called it. Jeanette also hauled me out for a hike through Muir Woods and to the top of Mount Tamalpais (elevation 2,517 feet) in Marin County.

One sunny afternoon when we were both free (thus presumably a Sunday), Jeanette took me on a picnic to the beautiful beach at Half Moon Bay. Ever since I was a kid, I'd tried unsuccessfully to get a suntan, but only ever got sunburns instead. Now, in the California sun, I thought I'd try my luck, armed with plenty of suntan lotion. It was a bit windy, which only made the surf better, and helped to minimize sweatiness – as well as any awareness of the possible effects of the sun's radiation or the waves' effectiveness in removing the lotion. Jeanette was content to stay on the beach reading, while I cavorted in the waves. She'd prepared my all-time favorite sandwich: a whole loaf of fresh San Francisco sourdough bread, sliced lengthwise, and spread with French's mustard, to which she added lots of amazing, thinly sliced, real Italian salami from the family's favorite Italian butcher, leaves of crispy lettuce and slices of fresh, sun-ripened tomatoes. Then she'd cut the whole thing in two and gave me the bigger half. Between that sandwich, my frequent jubilant headlong rushes into the breaking waves, and the cooling sea breezes, I was blithely unaware that my suntan lotion was long since washed and worn away, and that my skin was becoming quite red. I ended up with a second-degree sunburn on my chest and thighs, and it took a few days for the blistery furnace to subside.

Jim Gillingham and his fiancée Judy were getting married in early August, and Jim asked me to be his best man. Since theirs was also a Catholic wedding – a nuptial mass – it would be a kind of sneak preview for Jeanette and me, especially me. It followed all the traditions and customs that most Catholics and others seemed to find applicable, but it confirmed in my mind that it was most definitely *not* what I wanted. Although it didn't seem to bother Jeanette much, I knew with some considerable dread that it was what I was going to get. I still knew nothing about the role of a best man, but since nobody commented on my shortcomings in any way, I can in retrospect wonder whether those traditions that I failed to observe were fully developed in America at that time?

I naturally met Judy's parents at the rehearsal as well as at the wedding. Her dad was the senior sales manager at the venerable Chrysler-Dodge-Plymouth dealership on Van Ness. When I mentioned that Jeanette and I might be paying him a visit soon, as we would be needing a new car when we got married, he enthusiastically promised us a "terrific" deal.

Regarding our own wedding, the list of "must-haves" and "must-dos" was growing daily, all coming from sources other than Jeanette and me: tradition-dictated formulation and design of the formal and costly invitations, the seemingly endless list of people I didn't know who would be receiving them, registration for a china pattern (what the hell did we need bone china for?!) and a crystal glassware pattern, rental of that awful, stupid formalwear, the hiring of a photographer, a goddamn garter to throw, anything and everything to avoid keeping it simple, personal and genuine – and to avoid allowing Jeanette and me to be directly involved in choosing the style or the trappings of our own wedding; anything to avoid thinking that a wedding was supposed to be about love. The feeling of entrapment was growing. That's how it felt to me, but still nobody was asking.

Late one Friday evening after I got home from my pizza job – it was in early September, just under a month before the increasingly dreaded Big Day, and I'd already talked Jeanette to sleep and hung up – the phone rang. Assuming it was Jeanette again, I picked it up with a whispered "*Hi*". It wasn't Jeanette; it was Mary Lou. I was thrown completely off balance in astonishment. She said she was in town for some nurses' convention, and was pretty upset about Norm's marriage. She whimpered that she was all alone on a street corner somewhere up on Nob Hill and didn't know how to find her hotel and what could she do? I was too flustered to consider that I might just ask for her current location, then give her simple directions to her hotel. Instead, I told her to wait right there and I'd come and pick her up.

I'd had a soft spot in my heart (and a hard spot elsewhere) for Mary Lou since the first time I saw her in Oak Park, but now it was (I thought) a question of rescuing a damsel in distress out of pure gallantry, if not on a white steed then in a bashed-up white Corvair. In the time it took me to dress, jump in the car, and drive all the way to Nob Hill in the middle of the night, Mary Lou could have walked from where she was to her hotel and back a dozen times. The hotel was located halfway down Powell towards Market Street, and she was standing on a corner just a few blocks from Powell, on the same slope of Nob Hill, no more than five blocks away. (The Nob Hill area wasn't exactly seedy either.)

But I picked her up, and a minute later I found a parking space around the corner from her modest hotel. I'd forgotten how tall, lithesome, and doe-eyed she was. She asked me if I could please come up to talk – she was sharing a room with another nurse – but we could find a place to whisper, and we had a lot of catching up to do, and she had so many questions to ask about Norm and everything. I consented, feeling inexplicably nervous.

Inside the door to her room was a small vestibule with a door to the left to the bathroom (where we could whisper without waking her sleeping roommate in the bedroom through another door to the right). We tiptoed into the bathroom without turning on the light – there was sufficient light coming in through the large frosted bathroom window. She locked the door. I failed to notice that I'd parked my brain outside, around the corner.

The bathroom window was in a niche at least two feet deep, enough for her to climb into and sit comfortably. I stood in front of her. Her knees were at about the height of my hips and her lower legs dangled down from the ledge. Since we had to whisper, I kept close to the ledge, which meant that my groin was basically brushing against her knees which she moved slowly up and down, almost imperceptibly, not rhythmically, but with frequent adjustments of her position. At first, incredibly, I didn't even notice. Did she?

She did indeed have a lot to talk about and ask about. She was sad about Norm and wanted to know about the wedding and about Barbara, but I knew almost nothing myself. I told her that Norm was supposed to be the best man at my wedding coming up in a month, but that I hadn't been able to reach him or hadn't heard a word from him in months. I was beginning to have my doubts. (Decades later I would find out why. Norm was having an awful time, had just lost his job and was desperate. And he and Barbara were about to have a baby, born just a couple of weeks before Jeanette and I got married. I hadn't even known that Barbara was pregnant when they got married, much less that that was why.)

Once Mary Lou had all the information about Norm that I could possibly provide, she changed the subject. She said she'd always liked me very much too, and looked at me with those longing doe eyes, leaned forward slightly, separated her knees to bring me in closer, separated her lips and slowly planted them on mine. It didn't occur to me that I was being seduced. I had no thoughts at all anymore.

The customary cliché used to describe a progression of events characterized by irresponsible behavior is that "one thing led to another", which it did – Dad's sex advice to John was right on the money. After some minutes of increasingly sensual kissing, I unzipped her dress in the back, and she slid it off her shoulders while remaining seated on the window ledge. The dress fell down around her hips, as our mouths were locked together and she was reaching under my lips with her twirling tongue and sucking gently on mine. I unhooked her bra in the back and she whisked it away somewhere, raising her mouth from mine and arching her back to make sure my now freed mouth would find her breasts. After some minutes of euphoria, she pressed her body forward and flowed off the ledge, then stood pressing her pelvis against mine. I could make excuses (or simply delete this highly embarrassing story) and say that my initial acquiescence to her moves was a "cold feet" reaction to my imminent and dreaded wedding, or that it was a revolt against my powerlessness to shape how that wedding would be, but it would most likely be closer to the truth to say I lacked the character to think beyond that moment, and closer still to say I was an asshole.

At least, I reasoned (or rationalized later), we didn't have sex. The reason we didn't have sex was that when we reached the point where it was crystal-clear to me that she wanted to (her effortless removal of her girdle, her clinging to me while she was naked, and her copious wetness, which I felt with my trembling fingers, gave me those subtle clues, even though I remained fully clothed), I suddenly awoke from my trance, and asked myself what the hell I was doing. This sudden awakening and realignment of my moral position coincided with and was indubitably facilitated by the equally sudden explosion that had just taken place in my jeans.

I realized I had a brief window – a couple of minutes at best – before my raging libido would get me even deeper into a situation that my rational self didn't want. I awkwardly apologized to Mary Lou for doing most but not all of what we both wanted, hastily excused myself and hurried out, to my car. After all, I had to get up and go to work two and a half hours later.

I somehow got control of myself, managed to wake up after an hour's nap, got to work, and tried to banish the previous night's activities and near-activities from my mind. It would take me quite a long time to learn about the power of irrepressible memories.

Shortly thereafter, I got another late-evening phone call, this time from Los Angeles, from Linda. She told me she'd been moved by my letter and was sad, and she was down in LA visiting an aunt or somebody, and couldn't we please get together? Then she went into a long explanation of all she'd been through since high school – university somewhere, an unwanted and aborted pregnancy (before abortions were legal anywhere in the US), and some kind of protracted illness. I was feeling flabbergasted about all this sudden shower of attention from Mary Lou and Linda, the two girls I'd fallen for the hardest before meeting Jeanette (even though Mary Lou was more about lust than infatuation). And I realized more clearly than ever before that Jeanette was the one I wanted to spend my life with, the one for whom I could even endure the nightmare of a Catholic nuptial mass.

One or two Saturdays later (I think it was just a few days before my 21st birthday), I was heading for Jeanette's home on Seville Street after work, driving south in the heavy, high-speed traffic on the Bayshore Freeway. I got off as usual at the Geneva

Avenue exit, and hurried along Geneva to Munich Street. Seville, which didn't go through to Geneva, was one of several concentrically arced streets named after major European cities, and the arc of Munich was just outside the arc of Seville. I usually drove along Munich for three blocks to Cordova, then down a block to Seville.

This time, however, as I was slowly moving about halfway along Munich, steering slightly to the right the whole way to follow the arc, the Corvair suddenly only moved straight ahead. I jerked the steering wheel and nothing happened; it felt loose in my hands. I stopped the car in the middle of the small residential street – fortunately there were no other moving cars in either direction – and turned the steering wheel back and forth. There was no resistance; the car's wheels no longer obeyed. The steering wheel was as useless for steering a car as a lazy Susan.

I got out, sat down on the street, pulled with my hands as hard as I could on the inside of the right-hand side of the front wheel while pushing with my left leg as hard as I could on the outside of the left-hand side, in order turn the front wheels so I could work my way over to park along the curb. It took multiple steps and realignments to get there. Then I walked to Jeanette's home. Both Mike and Vic came out with me to have a look. If the car had had no other damage, it *might* have been worth repairing, but with its crumpled front end, this was clearly a case for the junkyard.

Somebody (I think it was Vic) had an extra car that Jeanette and I were able to borrow for a few days. We'd been planning to shop for a new car anyway, just as soon as we got married, but we weren't quite sure what to do for the immediate future. Then I remembered Judy's dad's offer. Jeanette and I got in touch with him, went down to the dealership on Van Ness. Judy's dad did indeed make us an offer we couldn't refuse: a brand-new (the outgoing year) Plymouth Valiant sedan for $2200, far less than we'd been expecting to pay for a decent used car, let alone for a new one. We were thrilled. Problem solved.

When Mom and Dad received their wedding invitation – the official printed one from Jeanette's parents – they wrote and told me they were hoping and praying they could come, but would like a personal request from me. They'd apparently forgotten my having already made *countless* written and verbal personal requests, starting when I first told them of our plans to marry, that I personally hoped they would come to our wedding. I had mixed feelings about having them come now, in view of their total lack of support for our marriage, their refusal to give their consent for the pre-21 wedding we'd originally hoped to have in June, their overt withholding of love towards Jeanette until she met their criteria, and Mom's propensity to ostentatiously display her profound disapproval of the normal behavior that non-Meeting people tended to enjoy – behavior that tends to be typical at weddings (even Biblical ones!), like drinking and dancing. I was frankly afraid they would make a scene if they came.

My brothers and their wives were coming (without personal invitations from me), as were crazy Aunt Marion and her two children (my cousins Winnie and Sterling, with spouses), whom I'd never had any contact with as an adult. I figured that it was quite possible that Aunt Marion might make a scene, but it's one thing if the groom's whacky aunt makes a scene, and quite another matter if the groom's mother does.

Aunt Marion *did* make a scene at the reception. She huffed and puffed her disapproval, sneered her rage, stuck her nose in the air and marched out in a flurry of outrage that went largely unnoticed. I have no memory of how or when Winnie and Sterling left the reception, nor of speaking with either of them.

But Mom somehow seemed to think they had a bargaining position and were now making their presence contingent on a further repetition of my explicit and personal welcome, my insistence that they come, despite their persistent refusal to grant us their approval. I concluded that while I would never tell them *not* to come, I earnestly hoped they wouldn't. They were offering me a cat-and-mouse game that I refused to play – and they didn't come. (Mom would keep telling me reproachfully many times over the years to come how they were waiting "with our bags packed" for that personal plea from me, until I finally got fed up with her whining about it and told her exactly why that plea never came, and how her sister Marion had behaved.)

Nor did Norm get in touch. With the wedding just weeks away without a word of contact from him, I asked Vic to be my best man, and Jim to be a man of honor. Marilyn was Jeanette's maid of honor, and she had three other bridesmaids: her sister Rosanne, her friend Carol and her cousin Maureen.

Jeanette and I found a pleasant and affordable apartment at #10 Pueblo Street, on the third floor of a small, three-storey apartment building, a couple of blocks off Geneva, not far from the Cow Palace.[8] The first floor was, in the usual manner of San Francisco dwellings, devoted to storage lockers and the garage. There were two apartments each on the second and third floors. Our apartment seemed huge to me after Fred's garage, but probably seemed small to Jeanette after the house on Seville. It was ours from October 1st, which gave us more than a week before our wedding to start moving things in so we would have a place to come home to after our honeymoon. Fred Bito kindly let me keep my room on Evergreen for the extra week, without rent.

Following the instructions of Jeanette's urgently middle-class family, we purchased a five-piece walnut bedroom set consisting of a queen-size bed, two night tables, a dresser with mirror and a chest of drawers. We'd already picked out and ordered our living-room set as well (a three-seat green-and-yellowish, brocade-ish upholstered sofa and matching armchair, two end tables and a coffee table, as well as a couple of monstrous table lamps), and had them delivered to our apartment days before the wedding. Our bedroom was small (but at least twice the size of my room on Evergreen); the living room was a bit larger than the bedroom; and there was a proper kitchen with space enough for a small Formica table where the two of us could sit for meals. There was also a small bathroom with a tub, as well as a fairly spacious storage locker on the ground floor, at the back of the garage.

Once again, putting up my paintings on the walls transformed the place into home – for Jeanette too. In addition to *Man with Guitar* and *Bottle*, I now had *The City*, which I'd had to leave in Oak Park. (Mom and Dad brought with them when they visited me en route to the LA Conference in December 1965.)

We weren't quite sure what to do about a honeymoon. Because of my parents' refusal to condone our marriage, we'd felt obliged to postpone a June wedding until a few weeks into the fall term (my own fault, as it turned out). Taking off more than a week was out of the question. We had little money, but we did want to go somewhere special, memorable, and to get away. There was heavy competition among several airlines for flights along the West Coast. We thought of Mexico (Jeanette was eager to visit other countries), but that was still too expensive. Canada – Vancouver – was close enough and cheap enough, yet sounded sufficiently exotic to both of us. Neither of us had ever been to Vancouver before and knew nothing about it; Jeanette had never even been

---

8 See drawing of the apartment in Appendix 1.

to Canada. Since United had budget shuttle flights to Vancouver, we decided that would be great. October being the off-season, we didn't think it would be necessary to make any hotel reservations (an arduous task in the days before the internet!). There was sure to be something; plane reservations would be enough.

The wedding day came, with blue skies and pleasantly balmy San Francisco temperatures. I was being herded around, told when to do what, mostly by Vic and Jim, who in turn were being told what to do, and what to tell me to do, by Rose and Marilyn. I felt like an empty barrel in a churning rapids, a man in a waterfall. I was in a complete daze getting through the hour-long nuptial mass at Epiphany; I just stood and kneeled and stood and kneeled as prompted, repeating words the priest told me to say. I wasn't saying anything *to* Jeanette and hardly heard what she said to me. It was like a bad dream I had to smile through, and I just wanted it to be over.

When the long, numbing, dumbing nuptial mass finally ended, and we emerged into the sunlight, we were again shuttled into position for a series of photographs, me feeling unreal in my rented gear, Jeanette beautiful despite the huge and elaborate white gown and all the make-up she'd been encouraged to wear (which I'd never seen her wear before). It all felt like an act, a masquerade, with uncreative scenography and choreography commanded by persons unknown. And then we were herded into cars to head for the Longshoreman's union hall at Fisherman's Wharf for the reception. All I needed was a couple of drinks. I'd had almost no part in making the arrangements, the choice of venue, the menu, the music, the guests, the apparel, nothing. Of course Jeanette was the center of attention, as it should be, but she also felt in many ways that she was just along for the ride. And I was just along for hers.

I know there was plenty to eat and drink. It was almost certainly good. I know there was dancing, and that I faked my way through the dances that were obligatory for me – including the first dance with Jeanette. She waltzed and I moved back and forth doing my best to avoid stepping on her feet or her dress while showing off all my non-existent dancing skills to everyone present. There were more traditions to fulfil: an awkward and mandatory dance with Rose, throwing Jeanette's garter for outlandish reasons whose origins nobody seemed to know, throwing her bouquet, possibly throwing other things.

I knew few of the relatively many guests from Jeanette's side, apart from her immediate family. (Michael was in Vietnam and didn't come.) From my side, it was John and Marj, Al and Nancy, and then Marion and her two kids (in their 30s). I remember that crazy Aunt Marion actually *stormed* out of the reception at an early stage, due to her outrage at the booze and dancing. Although these were explicitly the kinds of merriment Jesus contributed to at Caana, they were contradictorily the kinds of merriment that were wont to make my family and their Meeting ilk huff and puff for Christ's sake. Aunt Marion behaved in precisely the way I expected she would, which was in turn precisely the way I feared my mom would have behaved if she'd come – unless she started weeping and preaching instead, which would have been far worse. Mom's attitude, as expressed in her anniversary diary, made my parents' position pretty clear: "*May the Lord turn Stan's dark heart to see the light so he will be interested in his wife's salvation.*" (I was unaware that Joseph Conrad might have had someone like me in mind for one of his novels.) I was *greatly* relieved that they didn't come. I don't remember any speeches, but there may well have been a couple, or many, or none.

To me, a celebration had always entailed great, effervescent joy, whooping it up a little, uninhibited happiness. Our wedding felt to me like following rules, sticking to a script. But at last, at some point during the "celebrations", it was time for Jeanette and me to change out of our wedding costumes and take our leave to catch our plane. I have no memory of how we got to the airport (one or more of our siblings presumably drove us there), or of checking in, or of the flight taking off in the early evening. It felt like Jeanette and I had hardly spoken to each other all day. The noise level at the reception and our nerves throughout the day were not exactly conducive to normal conversation, much less anything affectionate, much less anything passionate or intimate. We were both exhausted and didn't try to talk much above the roar of the engines.

When we arrived at the Vancouver airport, it was raining. We splurged and asked a taxi driver to take us to a hotel downtown. The driver wanted to know which hotel. We didn't know, we said, any nice one that's not too ritzy. We took off towards downtown Vancouver, nerves about "doing it" for the first time again adding to our obscured perceptions. When we got to what was obviously the downtown area, our driver pulled up to a Holiday Inn (back in the day before they rebranded from their lower-end budget image) or a TraveLodge or some other chain with a name we recognized. He asked if it would be OK. We said it would be fine. We got out into the rain, got our bags from the trunk, paid the fare and hurried in to find the reception. No vacancy. The taxi had already gone. The receptionist made a couple of suggestions of other hotels or motels "nearby", and we headed off into the rainy night again, this time on foot, without umbrellas, carrying bags that had no wheels or shoulder straps, frustrated, beginning to sweat, thus becoming ever wetter both inside and outside our clothing. On our third try, we finally got a room.

The wedding night was pretty much of a disaster. Lots of marital advice books caution newlyweds not to expect the earth to move on the wedding night. Ours felt more like we'd been hit by an earthmover. We were worn out, nervous, frustrated, irritable, soaking, everything one shouldn't be and everything no one ever is on wedding nights in the movies.

I knew that Jeanette was a virgin and afraid; I was far from experienced and hardly fearless myself. We were pretty clear about the what-goes-where-and-how parts, but we weren't feeling much of the why right then. Jeanette understandably wanted to have a towel beneath her, to avoid embarrassment when they came to make up our bed in the morning. The towel wasn't the softest or sexiest; I didn't want to use a condom, but had to, to avoid the risk of immediate pregnancy, which happened to Marilyn. Like the wedding itself, get-it-over-and-done-with was the dominant feeling accompanying our fumbling attempts to make something worthy of calling love.

My parents' tacit opposition, the wedding experience itself, and two years of a no-sex taboo had taken a considerable toll on our relationship. We would now start to repair that damage, because we both knew that the love that was still in there somewhere had somehow survived the wedding.

CHAPTER 6

Escapades and other escapes

When we woke up in Vancouver on the Sunday morning after our wedding night, we actually looked at – and actually saw – each other. It seemed like it was for the first time in days, probably even weeks. The documents, witnesses and ceremonies merely proved that we were "married" in the eyes of the law and that Holy fucking Church. What mattered to us now was making each other happy, bringing joy and fulfillment to each other's lives, finding our own path together, building a future.

We were already able to laugh, even if nervously, about the previous night's fiasco. Jeanette was somewhat sore, and I was sufficiently sensitive and understanding not to require any convincing or persuasion that she needed to heal a little before we could begin to experience our now-sanctioned intimacy properly. Yet it felt to me that both of us had been hornier every evening for the better part of two years on her parents' front porch than we were now in our marital bed. Although it would gradually change, at this point we were suddenly more like friends than lovers.

We started to explore the downtown area together. Vancouver itself was almost as flat as Chicago, and was clean and beautiful. But immediately to the north of the narrow strait that formed the northern boundary of the city, there were mountain peaks, some of them tinged with snow. Back then there were few tall buildings to obstruct the view. We were enthralled by Vancouver, but for some reason we both immediately wanted something more, something else. We found a tourist office and discovered we could take a bus from downtown to the exotic-sounding harbor at Tsawwassen (exotic in name only), and from there take a ferry over to Swartz Bay on Vancouver Island, then take another fairly short bus ride to the provincial capital of Victoria, where we'd allegedly find a fabulous old hotel called The Empress. We bought the tickets for the next day and booked three nights at The Empress. Then our strolls in the downtown area took us to Georgia Street, past the venerable Hotel Vancouver, and on into the lobby. We liked the look of it and booked a room there for the last two nights of our honeymoon.

There were few tourists in Vancouver or Victoria in October (and far fewer inhabitants back then), in spite of the bright, almost balmy autumnal weather that alternated with days of rain. In Victoria, it felt like we had the huge Empress to ourselves, or maybe we just lost track of other people, the way we almost lost track of each other in the weeks leading up to, as well as during, our wedding.

We took a half-day excursion to the stunningly beautiful Butchart Gardens, set in an old quarry north of Victoria. It rained lightly all day that day, and we didn't mind a bit. Victoria itself was tranquil and dignified, so peaceful it almost felt like it had been perfected and then frozen in time. It also felt strangely British, or at least trying hard to be, despite the surroundings that were largely wilderness. On our last day, we took a bus to the edge of town to visit a replica of Shakespeare's birthplace (it was closed for the season). From Victoria, Jeanette wrote an irony-toothed postcard to Mom and Dad: *"Sorry you were unable to make it to the wedding."*

Back on the mainland, our experience at the majestic and venerable Hotel Vancouver was like at the Empress – and everything the motel of our first two nights was not. We had spectacular views of the mountains; we were told that it was the edge of a vast wilderness stretching as far north as north itself, yet close to a fairly pulsating city. We'd more or less picked Vancouver out of a hat as our honeymoon destination, but we agreed that we could hardly have picked a place we'd have liked better – certainly not on our budget.

Sex remained pretty much of a disappointment for both of us throughout our honeymoon. Perhaps the frustrations of all that religion-imposed, wait-until-we're-married crap contributed to unreasonably high expectations. Our almost total lack of experience (apart from my drunken revelries one night more than two years before) certainly didn't help, nor did our prudery make the need for me to wear a condom less awkward. It's unlikely that Jeanette got any more sex education than I did, which was next to none. We didn't know how to talk to each other about it, how to tell each other what we wanted or didn't, what felt good or not, how to express desire in that snowballing way that builds and stokes ever-greater passion. As a result, the honeymoon was totally lacking in the cunicular behavior that might otherwise have played a key role in making our honeymoon blissful.

We returned home to San Francisco to the news that the US had started a major bombing attack on North Vietnam, which of course ignited even more vociferous protests in various places around the nation, and raised the family's anxiety level about the welfare of Michael, whose location over there was unknown. (Our mailing address for him had nothing to do with his actual geographical location.) Where I was directly concerned, it also raised the level of anxiety about increases in the conscription rate, combined with the lowering of induction criteria and subsequent cancellation of deferments. Jeanette and I began talking about a need for contingency plans.

Returning home from our honeymoon also meant the start of our cohabitation at number 10 Pueblo Street, and all the major adjustments in daily life it would mean for each of us – in nearly opposite ways. I was now sharing living quarters with someone, after having lived alone for nearly two years; Jeanette was now sharing her quarters with *only* one person, instead of three or four, and hadn't experienced sharing with a *new* person since her kid sister was born. And we were both sharing a bed with someone, and would wake up with that someone, for the first time ever. Our respective habits and quirks quickly began coming to each other's attention and acceptance. New routines began to evolve on their own, or had to be invented.

In the physical sense, our apartment required no painting or wallpapering, but we didn't yet have all the things we wanted to make it feel like home. I decided to build a couple of bookcases to house all the books I was acquiring, largely through the unwitting largesse of The Emporium, others from prowling around cheap second-hand bookstores all over San Francisco. I also purchased a few new ones at full price at the college bookstore.

I got to use Jeanette's parents' garage, as well as Mike's tools, for my first real adventure in carpentry. My bookcase design was simple enough – two uprights about two and a half feet apart, and seven shelves between them, including a top piece and a plywood back for stability. With the help of Mike's router – a tool I'd never used before – I decided I'd try to make an impressive piece of furniture by routing out grooves in the inner sides of the uprights, slightly less than the width of the shelves, but of the shelf thickness, so as not to have the joints show from the front. Then I would simply insert the shelves from the back and glue or screw them in place. I measured carefully, then made nice clean grooves of exactly the right depth. But when I began to assemble the bookcase, I encountered a slight problem: on the one upright I discovered that I'd measured for the grooves from the top, and on the other from the bottom. Unless I wanted a bookcase with slightly diagonal shelves, I would have to get myself another upright and start over; Mike seemed to be struggling to minimize the look of derision on his face.

On the first day of the autumn semester in my course on modern British literature, Dr Robin Gajdusek claimed that we would find one of the most pervasive metaphors of modern literature to be the concept of synthesis, or lack of it, which he illustrated with the opening lines of W.B. Yeats' poem *The Second Coming*:

> *Turning and turning in the widening gyre*
> *The falcon cannot hear the falconer;*
> *Things fall apart; the centre cannot hold;*
> *Mere anarchy is loosed upon the world [...]*

I certainly felt like a falcon, soaring and solitary. I was just becoming aware of all the would-be falconers who'd always been seeking to entice and rein me in: my parents, Keith Sartorius, the Selective Service, as well as all the purveyors of fad and fashion, this-is-the-way-it's-done traditions, hypocritical middle-class morality and barbaric Biblical injunctions. I wasn't at all convinced that anarchy was a rational alternative, but exactly what need does a falcon have of falconers? Why not just fly free?

"*Principle doesn't relate to the individual*," Dr Gajdusek noted. "*Listening to one's inner voice, and being governed by it, relates to nothing else.*" There is no absolute, only dislocation – a torrent in the mind without words, no language to express the mental seething. And yet many of the late 19th and early 20th century poets we studied seemed to me to have found that language quite well. Wilfred Owen, in his poem *Dulce Et Decorum Est*, captured with chilling precision "the old lie", not only about the so-called Great War, but also about war in general. To me, it was scathingly pertinent about Vietnam.

Dr Gajdusek inflamed my passion for seeking out the symbolism in literature, from Thomas Hardy and D.H. Lawrence to Joseph Conrad, E.M. Forster, Virginia Woolf, and my first real introduction to James Joyce, all of whom became instant favorites. Overlapping that course I had another course surveying the "late period" of English (British and American) literature. I was thus becoming well immersed in this period. And I was fortunate to find that most of these authors' works were available in the book department at The Emporium....

As much as I enjoyed modern literature, I somehow felt that the place where all ladders started was the Bard. I'd been amply rewarded for every effort I'd made to work my way through a few of Shakespeare's plays, and now at last I had an entire course devoted to tackling many more. The plots that grabbed me by the throat – the profound tragedies of *Lear* and *Othello* – as well as the histories and comedies, were all cloaked in the most beautiful and witty language ("wit" in the sense of Alexander Pope's lines: *"True wit is nature to advantage dress'd,/ What oft was thought but ne'er so well express'd"*). My unusual background in King James' English enabled me to handle the form without difficulty and go directly for the content, letting the pure pleasure of it flow straight into my mind and heart.

Throughout the autumn, Jeanette wrote anxious, chatty letters to Michael and sent him stuff – cassette tapes with music, books, candy – just about every week. As far as I know, she was the only one in the family who strived to maintain anywhere near that level of contact. Nobody else talked about him much, at least not until Jeanette brought up the subject. It was a topic that made her family nervous and emotional, and they seemed to believe that one should avoid such feelings – and therefore such topics – at all costs. Jeanette paid a high price for her efforts. She became increasingly moody, often brooding, sometimes outraged at this or that or me.

The first time she screamed at me was the first time anyone close to me had ever screamed at me, and I was appalled and distressed, not knowing where or to whom I could turn. I was trying to make sense of it, to analyze it, to find the reasons for it, but since it was irrational, looking for rational explanations was fruitless. Not knowing what to do, I retreated to the bathroom. I was so upset, I was sweating profusely, so I decided to take a bath. All the while she was screaming angrily. I slipped my head down under the water to mute the sound and found it peaceful. While I was doing that, and not responding to her, she rushed in and dragged me up, thinking I was drowning myself. Her rage ceased abruptly.

But apart from occasional and totally unpredictable outbursts of rage or inbursts of brooding, she was often playful and happy. She was developing a real thirst for knowledge – reading many of my textbooks and literature and discussing them with me, trying to find out as much as possible about the miserable escalating war, taking cooking classes – and becoming increasingly hostile towards her parents for their having discouraged and dismissed her budding academic interests years before we met.

We went to her parents' two or three times a week for a couple of hours, but we were always happy to come back to *our* new home, where our own routines were slowly developing. Friday evenings were real end-of-the-work-week evenings for Jeanette, but since I started work disgustingly early most Saturday mornings, I didn't have quite the same feelings of freedom about them. Most Friday evenings, Jeanette would make delicious toasted sandwiches with bacon, lettuce and tomato, with just a touch of mayonnaise, and we'd have them on our couch, in front of our black-and-white TV. We mostly watched stupid programs, but the fascination I had with nearly anything that moved on a television screen hadn't entirely worn off since my prohibitionist Oak Park days.

The range of merchandise I was taking home from The Emporium was expanding beyond my own clothing and my rapidly growing collection of books. I also started getting nice clothes for Jeanette. Once I figured out her size and taste, I got her a couple of new outfits every week – and The Emporium offered a vast selection. Towels and sheets were no longer in short supply in our home. Gifts for family members? As long as they weren't too bulky, I always managed to get a terrific deal: fur collars for Mom and Rose, a sweater for Dad's birthday, things to send to Michael, and nearly all our Christmas presents. Jeanette seemed to find it as thrilling as I did; we were some sort of precursor to Bonny and Clyde (the film didn't come out until the end of 1967). And she loved the clothes that were coming her way.

Although I was getting a bigger and bigger kick out of it, and getting bolder all the time, I didn't like to use the word *stealing*. (Maybe I should have used larceny – Larson E – my middle name and last initial!) So I used all kinds of euphemisms, the type one hears in movies or TV dramas to glamorize cat burglars and sophisticated art thieves: pilfer, lift, swipe, filch, pinch, plunder, misappropriate, purloin or the five-finger discount. The risks were enormous and growing, and the stakes were monstrous, but I gave them no more thought than I gave to the traffic on North Avenue when I plunged into it to become Jimmy Brown scoring touchdowns while fetching the evening *Tribune*.

I was pretty good at rationalizing things, which basically meant using words to convince myself that my stupid actions were smart ones, thus having little to do with rationality – or morality. I told myself that by filching from The Emporium I was beating the Establishment: that nameless, faceless conglomeration of what was being called the industrial-military complex that for me included draft boards, decadent Emporium executives, lesson-giving priests, snobby exploiters of the poor, politicians hell-bent on foisting war on whomever they chose, racist bastards, grumpy grandfathers, holier-than-thou Meeting idiots, corrupt cops, phony-pitch-writing encyclopedia peddlers, and any other candidates that pissed me off on any particular day. I also told myself that I wasn't hurting anybody, except possibly depriving a few unrighteously wealthy Emporium stakeholders of some extra pocket change to spend on their opulent Marin County mansions. And I believed it. So did Jeanette. There might even have been an element of truth in it, in a convoluted, unlawful sort of way.

I had certainly lost my moral compass; or discovered that my old one had been *im*moral, based on now-obvious lies about a loving god, a sweet land of liberty, and a society that safeguarded the fundamental needs of all its members. Some day I would have to start finding a new compass.

Highly efficient stockroom worker that I was, I also developed a highly efficient method for siphoning off the merchandise I wanted. My isolated 5 AM Saturday starting time was the key. It was then I presumed I was on my own in the entire store for nearly two hours, with access to almost anything, anywhere in the store, as I swiftly pulled and pushed truck after truck of merchandise out to the correct departments. Since I worked fast, there was time left over for me to have a quick look around in every department, at anything that might be of interest to Jeanette and me. Size was the only limitation. I could then make my selections, placing what I wanted onto the one truck I would take back to the second-floor stockroom with me before anyone else arrived for work. I stashed my items on obscure shelves or, in the case of the books (not in the bookcase), on the floor under one of the shelf racks.

I could then conceal one round of merchandise at a time under my clothing, whisk it out of the store, hurry to my car parked a couple of blocks away, and deposit it there on my morning coffee break. My next round was at lunchtime, and a third round was when I left work in the afternoon. Then there were two rounds on each of my evening shifts. That worked out to be a lot of merchandise I was getting away with every week.

I usually just wore the men's clothing out of the building, under my loose-fitting, greenish-gray raincoat, walking right past the security guard just two feet away from me as I exited the building via the employees' entrance. Two or three shirts at a time was no challenge. A couple of sweaters or a sport coat or suit jacket were amazingly easy. Pants (unless I was exchanging a worn-out pair for new ones) had to be folded up and tucked under my belt, inside the pants I was wearing, and then I had to suck in my belly and lean forward slightly as I prepared to leave the building without showing any bulge. And I took care to adopt the same forward-leaning posture on entering and re-entering the building as well, just in case. (I must have looked like Groucho Marx!) Shoes involved the same procedure, as did handbags for Jeanette, who began to acquire a small collection of bags in luxurious alligator. By Christmas 1966, we'd begun to attain a standard of living – as least in terms of the clothes we wore – that no longer bore any relationship to our paltry incomes. And it only got better throughout the spring of '67.

Being well-trained as a loner, I didn't feel compelled to boast of my triumphs to anyone; Jeanette was the only one who knew, although her family may have sensed that something was going on, along the lines of Mike's relatively rare fell-off-the-back-of-a-truck bargains. But I never breathed a word of it to anyone. Even when a bunch of my workmates were describing a few minor feats of their own, I didn't allow myself to get drawn into a contest that I would easily have won. And when I brought the second round of six pairs of high-quality slacks and suit pants to a tailor to have the lengths adjusted, and he looked at my otherwise highly non-Kuppenheimer personal style and asked something about the back of a truck, I just smiled uncomprehendingly at his insinuations.

Michael was supposed to be coming home in February or March, if he survived that long. His letters told nothing at all about where he was or what he was doing; they probably would have been censored if he'd indicated any such stuff. He was to some extent aware of the growing opposition to the War at home, but the information he got may have been filtered and slanted too. We suspected he was doing everything possible just to keep his head down and survive. Several thousand young American men had already fled to Canada, whose extradition treaties with the US didn't cover draft-dodging or desertion. In January, newspapers reported about a few army guys who deserted to Sweden ("*Just like Orr in* Catch-22," I thought), but that kind of action was never going to be Michael's.

In the meantime, Jeanette was engaged in the first of several cooking classes she took together with her friend Elsie, in order to broaden her repertoire from an already impressive range of Italian dishes she learned from her mother. She was vivaciously ambitious and seemed to love preparing new Mexican, French and Chinese creations for me every week, and I loved eating them. She was becoming a marvelous cook.

The only perceivable problem between us was her occasional bouts of nearly insane jealousy, sometimes triggered by my involuntarily letting my eyes rest a split-second too long on a pretty girl; sometimes because I listened with as much attentive amusement as she did to the rhythmic thumping sounds and moans occasionally coming from the bedroom in the apartment below us; and sometimes for no perceptible reason at all. Perhaps both of us naively thought that a wedding ceremony would somehow magically bestow immunity from attraction to anyone else. I realized she probably felt some underlying insecurity, and I probably had a problem with unfulfilled lust, but neither of us understood ourselves enough to have a clue about what was going on or knew how to deal with it. Jeanette had no sympathy for the don't-care-where-he-gets-his-appetite-as-long-as-he-eats-at-home point of view. However, she usually knew when she'd gone too far, when her jealous rage drove me crazy to the point of my becoming distraught. Then she would back off, and it would be over for a while.

Once or twice she made a remark (or a slip of the tongue) about how her father could be "pretty rough", but I wasn't sure whether he'd been rough with Jeanette, or if she'd witnessed her mom or siblings being treated roughly. She refused to talk about it or clarify any further.

America's escalation of the War continued, and the obvious need for more and more troops sharply contradicted the Pentagon's claims of imminent victory and lopsided enemy body counts, which apparently included Vietnamese civilians. In April, Muhammad Ali was stripped of his heavyweight boxing titles for refusing to be drafted, and suddenly "brash young Cassius" became a real champion to me and many others. Dodging the draft through deferments and appeals was one thing, but would I be willing to take a stand like that against the War if all my appeals were rejected? Did I have the guts to do what Ali was doing?

The number of young men being drafted seemed to be increasing daily, and it meant a near certainty of being shipped off to Vietnam, as in the case of Michael. Student deferments were becoming harder to get, but for the time being, my heavy course load and good grades kept me out of danger. Rumors were flying around (if you were married, you'd be OK; then no, you wouldn't, only if you had kids) and were constantly changing.

There weren't that many options available to me, as far as I could see. The first would be to wait to get drafted and sent to an insane and unjust war in Vietnam, where I might have to kill or be killed. If the former, it would be something I'd have to live with, without any guarantees that I could. If the latter, no more options on anything, ever again. The second option was to refuse to be drafted, like Ali, who in June was sentenced to five years in federal prison. Or I could desert once I was in the army, which might be much more difficult and for which punishment would be much more severe. (Although it hadn't been used for such a crime since 1945, the death penalty was still on the books.) The third and final option would be exile. It was becoming widely known that more and more draft-eligible young Americans were heading for a new life in Canada. Although they would not face extradition, I never heard anything about a statute of limitations for draft evasion. The period of exile thus could and probably would last a lifetime.

A lot of people – still the majority of Americans, including all the fat cats who managed to pull strings to keep their sons out of the War – derided draft-dodgers and deserters as cowards. They clearly had no clue about how much courage it takes to be a Muhammad Ali or a deserter or a draft-dodger and stand up to an incredibly powerful Establishment against a stupid and wrongful war, to face a harsh prison sentence or to leave behind everything and everyone you've ever known, possibly never to return.

Just as my unusual upbringing gave me an advantage in understanding Shakespeare, and in unintentionally teaching me – obliging me – to question what I was told, I had one further advantage: by having been forced to be an outsider, I'd already torn up most of my roots when I left Oak Park and had few left. In that sense, I wasn't new to the game.

For the first time ever, I found the spring 1967 term at San Francisco State to be a lot more boring than what was going on in the real world – both the external one and its war and struggle for civil rights, and my internal one with its chaos of major changes, risks and decisions. I took a humanities course, but it seemed like a hippie-style parody of courses, a hippy-dippy absurdist joke. I quickly figured out how to play the game and get an A, but it taught me absolutely nothing. My philosophy courses covered Descartes, Leibnitz and Spinoza – potentially exciting stuff – but I got much more out of simply reading the writings of the philosophers themselves than anything the classroom sessions had to contribute.

Two of my English courses – one covering Jacobean and Caroline literature, the other covering Augustan literature – were supposed to offer greater depth than the other courses I'd already had, which touched upon the likes of Dryden, Defoe and their contemporaries. But they didn't. The former began with a look at the King James Bible (I'd heard of it). I remember astonishing the professor with my analysis of the metaphor about the effects of aging on the human body in Ecclesiastes 12 that he seemed to know astonishingly little about. Of course Dryden *et al* were masters of their craft, but I'd already gone into more depth with them on my own in connection with the previous introductory courses. Not much was new there.

My so-called junior seminar did provide a stimulating forum for more in-depth literary analyses. My assignment covered an interesting cross-section: a Shakespeare sonnet, a Robert Frost poem, a Wallace Stevens poem (my first encounter with that poet), a short story by James Joyce, a short novel by Henry Fielding, and a play by Bertolt Brecht. I realized I got a great deal more out of trying to figure out an author's explicit and implicit messages in a work than I got out of studying the author's biography (not to mention what the critics of the author or the critics of the author's biographers might have had to say about the literature that it was all about in the first place). An *auto*biography might have been a different story – or am I biased by what I'm currently working on?

The one course in the spring of '67 that I fully enjoyed was a study of literature and society – how a number of authors, starting with Dickens, used their art to render scathing portrayals of the contemporary societal wrongs. In *Pickwick Papers*, Dickens attacked the courts, the newspapers, the prisons and just about every social institution of his time. From the mines of Zola's *Germinal* to the would-be manipulators of Ellis' *Invisible Man*, to the library steps of Amis' *Lucky Jim*, writers were playing key roles in illuminating tragedies and satirizing absurdities.

Of particular and immediate interest to me was Remarque's *All Quiet on the Western Front*, a short novel of the First World War about which I wrote a term paper titled "War and the Individual". My paper included intimations of personal observations:

> *The war into which the individual is thrust will continue to control his life even if it fails to take his life. [...] It destroys his values and his morals. It destroys his hopes. It destroys his relations with others. It destroys the individual as an individual, and finally, war may destroy his life.*

I wrote that paper not long after Michael returned from Vietnam. The family's sense of relief was enormous. Michael still had all his limbs and appendages, his eyesight and his hearing. There were no broken bones, no cuts, no wounds or other scars, at least nothing visible.

If Michael seemed laconic before he left, his reticence not only survived the war, but was greatly strengthened by it, except that it didn't come across as the strong, silent, Gary Cooper type of non-verbosity. Naturally, everyone in the family had loads of questions to ask about Vietnam. *What was it like over there?* It was all right. *Did you see any action?* Naw, we were just in a base camp. *Did you make any friends?* Not really. *Did you ever feel you were in danger?* C'mon, can we talk about something else now?!

Michael broke into a cold sweat, an almost Pavlovian response, at the mere mention of *Vietnam*. No probing was allowed. No information was forthcoming. Most of the time, he parked himself on the easy chair in front of the TV in the Seville Street living room and watched one sitcom or gameshow after another. If anyone outside the immediate family came to the house, he would instantly retreat to his room upstairs, shut the door and spend hours reading and listening to music. Simon and Garfunkel were particular favorites. He retreated there more and more frequently, as questions from the immediate family persisted.

He had no interest in resuming his studies at San Francisco State, in biology or any other -ology, nor did he show any interest in getting a job. He seemed to have no friends or even acquaintances and he never went out. The photos he'd taken in Vietnam were all in the form of slides, and he said he didn't want to show them to anyone until he'd organized them, which he showed no interest in doing. Looking at him from across a room, one would probably have no idea that anything was amiss. He looked pretty much like a normal guy, except for the cold sweat that burst forth every time *Vietnam* was uttered.

His parents didn't know what to do, and like most parents (like most *people*) they didn't *want* to think anything was wrong. They decided the best thing would be to give him some space, not to push him into anything. There was no follow-up from the army, no counseling, no shrink. It's possible that such things were offered and that Michael declined them, but he got no help. PSTD had not yet been identified and went untreated. Michael and probably tens of thousands like him were never included among the statistics of the casualties of the Vietnam War. Similarities to Paul Bäumer were remarqueable. (Sometimes, no matter how grave the situation, I find punning irresistible. I apologize to unknown readers for any unintended offense and to others unfamiliar with the works of Erich Maria Remarque.)

In Stockholm in May, the international Russell Tribunal (mostly comprising

Western doctors, historians, scientists, legal experts and celebrities) publicly condemned US aggression in Vietnam. Although the tribunal was not part of the Swedish government, it seemed to have its tacit support, and was the first time I'd heard of anyone on "our" side of the Cold War condemning "our" actions. The right-wing media was huffing and puffing about outsiders sticking their noses into what didn't concern them, failing to realize that a war does concern peace-loving people everywhere, and that getting involved in another country's actions by issuing a condemnation of their violence could be considered preferable to and less invasive than actually invading and bombing another country.

Anti-war demonstrations throughout the US, especially in Berkeley and San Francisco, were intensifying. At the same time, there were race riots in Tampa and Cincinnati, as frustrations about America's racial oppression continued. On June 5th, Israel launched what would come to be known as the Six-Day War, which included an attack on the *USS Liberty* in the Mediterranean, killing 34. But the Israelis were our friends. And China got the H-bomb.

(The news that spring wasn't all bad. Like a parenthesis among all the war bulletins, the State of Tennessee repealed the Butler Act, which had criminalized the teaching of evolution in the schools that had led to the infamous Monkey Trial. And the US Supreme Court at last struck down all legal bans on interracial marriages.)

The school year was at an end; I had just one year left on my Bachelor's degree. Then it would be grad school for a number of years, and presumably an equal number of years of extension of my student deferment. Since I saw a clear path ahead, including only slightly more than normal course loads for my final two semesters, I decided to skip night classes that summer too. Besides, the perks of working full-time at The Emporium that summer would give me all the excitement I needed. Fortunately, summer evenings in San Francisco could be quite cool, and sometimes rainy. It would thus be perfectly normal for me to bring my trusty raincoat with me to work every day.

Jeanette and I did manage to take some vacation time that summer. As soon as school was out, we went camping in the wilderness of the Rogue River National Forest on the slopes of Crater Lake in Oregon. Neither of us had any experience of camping (except for a few nights I'd spent in a couple of middle-class Oak Park backyards as a kid). We bought a couple of sleeping bags and some mosquito netting and a few provisions. I also had a large and beautiful Bowie knife, courtesy of The Emporium, to fend off whatever might need fending off.

The scenery along our way north was wonderful, with the pine and cedar forests, mountain ranges, and spectacular volcanic mountains, such as Mount Shasta, that are found at irregular intervals all the way up the American West Coast.

The beauty and wonder of the mountains, rushing rivers and wilderness woodlands increased as we entered Oregon, and by the time we saw the signs for Rogue River, it was sensational. As the road started to climb the slopes of Crater Lake, the early summer gradually receded into spring and then into early spring, with a good deal of crusty snow remaining along the sides of the roads, until we reached an almost deserted campsite in the Rogue River National Forest. It lay along one side of the raging river itself, a turbulent torrent of rapids and waterfalls that raced along one of the old lava flows from Crater Lake. Stones of both lava and pumice were to be found in abundance. If only I'd learned a bit about minerology, I'd probably have seen much more.

Individual campsites had been set up in the woods by the Park Service, each with a parking place, picnic table, wood-burning stove, and campfire pit. In several locations at the site there were generous supplies of split cedar and pine logs, all provided free of charge. The entire campsite was empty except for one camper parked at the far end. Nobody else was in sight. The whole place was as perfect a campsite as we would ever see.

On getting out of the car, we could feel a thick soft carpet of needles beneath our boots, smell the cedars and pines in the crisp, cold air, as well as the faint smell of our sole distant neighbor's campfire. The roar of the river – just some 40 feet from where we parked – drowned out most other sounds except for a single "*Aaarooo*!" from the direction of the camper. If we'd been anywhere near the sea, we would have guessed it was a seal. Instead, it turned out to be a basset hound, and its single cry sufficed to alert its master, an elderly, slightly grizzled outdoorsman who opened the door on the side of his camper to have a look at what was happening outdoors. When he saw that he was no longer alone at the campsite, he extended one arm towards us in a big, slow wave to acknowledge and accept our presence. We returned the gesture, and he returned to the interior of his camper. The dog followed him.

I set about making a campfire – a task that was totally new to me. First I looked for some small, dry pieces of wood that I could use as kindling. It was great that the Park Service provided all those big split logs, but we had no ax or hatchet, and thus no way to make them any smaller. I tore and crumpled up some pages from a newspaper we'd already read, and placed them in the center of the campfire pit. The pit consisted of a number of large rocks or small boulders in an irregular circle that numerous previous visitors enabled me to identify as the place in which to make fires for keeping warm or barbecuing things on hand-held skewers. There was also a stone stove with a thick iron griddle on top, suitable for pots or pans, provided that one figured out how to get a fire roaring in the chamber beneath the griddle. The chamber had a small door through which none of the logs I saw lying about could possibly fit.

I started with the pit, since we were both pretty cold. I added a few dry-ish twigs and sticks around the paper, lit a match and, while the paper was rapidly burning up, I was bent over and blew frantically until my face was red and the paper was consumed – without having ignited a single twig. While repeating this procedure several times, I caught a glimpse of our neighbor and his dog emerging from the camper across the way. He took a seat on the steps and puffed gently on his pipe. As I was repeating the procedure for about the fifth time, I saw him slowly getting up and moseying our way, the basset waddling along just behind him, occasionally casting its big forlorn eyes upwards at its master.

I was embarrassed about my pathetic efforts to light a fire, but I had no idea how to go about making my efforts any less pathetic with little else to burn but those large split logs. "*Not used to making fires?*" he asked softly (and rhetorically, since he didn't wait for an answer). He then took the single remaining sheet of newspaper, crumpled it, put a few twigs around it, and lit it. But instead of waiting for the twigs to start burning, or blowing at them like a fool, he immediately started grabbing one big split log after another, propping them up against each other like a teepee, piling them quickly and carefully around the burning paper, while my jaw dropped and I thought there was *no way* that would ever burn. He just drawled, measuredly and without a trace of disdain, "*Got to keep the heat in.*" Then he turned and headed back to his camper. The basset followed him, occasionally looking over its shoulder to check us out. The old man didn't need to check the fire. It was roaring before he reached his camper.

So we had our fire and could thaw out. We ranged a little further afield and found more small sticks with which to try our luck with a fire in the stove, and found it surprisingly easy. We had a package of hot dogs and some buns, and made our evening meal on the griddle. There were no lights anywhere, of course; we would have to get everything ready for the night before it got completely dark. The ground was a bit damp, either from recently having been covered with snow or from the constant mist from the ever-churning river. We put down an old army surplus blanket on a flat patch of ground that was covered by a thick carpet of pine needles, then spread out our sleeping bags. Since they were barely insulated, we had to sleep in our clothes too. We rounded up four sturdy sticks about three feet long each, and stuck them in the ground towards the head of our "bed" and spread out the mosquito net over them. It was probably too cold for mosquitos anyway, but not for bears – an eventuality that never occurred to us. If it had, there'd have been no camping at all.

Very early the next morning, before dawn had gone down to day, we awoke to the sound of approaching footsteps, and were startled to see our neighbor, carrying a load over his shoulder. As we hurried out of our sleeping bags to greet him, he lay down his burden on our picnic table: some 8-10 newly caught rainbow trout, each about ten inches long. Before he turned and left, he commented in his taciturn way, "*Thought you might like something for breakfast.*" We were so flabbergasted – at the suddenness, the other-worldliness, his generosity, his bizarrely laconic manner – that we were unable to speak. We just stood there, staring, at each other, at him, at the beautiful fish, and at our weird accommodations. Then I made a new campfire.

Later that day, we went over to thank our neighbor and ended up having a nice long chat with him. He had a wife and children and grandchildren whom he loved, but sometimes he loved solitude more. His basset seemed to share his temperament. He told us that his grandchildren sometimes tried to ride the dog and it never complained. And they discovered that when one of their toddler grandchildren had just been reprimanded for something, he would bite the dog, and the dog endured it all. The only sound we ever heard it make during our stay in that magical place was when it alerted its master to our arrival with that single "*Aaarooo!*"

In the real world, the summer was short on good news. A civil war started in Nigeria, and reports began appearing in the papers of the most horrendous atrocities committed against the Biafran rebels and people. In early August, Johnson announced he was sending 45,000 more troops to that other civil war, in South East Asia. The escalation showed no signs of slowing down, and I was pretty sure there would be implications for my chances of continued student deferments. Escaping from new and higher levels of anxiety was becoming a matter of survival and of maintaining sanity. Jeanette and I were paying a lot more attention to the stories of young American men moving north to Canada.

The pleasure our Rogue River experience gave us called for more. We had two whole weeks' vacation coming up in early August, which we could devote to a real camping trip, not a mere excursion. We both loved the wonderful combination of deep evergreen forests, rugged mountains, temperate climate and ocean that was unique (in the US) to the Pacific Northwest. We hauled out a map and started planning. Why not do the whole thing? We decided to drive all the way up to the Olympic National Park in the northwesternmost corner of Washington, follow our noses, stop and see what we liked, take any road that looked interesting, and try to stick as close to the coast as possible on the way back down to San Francisco.

Since we camped in our sleeping bags the whole way, avoiding towns except to replenish supplies, the total trip cost astonishingly little (gas was still cheap back then). We felt that our sleeping bags would be enough, but just in case, we brought along a big sheet of opalescent construction plastic film we could use as a tarp (using our long rope to hang it on between two trees) to give ourselves some protection from possible rain. I also decided that for the duration of the trip, I would abandon the tiresome and unpleasant process of scraping my face every morning, in the hope that the skin irritation shaving always caused me would not result in other kinds of irritation. Fortunately, Jeanette liked both the idea and the result of my growing a beard.

The trip was fantastic. Nearly everywhere we went, we were completely alone. We managed to find the most beautiful and isolated campsites in the National and State Forests, where the ground was a soft loam of pine needles and the smell was paradise. Even the simplest fare cooked over a crackling campfire tasted wonderful. We heard the flittering and calling of birds and the dripping of raindrops from the huge trees and ferns. Jeanette and I both remarked to each other that we felt so incredibly much on the same wavelength that it sometimes felt like we were the same person. We were highly affectionate towards each other, and yet sex still played no more than a minor role.

The unspoiled (in 1967) and isolated beauty of the Olympic National Park took our breath away, and at most of the vista points our views were only shared by some large ravens hopping around and foraging on the remaining mounds of melting snow. We drove all the way up to the tiny fishing village of Neah Bay, which was as far northwest as it was possible to drive in the lower 48, and we hardly ever encountered another car. Most of the few hundred people in Neah Bay seemed to be poor Indians. This was another world, another America. A sign claimed it was possible to see across the water to Vancouver Island on a clear day, but few days were ever that clear.

We had to drive quite a long way before we could hook up with a southbound road that would afford us some views of the Pacific Ocean. Once in a while, we'd spot a sign indicating a hamlet that our map showed to be on an Indian reservation, and we decided to have a look. Near the coast along our way home, we ended up going to three or four reservations, some accessible only by long dead-end roads. Conditions in all of the reservations were appalling. There was hardly a dwelling that wouldn't instantly be condemned if it were in an urban slum. The few people we saw looked apathetic. They were clearly unused to having visitors from the Outside World, and few seemed to speak English, or perhaps they chose not to.

In several places, we noticed stacks of hand-crafted baskets on the ramshackle porches. Since the baskets appeared to be new and might possibly be a source of income for the people there, we asked if they were for sale. We ended up buying as many as we felt we would have room for in our apartment, at shamefully low prices. As we drove along, all the agony and disgust I felt as a child about the mistreatment of the Original Americans at the hands and guns of the White Man came rushing back to me. I shared all my feelings with Jeanette, the story of Colonel Chivington, Manifest Destiny, the ruthless confiscation of land and displacement to whatever confined parcels were left after the White Man took more than his fill of the best.

I'm sure I had at least 100 times the passion in my voice as I'd ever had in my asinine attempts to tell her about the Lord. If the Indians had been paid just one percent of the value of the land stolen from them, they would surely all be wealthy. Stealing some paltry merchandise from The Emporium was absolutely nothing compared to the self-righteous and systematic theft from the Indians on the part of my fellow white men – not to mention the unspeakable things that the Whites did (and to some extent were still doing) to the Blacks. I felt ashamed to be white and ashamed to be American, except for that little part of me that was allegedly Cherokee.

When we got home to San Francisco, Jeanette's family members were mildly shocked by my new beard. Beards were primarily identified with hippies and beatniks at that time, despite the fact that few people would be able to produce photos of beardless great-grandfathers, not to mention the artistic renderings of Jesus, his dad, and most of the Catholic Saints, except for those of the female persuasion. I did look a little wild, and however appropriate that look may have been in terms of the chaos inside me, I made sure I trimmed my beard neatly before reporting back for work at The Emporium.

Only one other employee had a beard at that time: the window dresser, the man responsible for the design and execution of the Big E's important large display windows along Market Street. His artistic role was considered unique, and he was therefore granted unique exemption from the unwritten no-beard rule. The only other semi-exception concerning facial hair was Vince Noli, my second-floor-stockroom workmate, whose David-Niven-style pencil-line mustache was also permitted.

On my first day back at work, my colleagues did a double-take when they saw me. A few spluttered some sort of comment about whether I was allowed to have a beard. It wasn't until the second day back that a delegation of my boss's bosses marched up to me and challenged me directly and aggressively. "*What are you doing with a beard?*" demanded Squires (with McNut at his side, nodding vigorously in approval of the question). I told them that it was to get relief from the skin irritation I got from shaving, and that I intended to keep it well trimmed, and besides, the window dresser had one, and besides, I had little or no contact with customers, and besides, I was about to start school again, which meant only part-time work again. Having no counter-arguments, they presumably decided (with obvious reluctance) to look the other way, and they marched off. There was apparently no written store policy prohibiting beards, and I'd argued my case pretty forcefully.

As soon as I got their tacit approval, or abnegation of overt disapproval, I shaved my beard off. But as soon as I did so, I found that I missed it (my face felt cold!), and I let it grow back again, this time as a neatly trimmed goatee and mustache only, the so-called Van Dyke style, along the lines of V.I. Lenin, albeit with a contiguous beard and mustache – and only salvaged traces of the philosophy that lurked behind his beard.

In the late summer, we made another trip "up the River". While San Francisco maintained a pleasantly cool temperature throughout the summer, it was hot in Guerneville; the river beckoned. Every summer, the town put up "summer dams" in the river, to retain enough water for recreation purposes. I soon discovered I could stand at the base of the Johnson's Beach Dam, where the water depth was about chest-high just beneath the "waterfall" from the overflow. There I let the falling water blast away at my neck and shoulders like a powerful water massage. I stood there for as long as half an hour after finding the right angle, without getting knocked over by the mass of water. On this particular day, when I at last came ashore, something was missing. With an enormous sinking feeling, I discovered that my wedding ring was gone. I spent the next hour vainly trying to search the riverbed silt for that hoop of gold. Perhaps someone downstream would someday pan for gold and find it, but I never did.

Apart from finding a new wedding ring for me, we found another kind of gold that autumn: incredibly cheap season tickets to the new American Conservatory Theater on Geary Street on Nob Hill. This remarkable troupe staged an astounding variety of plays, from Shakespeare, Molière and Chekhov, to Samuel Beckett, Edward Albee, Tennessee Williams and Arthur Miller. We thoroughly enjoyed every performance we could get to, and I was constantly amazed by the memory capacity of the actors, not only to learn all their lines – any given actor could have roles in several different plays over the course of just a few weeks – but to deliver them articulately and convincingly.

My fall semester at San Francisco State felt different because it was now time to start applying for graduate school. My intention was still to go for a doctorate and eventually teach at university level. I asked a few of my English professors for advice or suggestions, and they were pretty much in agreement that I should apply to Princeton (in New Jersey, not awfully far southwest of New York City) and Yale (in Connecticut, not awfully far northeast of New York City). Their graduate programs sounded good to me, and there didn't seem to be much doubt that my grades would enable me to get in, but there was that other big threat to consider. To be on the safe side, I therefore applied to McGill University (Montréal), York University (Toronto) and the University of British Columbia (Vancouver). Then I just had to wait to find out where I might be accepted and thus what my choices would be when the time came. Combat in Vietnam was *never* going to be an option I would consider.

The fall semester was also unusual in the sense that it was the only university term in which I had no English courses; the remaining three I wanted in order to complete my major weren't being offered until the spring. I basically just wanted to get through the term; I had enough on my mind already, and at least half of me was already living in the unknown beyond graduation. I chose several "light" courses.

One of these was the continuation of the humanities "non-course" I'd stumbled into in the spring. Another was an introductory course in philosophy that I was surprised they allowed me to take, considering I'd already completed most of the courses I needed for my minor, but they seemed to be counting credits, not content – as I was in this case. A third was a course in metaphysics, also part of the philosophy program, with a lot of emphasis on Aristotle, Kant and Berkeley. To me it was high-level intellectual gymnastics, building weird mental muscles that had little purpose in the real world. Years later I would whoop with delight when I read this statement by Bertrand Russell: "Aristotle could have avoided the mistake of thinking that women have fewer teeth than men, by the simple device of asking Mrs. Aristotle to keep her mouth open while he counted."

But there was one philosophy course – aesthetics – that had much greater relevance for me, with its big and insoluble questions of what art is (or is not) and what makes art good (or bad). Just as my ethics course demonstrated the impossibility of settling the ethical question of defining such seemingly simple words as *good* and *bad*, a review of the historical attempts showed them to be equally futile in arriving at a universally satisfactory definition of art.

I tended to be more active in the classroom discussions than the rest of the class (combined), possibly because I was the only one in the room who not only aspired to be an artist, but was one. The professor and I disagreed on a lot of things, and our debates were intellectually stimulating, but it was clear that she often felt challenged – not a feeling she craved. Towards the end of the term, she outlined the basic arguments of an academic paper on which she was putting the finishing touches – yet another attempt to establish criteria for "good art" versus "bad art". I listened, thought for a while, and then asked a couple of simple questions: "*Why does art have to be either good or bad? Why can't there be degrees, a continuum?*" And she just stared at me, dumbstruck, with her mouth open. I felt like the little boy in *The Emperor's New Clothes*. At last she burst out with a scowl, "*Damn you!! Now I'll have to redo the whole damn paper!*"

The last of my courses during the fall was French. I'd always liked the sound of *la belle langage*, and welcomed the idea of learning another language, despite not having been that eager to learn Spanish in my first two years of high school. But perhaps the biggest factor in the choice of French was the increasing relevance of a possible move to Canada. And if it turned out to be McGill for grad school, then French might become more of a practical necessity that just an intellectual exercise.

We had, in fact, a good reason to take the matter of exile much more seriously now. The Selective Service had just sent me a letter informing me that they had changed my 2-S student deferment to a new classification, 1-S (C), a deferment would only remain valid until the end of the ongoing academic year, after which I could not even apply for a further student deferment, but would automatically be re-classified 1-A: eligible for immediate induction. The rumor mills suggested that appeals were unlikely to succeed; the military's need for cannon fodder was becoming too great. But in Canada we would be safe from Vietnam, safe from federal prison, safe from the homeland that was shoving those two – and only those two – alternatives at me.

A few of my classmates told me that some of their friends who, having fled to Canada to avoid the draft, had no regrets. We found that San Francisco had a Canadian Consulate in an austere office, yet full of promise, down in the Financial District. We went there to make some inquiries about the possibility of immigrating. For me, asking such questions was extremely emotional; I could barely speak. For them, my questions were everyday matters, mere office routines. They gave us the forms.

We discovered that we would be applying for something the Canadians called "landed immigrant status" (not quite the same as landed gentry), a new and odd-sounding term to our ears, but at least we wouldn't be "aliens" or extra-planetary monsters. The forms were rather simple and straightforward, but for us the step was monumental, a watershed. Although there's no way of ever knowing, I seriously doubt that the thought of moving from the US would have ever occurred to us, at least not to me, had it not been for Vietnam.

The Canadian immigration people didn't seem to have a problem with our not having already arranged for jobs and housing there, nor the fact that we still had no idea of where in Canada we would be heading. For Jeanette, secretarial jobs seemed to be readily available, and the fact that I had already applied to three Canadian graduate schools seemed to satisfy the immigration authorities where I was concerned, but we decided to hold off for a while, and see how things went.

The War was certainly continuing, as were the protests, with an enormous march on the Pentagon in October. In November, General Westmoreland announced with "absolute certainty" that the enemy was losing, although fewer and fewer people – including the enemy – seemed inclined to share that view.

One evening in the late autumn, Michael finally relented, and agreed to show the family selected slides from his sojourn in Vietnam. Most were scenes from the base camp where he insisted he spent his entire time. There were also a number of portraits – close-ups of his army buddies. The slide-show banter quickly took on a monotonous (and morose) character: *What's his name?* Joe. *Do you still have contact with him?* No. *Why not?* He's dead.

The only variation, for face after face, was the name of the buddy. They were all dead, yet Michael still insisted he saw "no action". And he still broke into a cold sweat whenever *Vietnam* was mentioned. As far as Jeanette and I ever knew, that one slide show was the only one Michael ever held.

In late November, Eugene McCarthy, a US Senator (and part-time poet) from Minnesota, announced he would be running for the Presidency as an anti-war Democrat. Although his chances were thought to be miniscule, at least there was someone out there of that stature standing up against the War, and born optimists like me took heart.

Meanwhile, back at The Emporium, the summer emboldened me to shift into high gear and open up two new fronts in my increasingly reckless campaign. One was to start going for bigger stuff, both in size and value. The other was to acquire all kinds of clothing for the Indians.

We'd been greatly disturbed by the abject poverty we saw on our visits to the reservations. We were also ashamed of the dirt-cheap prices we paid for their hand-woven baskets. Consequently, we got a few large empty moving cartons which we had in our ground-floor locker space on Pueblo Street, and began filling them with shirts, sweaters, pants, of all sizes, even shoes, courtesy of The Emporium. When a carton was full, we'd ship it off to one of two or three reservations we had the addresses for. We sent the cartons anonymously. We weren't looking for their gratitude; there was certainly no need for them to thank white people! We simply wanted them to have some clothes to keep them warm. I think we shipped five or six big cartons during the fall.

The other front was the polar opposite of the first – a gesture of spite towards the fat-cats, the filthy-rich executives and owners of The Emporium who treated lowly employees like commodities. I got a mink hat for my mom, another for Jeanette's mom, several for Jeanette, and lots of nice alligator wallets. As a supervisor, I now had access to the small locked storage area that belonged to the store's silverware department. It was pretty common for young people to pick out a silverware pattern to go with their bone china pattern when they registered prior to wedding showers. We never got that far, but perhaps it was time to have some nice silver not to use with the bone china we'd already never used. I brought home a place setting of a Wallace Sterling pattern called "Grand Baroque" for Jeanette to have a look at. She liked it too. Silver was easy – it didn't take much space, although I had to be careful to tape things together to prevent dinner knives from rattling and silver spoons from sliding down my pants leg just as I was passing the security guard.

Once I acquired a complete set of 12 place settings and various serving utensils, I thought it could be good to have the box to put them in – a simple, rigid wooden box lined with velvet, with lots of slots specifically designed for silverware. The box had a lid that was hinged along the back, as well as a drawer for the serving utensils. It was 17 inches long, 6½ inches high, and 11½ inches deep. The challenge of stuffing that monstrosity into my pants and under my shirt, then concealing the monumental bulge under a loose-fitting raincoat by walking past the security guard with a forward-leaning slouch, was more than daunting. It was a conjuring trick. It was insane. And the box itself wasn't even worth that much. The ability I had as a kid to suck in my entire abdomen almost to my backbone was now being put to the ultimate test. And I passed it. (To this day, I find it hard to believe that I would even try, much less that I'd succeed. I still have the box, and have added a bit of a paunch.)

Naturally, that feat emboldened me further. I got Jeanette a luxurious, thigh-length mink coat. By complementing my ordinary pants belt with two extra belts strapped around my midriff and chest, I was able to walk out with a total of nine Persian throw rugs (including one for Jeanette's parents), one at a time. But perhaps the most absurd caper of them all was a full-size cowhide, also from the rug department, that combined the impossible dimensions of the silver box with the awful bulk of the Persian carpets. For that I even wound twine all around my torso. I was out of control.

One bulky item that I sneaked out of the store turned out to be a hilarious waste of time, trouser space, and risk-taking. I'd noticed that the perfume department (from which I kept Jeanette well supplied with her three favorites (Arpége, Calèche, and Chanel No. 5) had on display a gigantic bottle of Chanel, probably at least a gallon. Naturally, I took it home, only to discover that it contained colored water. It was a goddamn display dummy! Jeanette and I howled with laughter.

By the end of the year, the number of volumes in my book collection was well in excess of a thousand (*not* all from The Emporium; I'd purchased many of them at second-hand bookstores, as well as a few I bought at full price at the university bookstore). I also received letters of acceptance from all the graduate schools I'd applied to, including Simon Fraser (in greater Vancouver), which I added at the last minute in order to get a second choice in the Vancouver area. We were already leaning strongly in the direction of UBC, mostly based on the venue. Because we happened to spend our honeymoon in that beautiful city, it was the only one that was not a complete unknown to us. We also felt more at ease with access to the sea, forests and mountains. I wasn't thrilled with the idea of again subjecting myself to the harsh Chicago-style winters of Montréal or Toronto (or Greater New York if I wasn't drafted after all). And we thought it might be nice to stay on the West Coast where most of our family members were: all Jeanette's family, as well as John and his family. Al was not going to be staying in Iowa after getting his doctorate; he thought he might be looking at options out west after graduation in June. Keeping some familiarities close by might make it easier to make the huge step that self-imposed exile was certain to entail.

The sharp decline in my correspondence with my parents since the beginning of 1966 was precipitated by their meeting Jeanette at Christmas '65, or perhaps it would be more accurate to say that they had the *opportunity* to meet Jeanette, but declined to take it, preferring only to meet the Lost Soul they imagined they were seeing when Jeanette the person was standing and sitting right there in front of them. No matter how well-intentioned their subsequent letters to me and to Jeanette might have been, at best they gave little to respond to and at worst they were rude and insulting. The breaking point was denying me their approval to marry Jeanette.

Even after our wedding and their pathetic flurry of last-minute excuses for not attending, we found little to write about. How could we? Dad seldom wrote; and Mom seemed unable to write without sermonizing and ranting about the Lord. Perhaps the fact that my relationship with Jeanette was so close and gratifying on most levels contributed to my lack of interest in trying to find ways to reply to letters that gave me nothing to reply to. Mom had no questions; nor did she have any answers – only <u>Answers</u> – the kind that may not be questioned. I knew their world all too well and was pretty much done with it. They knew almost nothing of my world and expressed no interest in wanting to know about it. I loved my mom and dad and told them so. I didn't love them *if and only if* they would think like this or believe like that or any other terms and conditions. I just loved them. Why couldn't they do the same for me? And where could we go from here?

During this period, I was giving my brother John a hard time by mail, for once not about religion, but about another of his indefensible positions. I discovered that his current job as an engineer involved designing weapons systems for the helicopters that the US was using to fill Vietnamese hearts with terror, lead and death. Normally I rejoiced when he let his pragmatism (or hedonism) overrule his inherited, force-fed principles, but that was because those principles were rooted in ancient nomadic writings of highly questionable accuracy. This time, I was hoping that he would allow his principles of humanity to overrule his pragmatic desire for a secure job. He eventually decided he couldn't continue contributing to the War effort, and found a non-military-related job (although that sequence may have been reversed).

The spring term of 1968 – my last semester at San Francisco State and the last semester for the completion of my degree – paled beside the other major events that were going on in our lives, but still offered some good courses. I continued with my French course, which I enjoyed thoroughly, and eventually developed enough skill to be able to read (albeit with considerable effort) Camus' *L'Etranger* in the original. I was also able to carry on a discussion in French at a level well beyond the needs of a tourist.

My final philosophy course was in advanced ethics, under Dr Donald Provence. Most philosophers try to look at ethics rationally, "*but does 'rational' mean 'unfeeling'?*" our professor asked rhetorically? "*There's no reason to think so. How people feel is a very important consideration in ethics.*" Nor is *rational* the same as *objective*, and trying to find objective criteria for ethics remains a conundrum. The excellence of a thing might be said to have objective criteria, but only in terms of the purpose of that thing, but what is the "purpose" of a person? Ethics is more about obligation; it's necessary to know the grounds for telling a person what he or she ought or ought not to do. Wrestling with questions that may not have any final answers is much more difficult than simply claiming to have the answers and then stifling all the questions!

I had three English courses that final spring. One covered more of Chaucer – a pure delight again – and another covered American literature from 1840 to 1912, thus including Longfellow, Emerson and Thoreau, as well as Hawthorne, Melville and Emily Dickenson. In my term paper, on the subject of evil in *The*

Scarlet Letter and *Moby Dick*, my thesis was that the obsession (Chillingworth's and Captain Ahab's respectively) to avenge and destroy evil was in itself the greater evil and led to greater destruction. I might have had some other people's obsessions with evil in mind.

The final course was entirely devoted to James Joyce, who'd already become one of my favorite authors since I read *Portrait of the Artist as a Young Man* and *Dubliners*, but this course focused on *Ulysses* – a work that ambushed me with its magical use of language and styles. Our professor, Albert J. LaValley, was also among that rare breed who could truly captivate and inspire, and it was rewarding to have my undergraduate studies come to an end on such a positive note.

Other things were also coming to an end, but my Emporium escapades were continuing. However, space limitations and the prospect of having to move at the end of the school year were making me more selective. At the same time, I was convinced that my purloining skills were honed to perfection – *hubris* was not a problem for the likes of me!

In mid-January I noticed a sumptuously warm sheepskin coat, dark brown and full length, in Jeanette's size. I knew Jeanette would adore it, and I managed to get it out, although it was almost as bulky as the cowhide. Otherwise, I was mostly just adding to my book collection.

On January 30th, the North Vietnamese and Viet Cong launched a major attack – the so-called Tết offensive – which rocked American public opinion, especially among those who were still clinging to the illusion that the US couldn't lose the war, and that the enemy was already beaten into submission. (By this time the US had nearly half a million men in Vietnam.) Two days later, Nixon announced his candidacy, and two weeks later again, the US decided to send an additional 10,000 troops to the bottomless casualty pit that Vietnam had become.

As I was leaving work for the day in the afternoon on Saturday, February 17th, with about five books under my belt, two new hotshot house detectives (I'd seen and identified them at a distance a couple of times before) were entering the employee entrance as I was leaving it. They'd just apprehended a shoplifter, and they were beefily marching him to an interrogation room, forcefully restraining him. I thought they were looking at me in a funny way, but I dismissed the thought as excessive paranoia.

When I arrived at work on Monday evening (two days later), Mr Eliot told me I was to report at once to the security guard at the employees' entrance. He didn't say why, and I made no connection to what didn't happen on Saturday. I was "invited" to step in, behind the counter, and enter a brightly lit little room to one side, furnished with a small table and three or four chairs. I was further invited to take a seat. I started to feel a little nervous, and every ten seconds or so I noticed that the nervousness I was feeling was ratcheting up at a rate I couldn't control. But I made every effort to remain calm, or at least *appear* to remain calm.

Within what I presume was a few minutes (my grasp of the passage of time had suddenly abandoned me), the two hotshots entered the room and took up aggressive positions on the opposite side of the table from where I was seated. The bigger, burlier one stood straight up behind the table, with his arms folded across his chest and stared down sternly at me. The slim one, with glasses, put one foot up on one of the chairs and leaned slightly forward towards his knee and across the table towards me, with his hands spread out on the table, like the stance of a lineman just before the snap, or a sprinter just before the gun, peering at me intently as if my face was in some way legible. I suddenly realized that this was the moment I would have been dreading if I'd had enough sense to allow myself to be aware of the insane risks I'd been taking. But I'd had no sense, so here they were, charging at me like an avalanche down a ravine.

Their interrogation was fairly textbook, or at least vicariously familiar to me from a wide variety of TV crime shows I'd seen. "Do you know why you're here?" *Think, Stan, think!* Their voices were stern and authoritative. They looked confident, even cocky. *Shit! They know!!* This wasn't about suspicions; they had evidence. *Shit! Think!* No use pretending I didn't know why I was there. Now it was about damage control. *Think!* They couldn't have a lot of evidence over a long period of time, or they'd have collared me long ago. It wasn't as if they were breaking up a ring or something. They seemed to have only the most recent evidence, maybe the past week or two. *Can I remember everything I'd taken during that time? Think*! All that was racing through my mind in a second or two while I gulped nervously after hearing their question. I *wanted* them to see that I was nervous. I allowed my lower lip to tremble, or perhaps I made it tremble. Yes, I had a pretty good idea why I was there, I answered, my voice breaking.

"*You wanna tell us why?*" My brow wrinkled as I looked up at them earnestly, with tears welling in my eyes, and I said that I'd done some bad things, really bad things, and I felt terrible about it. They turned briefly to look at each other, nodding and smirking ever so slightly in smug, aggressive, triumphant satisfaction.

"*So how long has this been going on?*" A couple of weeks, I ventured, and they seemed satisfied with my answer (I'd guessed it right!). Then I got a flash of memory, of having seen the slender one at a distance on the second floor of the stockroom around ten days earlier. When he saw that I saw him, he abruptly disappeared down a corridor, and I didn't see him again. How much did they know about my procedure for getting merchandise from the shop floor back to the stockroom for later removal from the store? They're going to ask me about that next. I've got to assume they know something, and if I tell them a bit more than they're asking, they'll know I'm collaborating.

"*How are you doing it?*" I told them that for the past couple of weeks when I pushed the trucks out onto the shop floors early on those Saturday mornings, I put some books and a few other things onto the truck (at this point they looked at each other and nodded again) and then I stashed them under a shelf, and took them out of the store under my shirt, a little at a time.

"*Under which shelf?*" I realized that they'd probably made a note of the titles of the books I'd stashed there two days before, or more likely that they'd seen and recorded the books on the truck, but still didn't know where I stashed them. I gave them clear directions. Then they suddenly stopped and said we'd take a short break. I had pretty well figured out that the break in my interrogation was to allow Slim time to run up to the stockroom and check my story. During this time, Burly, who seemed unused to conducting interrogations on his own, was alternating the roles of good cop, bad cop, all by himself, giving me time to figure out another crucial strategy: I had to keep them – at all costs – from wanting to get a search warrant for our apartment and keep them from involving the police! But how the hell was I to do that?!

When Slim returned, he again nodded at Burly, and mumbled to him – *chk'sou* – my story checked out. I remembered that he would have been able to confirm that it was the right place because there were still a few books under that shelf awaiting my removal. I started weeping, I said I didn't know what came over me and that I felt miserable about it all, and just wanted to bring back all the stuff – *all* of it – and turn back the clock and make it all go away. My life would be coming to an end if I couldn't and my wife would leave me and I wouldn't be able to graduate, all because of a few books and some clothes. I could see that they were starting to feel sorry for me.

"*What clothes?*" Whoops! They were suddenly *highly* suspicious again. They appeared not to have known about the clothes, and I realized I would have to tread carefully so as not to broaden the scope of my escapades any further. I remembered a few of the latest unnecessary things I got for Jeanette, some of which hadn't been exactly to her taste, plus a couple of entirely unnecessary shirts for myself. I described them, and begged to be allowed to bring them all back; I wouldn't be able to sleep until they were returned, I told them. I could bring them back that same evening if they wanted. Tears were streaming down my face now, and I was shaking. I looked and sounded like a complete wreck.

Slim and Burly looked as if they were prepared to go a little easier on me, but first they had a couple more questions. "*Have you taken – or seen – a full-length dark-brown sheepskin coat?*" They didn't have the same already-know-the-answer cockiness when they asked this question. Should I confess to this one? Then it occurred to me that this would be a floodgate I *absolutely* didn't want to open. If I admitted to walking out with something that big, that bulky, it would put all my escapades into a completely different league, and there might not be any stopping it. I said I didn't understand the question, and as they repeated it, I tried to look like I was trying to remember something I knew nothing about, and would gladly have helped them if only I could, but I couldn't. And they bought my story. Obviously, getting a coat like that out of the store would have to be the work of an expert, not some pathetic amateur like me. They were satisfied that they had all the answers I could give them, and that I truly saw my stolen merchandise as an infected sliver in my finger that I truly wanted to get rid of. They agreed that the next day, at 11 AM, I would report back with all the merchandise I took.

I knew that this was a test. I correctly guessed that they knew exactly which books I took the previous Saturday, at least. I had to do everything in my power to remember every single book I'd taken in the past two weeks, and perhaps a few more to bolster my image of sincerity. I scoured my bookshelves at home that evening and found that my memory was good; I'd unconsciously mentally catalogued everything, which enabled me to pick 20 or so volumes of the most recent acquisitions off my shelves and place them and the clothing in the two big paper shopping bags Jeanette rounded up for me. She was also nervous, but not nearly as nervous as me. (I was terrified.) I added a few more books and garments we didn't much want anyway to the bags (except for one book; I reluctantly returned a slipcase edition of *Giacomo Joyce* by James Joyce) and sheepishly carried them through the employees' entrance just before 11 the next morning. Slim and Burly were waiting for me.

After carefully going through everything, occasionally referring to a paper they had (I guessed it was their list), and listening to my tearful expressions of relief to get that infected stuff out of my life, they sat down at the table opposite me. I suddenly realized that whatever decision was to be made about my fate, it wasn't theirs to make, and that it had already been made, higher up. They had a paper, a form, already filled out, ready for me to sign. "*You understand that you can't keep your job – we're firing you – but we're not bringing the police in on this one. It's not good for the store. So sign here* [I signed] *and we'll give you a copy* [they gave me the green copy], *and good luck to you.*" I was free to go, with no goodbyes to anyone. (After Jeanette and I got married, we had little contact with Jim Gillingham and his wife, and my shame prevented me from making further contact him. He phoned me once many years later. As far as I know, he never knew about my "adventures" at the Big E.)

It wasn't until my increasingly quivering legs got me to my car, and I was sitting there in my parking space, that the full impact of the narrowness of my escape hit me. They could easily have called in the police and gotten a warrant to search our apartment, where they would have found merchandise that would almost certainly have led to a felony grand larceny charge. I calculated that the retail value of the merchandise I'd taken was far more than $30,000 (1967 value), roughly eight times my annual income…. I could have forgotten about graduate school and Canada. I might well have faced a judge who would offer me one of those punitive enlistment choices – prison or Vietnam – that many of my peers were talking about. Either alternative would likely have destroyed me, not to mention the terrible impact it would have had on Jeanette. But I was suddenly without health insurance in the country that more than most others professes to follow the teachings of Jesus, and to be democratic, yet refuses to ensure care for the poor and the sick. The only hypothetical reaction I could foresee from my parents would have been some we-told-you-so variant, "*Be sure your sin will find you out*", one of their favorite Bible quotes, from Numbers 32:23. Interestingly, this is the chapter immediately following the one in which God is angry with the Israelites for not slaughtering all the women and children of the Midianites; the "sin" that found them out was their failure to obey His bloodthirsty commands to commit genocide.

I once aspired to be an actor, and I'd just pulled off the role performance of a lifetime. But the *need* for my Academy-Award performance was so utterly stupid, so mindless, I could hardly grasp it. I'd risked nearly everything – my entire future, and Jeanette's – for what? A bunch of clothes? A few shelves full of books? Some silverware and carpets we didn't need? Any guilt that I felt was far overshadowed by the shame of having been so incredibly brainless.

It might seem difficult to understand how an honors university student with a good analytical ability could come within a heartbeat of ruining his life and probably the lives of a few others by pursuing – for the sheer thrill of it – some idiotic course of action. And yet. How many seemingly smart people with the capacity to weigh real evidence against centuries and millennia of foolish superstitions use their brains to do so? How many people in positions of power take a course of action that will lead to the greater good of mankind rather than feathering the nests of the already rich? These thoughts might be brushed off as lame excuses, pathetic rationalizations. But they are not – which in no way excuses me! They are merely examples of other nauseatingly real and commonplace instances of stupidity and ignorance.

The day after my dishonorable yet fortunate discharge from The Emporium, a guy named Olof Palme, a member of the Swedish Cabinet, made headlines all over the world for marching in Stockholm in a protest demonstration against the war in Vietnam. This was, as far as I know, the strongest public opposition voiced against the War by such a prominent political figure from a Western democracy.

On March 12th, the anti-war candidate Eugene McCarthy shocked the US political establishment by coming within seven percent of President Johnson in the New Hampshire primary. (Just four days later, American soldiers slaughtered and raped civilian Vietnamese in what would later be known as the Mỹ Lai massacre, although it wouldn't become publically known for another year and a half.) The only conviction eventually resulting from that massacre was three years of house arrest for the commanding officer who ordered and oversaw the carnage. I, on the other hand, could have faced many years in prison for taking extra profits from a few fat cats. It's always nice to have some sense of proportion.

Later in March, after Robert Kennedy also announced his candidacy, LBJ announced that he wouldn't be back for another term. On April 4th, Martin Luther King was assassinated by a racist sniper, just a week before Johnson signed the Civil Rights Act that Congress at last passed. If only changing people's hearts and minds were as easy as signing a bill into law.

I thought a lot about all the misery people perpetrate on one another in the form of prejudice and discrimination; all the hurt that people cause through greed and injustice, systematic and systemic inequality, might-makes-right subjugation and servitude; all the violence and mayhem that cause endless and untold suffering and scarring. Could those thoughts at this time have something to do with my inability to feel guilt about my Emporium escapades? Of course I realized the stupidity of the risks I took, but risks often have little to do with right or wrong. Or was I just good at rationalizing, making excuses, failing to own up?

By early April, we completed our required medical exams for immigration to Canada; there was just some final paperwork left. As it turned out, the fact that we delayed submitting our applications until March was fortuitous. It meant that in the sections of the application where I had to account for how I spent my recent years, I could truthfully list high school 1959-63, Link-Belt 1963-64, San Mateo 1965, San Francisco State 1966-date. No years unaccounted for, no need to mention The Emporium, no fear of devastating references.

Jeanette's parents made it clear to anyone who was listening that they considered our move to Vancouver a totally hare-brained idea. Jeanette and I were not among those listening. Mike and Rose learned, long before I realized I'd taught them, that entering a fray being fought on intellectual grounds was not going to prove fruitful for them. After all, what alternatives did we have? I could let myself get drafted and shipped off to Vietnam like Michael. They certainly didn't like it when that happened to him, however little they might have protested it happening to me. And it would have been horrendous beyond words for Jeanette. The second option was up to five years in Leavenworth or some such penal institution of lower learning. The only other alternative was exile: Canada. The fact that the best alternative could at the same time be totally hare-brained was a conundrum they hadn't figured out in their own minds. Instead, they bit their tongues.

A report in the paper in mid-April told of an accident with nerve gas near an army facility in the desert in Utah, in which thousands of sheep died convulsive deaths. I thought of my friend Ken, the one who bought my painting *Hands*, who was drafted in '64 after getting his degree in biology and was on his way to an army facility in Utah.

Some days later, I noticed in the paper that a Liberal politician named Pierre Elliot Trudeau had just become the new Prime Minister of Canada, an article I wouldn't normally have noticed, but now he was soon to be *our* Prime Minister.

One lazy Saturday morning in April, now that we had lazy Saturday mornings in my post-Emporium days, Jeanette finally decided it was time to put her inexperienced and inattentive husband in the picture about something that was a growing concern for her. She informed me that, contrary to her own expectations about how things were supposed to work, and despite coitus feeling good, vaginal stimulation was not enough to bring her to full sexual satisfaction, which both she and I ignorantly presumed would be the case, since she had experienced that nearly every time we met at my apartment on evergreen, despite abstinence from coitus. Neither of us had a clue that it might not work that way for a lot of women, nor that there was nothing abnormal about it.

She didn't express herself in quite that way, however, but only told me, with great concern, that for her the non-coital sex before we got married was better than the coital sex afterwards. Once that particular conversational door was finally opened, I could ask questions and get answers, which eventually led to major improvements, experiments with new positions and we at last began to enjoy having sex. But unfortunately it didn't do a lot to solve the problem of her bouts of inexplicable jealousy that could drive us both to desperation, albeit via diametrically opposed routes.

May was a month of good news. We got our formal immigration approval from Canada. All we'd have to do was present our official immigration identification cards at the border. A guy in my American Lit class at San Francisco State (who was interested in the sensual, auburn-haired girl who sat next to me, she being interested in me, not him, but whom I was not interested in) was – thanks to his activism against the War – perhaps interested in helping me with our plans to move to Vancouver and did so by giving me the phone number of a guy named Vince, an American in Vancouver who (my classmate said) was helping other Americans get settled there. Besides Vince's phone number, the only things I knew about Vancouver were what Jeanette and I saw on our honeymoon about a year and a half earlier, and that the University of British Colombia had accepted my application for graduate studies in the English Department. My classmate thought that Vince could offer some help or advice about finding a "pad" (the "cool" jargon of the day for an apartment; doesn't outdated slag sound weird?) in Vancouver.

I also began looking into options for moving our stuff. The established moving companies like Bekins (the only company whose name I knew) turned out to be far more costly than we could afford: at least $700. But we found we could rent a 12-foot U-Haul van at a more affordable $200, plus gas, and do the job ourselves at well below half the cost.

We started making some detailed plans. I would drive up to Vancouver on my own, immediately after graduation, to find us an apartment. (Note that I didn't say "try to find" – my optimism admitted no impediments.) Then we'd take most of the month of June to pack our stuff. Jeanette would continue working at Bank of America until the end of June, because we needed the money. Just before the end of the month, Michael and I would load the van, drive to Vancouver, unload it, and drive back down to San Francisco, and turn in the van. Then on the second of July, Jeanette and I would drive to Vancouver, arriving the next day.

On May 10th, the first day of Vietnam peace talks began in Paris. Once again there were rumors of hope for a quick end to the War and the draft, but only for the most wildly optimistic; I lacked the "wildly" part. However, the liberal reforms that were being announced in Czechoslovakia by the new leader, Alexander Dubček, were a breath of pure oxygen; the liberal "Prague spring" was bursting into bloom, earning the fervent praise of American liberals and conservatives alike, and optimists everywhere were confident that the Iron Curtain might be crumbling and the Cold War might be coming to an end. Then when Eugene McCarthy won the Oregon primary, to the delight of many of the most liberal Americans, optimists like me naively believed that the country might be waking up to the mistakes they'd made by failing twice to elect Adlai Stevenson, for whom I now realized I would have voted had I known then what I knew now, plus the small matter of having been born more than a decade too late to have been eligible to vote in 1952.

The last of my final exams at San Francisco State was on June 3rd. I started my trip to Vancouver in our bronze Valiant that same afternoon, aiming to get as far north as I could before stopping somewhere along the highway for a few hours' sleep. Once I had both the Bay Area and the wine country behind me, there was mile after mile of mostly beautiful forests and grasslands, mostly ugly towns and occasional volcanic peaks that rose up white against the horizon in the kind of magical way I would one day associate with Sacre Coeur in the evening in Paris. Jeanette and I came along this way on our camping road trips, when I first let my beard grow the summer before, raising eyebrows and rankles at the staid Emporium. After nightfall, the driving and the tension began to get to me and I just had to stop for a few hours' sleep by a roadside picnic spot somewhere in northern Oregon.

Along with the sun, my bladder and my hunger awoke me early the next morning, I had only a relatively short journey ahead of me, because I was going to meet Al in Seattle, in connection with a job interview he had been called to at Boeing. Apparently his mathematical skills were of great interest to the aerospace giant, and they flew him out and put him up at the prestigious Olympic Hotel (later called the Fairmont Olympic), where I surprised him in the hotel corridor outside his room after his interview on June 4th. We went for delicious fried clams at Ivar's street kitchen down in the harbor and talked a lot about the future – Al had reached a deal with Boeing, so he and his family would soon be living in Seattle and we'd be living in Vancouver. I'd brought along my football in the car, knowing I'd be meeting Al, so we threw it around for a while among the parked cars under the overpass across the street from Ivar's before going back to Al's room to talk for the rest of the evening. I gate-crashed and spent the night on the couch in his room.

Late in the evening we watched some TV and saw Bobby Kennedy's speech following his victory earlier that evening in the California Democratic primary. As soon as his speech was over, we turned off the TV and fell asleep. Al was going to fly out of Seattle the next morning, and I would drive him south to the SeaTac airport before once again heading back north, beyond Seattle, beyond Vancouver WA, to Vancouver BC.   When we woke up and turned on the TV to catch the morning news, we were shocked to learn that Bobby Kennedy had been shot the night before, just minutes after we'd turned off the TV. He was in critical condition. Dazed by that awful news, we headed to SeaTac and found a patch of grass where we could again throw the football around for a while, till Al had to check in; throwing around a football together had for some years been a lot easier for us than throwing around ideas. The extent to which I had and he hadn't strayed from The Path was now painfully apparent. It was equally apparent that I hadn't taken any new positions – nor refused to challenge any premises – that I wasn't prepared to defend or modify regarding matters of faith, religion or politics.

That great rupture one Thursday nearly seven years before – the Thursday Night Massacre, when my brother as I knew him died, and I was faced with the prospect of choosing his kind of living death or a great living unknown – continued to hound me, plague me, mock, prod, stimulate and shape me. Yet despite the estrangement that followed the Thursday Night Massacre, there remained a strong emotional bond between Al and me. But that bond was often painful, as our diverging worldviews invariably and inexorably manifested themselves. And here I was, about to move to Vancouver; and Al would be moving to Seattle in late January. Al would then be our closest family member, geographically speaking, while Jeanette and I would be farther away from him, and closer to each other, than ever.

I headed north from Seattle, first towards Bellingham, then on up to the US border crossing near Blaine, about an hour's drive south of Vancouver, with Vince's phone number in my pocket. I was half expecting FBI agents to pounce on me at any time, demanding to know where I was going and why. My paranoia peaked before I reached the Canadian border, but crossing it still gave me a great sense of relief and of newfound freedom.

One of the first things I did on reaching the Vancouver area was to phone my contact person. Vince seemed to be not entirely aware of or eager to embrace the role my classmate assigned him, but he nevertheless offered to do what he could to help, and told me I was welcome to "crash" at the commune where he was staying in the northwestern part of Vancouver. The commune was a motley collection of a dozen or so displaced Haight-Ashburyites who were doing their best to create as groovy an atmosphere as possible in a big, slightly run-down and messy Victorian house, architecturally similar to some of those I'd glimpsed in the Haight-Ashbury. My button-down Pendleton and annoying way of speaking in complete sentences didn't meet the strict norms of the Unique, and they looked me up and down with strained casualness and keen disinterest, like I was some kind of freak, man, but everything was cool when I explained I was, like, dodging the draft, man. They let me unroll my sleeping bag on their floor, and Vince talked me through the first shock of what I could expect from Vancouver's housing situation: "*Yeah, man. It's shit, like. Ya just gotta, ya know....*"

Vince had the Sunday newspaper with all the classifieds for apartment rental – most apartments were called "suites" in Canada – and I quickly discovered to my horror that the rents at that time were double or more than the average for San Francisco, where rents were already high for our budget. A place as simple as what we were renting on Pueblo Street might cost up to three times as much in Vancouver. We had no jobs, nor any guarantee of income. Our joint US income for the first half of 1968 was a mere $3676.

Struggling not to lose heart, I phoned Jeanette about the situation. She cheerfully made it clear that she would have no problem with a significantly lower standard of living; the important thing was that we could move there and be together, and hopefully have room for our stuff. She told me to go ahead and make any decision I felt necessary, and she would be fine with it.

With the rent level as my first criterion, I continued scrutinizing the classifieds until I came up with several possibilities. A couple of them were in locations that Vince felt I shouldn't even bother to look at. However, one cheap place – even cheaper than our apartment in San Francisco – was advertised as a "basement suite" located at 4520 Ross Street, near 29th Avenue, in the middle of a vast and modest residential area in the geographical center of town (downtown was close to the water along the northern edge of town), and Vince said that it might be all right. I phoned and talked to the owner of the house, a man named Mario Falcone, who spoke with a heavy Italian accent. Vince came along to guide me when I drove out to have a look at the place.

Vince hadn't adopted the hippie uniform along with the jargon, but Mario – an Italian immigrant, the man and owner of the house, my would-be landlord – was initially somewhat distracted by the presence of *two* males, thinking perhaps that Vince and I wanted to rent the place together. Mario's problems with English required several attempts on my part to clarify the situation. At last he understood that Vince was not involved in any way beyond helping me to find the address, and that I was going to be moving to Vancouver with my wife – whose mother's family, by the way, was Italian.

I'm sure Mario was mesmerized by my command of *grazie, prego,* and *molto bene,* which I threw into my questions and comments to ingratiate him. My amazing intuition told me that certain other words I'd picked up from Jeanette and her family, like *bruta bestia* and *figi butana* (that was how it sounded to me; I may have misheard, or it could have been an Italian dialect for *figlio di puttana*, son of a whore) might not make the impression I intended, particularly since Mario's wife Maria was also present, standing in the background with the earnest, strained smile of one who would have been unable to comprehend anything other than what my approximation of the Italian words meant, not my best intentions, if she heard me utter them.

The suite in question was in the basement of the Falcones' small, well-worn single-family dwelling that reminded me a little of Norm's parents' home in Elmwood Park. After a brief viewing, with Mario explaining what parts of the basement would comprise our suite and what parts would be off-limits, and that the rent would be just $85 Canadian a month (about $65 US at the time; we were paying $110 in San Francisco), suddenly the notion of a basement suite didn't take as much getting used to as the inflated rents of everything else. Moreover, there wasn't time to shop around in a strange city where they called apartments "suites". After quickly taking some visual measurements to try to determine whether our furniture and other things might fit into the place, I decided that they *would* fit or had to fit. And thus it was agreed – within about 20 minutes of having met Mario – that Jeanette and I would become his next tenants. I then drove Vince back to his pad, thanked him, phoned Jeanette to tell her the news, and set off on my way back south.

I got back to San Francisco on June 6th, the day Bobby Kennedy was pronounced dead, the same day that – four years earlier – Norm and I got on the Greyhound bus in downtown Chicago. Would Jeanette approve of the home suite home I'd picked out for us once she saw it? How well did we actually know each other? How well does anyone know anyone else? Is it even possible? (Such questions were grabbing my guts, nuts and throat at the same time, so hard that I hardly dared to go on pursuing them because I couldn't find a way to do so without seeming intellectually pretentious by my own self-imposed norms, or facetious in terms of those who impose no norms at all on their intellectual and/or pseudo-intellectual meditations. (And what's the difference? – answer that and you're a long way already!)

I revisited in my mind all that had happened *to* my mind since Oak Park. There was, of course, the initial euphoria of freedom – breaking as many of the old rules as possible – smoking, drinking, the thrill of getting high on alcohol, the disgust of getting sick on alcohol, getting laid at last, going to movies whenever I wanted to. Then there were the silly "compensations" – acts of deference to my parents – like briefly joining the Baptist Church (under false pretenses), all of my groveling letters to my parents that were never enough anyway, until at last I cast them all aside. Splitting up from Norm might have been inevitable at some point, but the way I handled it, and my *reasons* for the sudden rift, were beyond stupid. Meeting Jeanette, however, was the one great thing, the extraordinary thing, the thing that was worth fighting for, worth everything.

Together, we explored what religion meant – and meant to us – and we found emphatically that religion came up short, its history brutally besmirched, not only as it had been practiced by fallible men, but in the brutal immorality of its very premises and treatises. Once we had that compulsory wedding behind us, we cast off from organized religion altogether, to find our way in the world without a faulty roadmap.

My first night-school courses at San Francisco State's Downtown Extension thrust me into Camus and Sartre, and even Hemingway in a way that Oak Park never did to anyone. Since I was planning to study art, but the Extension didn't offer art, I tried English, where the Faulknerian William Walsh told us of Hemingway's claim to having learned to write by studying paintings. I realized clearly now how that changed the entire course of my academic pursuits. I remembered the rotund Henry Gardner thrusting me headlong into Sisyphus and his cohorts.

Why have so few of the truly great writers studied writing, or so few of the great painters attended art academies? In my studies of philosophy we could never even arrive at a clear and universally acceptable definition of art. Or of good and bad, right and wrong. It seemed to be harder to say what it is than what it isn't. And for most people, it seemed to me, the hardest thing of all was to say "*I don't know*."

I knew that stealing from The Emporium was wrong, but by what measuring stick? The law? Then remember that the law was sending people to Vietnam to kill and slaughter; the law in certain states was persecuting black people; the law had stolen everything from the Indians. And yet there have to be laws.

Is the Bible the measuring stick of right and wrong? The Bible describes a God who commands killing and slaughtering and mayhem left and right, who orchestrates the human sacrifice of His own Son (who was another aspect of Himself, part of Himself?! Huh?!), who persecutes those He labels as heathens and then steals their lands. My stealing had no discernible victims, but it was still wrong; I felt it and I knew it. But I couldn't find the measuring stick for it. I only knew that the Bible wasn't it.

For as long as I could remember, I'd always had some kind of howling longing inside. There's most likely nothing unusual about that. Maybe everyone does.

But most people don't let on, nor do they let on that they realize they might experience such longing. Psychologists can tell you where it comes from and that it's normal and all. Anyone can tell you that if you drop a glass on a concrete floor it will break. But learning that doesn't stop the breaking, does it? How could I ever know what drove me?

I knew a lot of people who liked to talk about "free will". Defenders of various faiths *loved* to talk about free will, and used that chimera to excuse the treacheries of their gods, a ludicrous defense for the Creator of All Things, who thus also created hell, and birth defects, lethal genes, gruesome predators, psychoses, parasites, all of them. Most Christians I'd spoken with liked to claim that God couldn't be expected to save *everybody*. Why the fuck not, if he could be bothered to create everybody?! Who would stop Him from being kind and decent to everyone?! Ah, they protested, our praise of Him, our only purpose for existing, would be of no value unless we *chose* it, by exercising our free will. It was all designed to give each individual total accountability, as if anyone could possibly be accountable for the actions of other individuals or entire societies with whom one is obliged to interact. Who the hell has "free will"? Who chose to be born, when to be born, where to be born, to what parents and with what genes? Who can lift his or her arms and fly away, no matter how much you try, no matter how strong your will? Free will may put you in the driver's seat, but you're driving in the dark on an unknown and treacherous road, in a car that doesn't work, the steering wheel spinning uselessly in your hands, the brakes laughing at you.

And what happens then, dear Christians, when you get to heaven? That's where you'll be doing nothing but praising Him for all eternity. But to be of value, it would still have to be by choice, wouldn't it? You would still need to exercise your free will, daily, hourly, constantly. And wouldn't that have to mean that you would have to be free *not* to continue praising Him? And wouldn't that get you booted out of heaven and sent on a one-way ride to hell after all? So much for Eternal Security, folks. Sorry you wasted your lives.

On the equally bizarre but opposite end from free will, others like to talk of "Fate". Everything is predetermined, we don't know what's coming, but it's all been decided. Fate removes *all* accountability; you cannot choose anything that Fate has not already compelled you to "choose". You are not the driver, you are being driven. You are behind an equally worthless wheel of a car with automatic fuel injection, pre-programmed brakes, uncontrollable steering. You're sailing along roads you haven't chosen, whether past lovely scenery or over a cliff. Even if you think you have made a choice, it's just Fate making you feel that you have chosen something you had no choice but to make.

But why should it have to be *either* free will or fate? What about a combination? Or a continuum? What about chaos, randomness, chance? You can perhaps make some choices, but only within the limitations of the cards you've been dealt, not the cards you would have chosen. How can you *know* whether the action you think you've chosen is not the result of some aspect of your personality that was formed with little or no conscious influence on your part?

Did I choose to be born into a Meeting family? Did I choose to be born in the US, and to be raised in ultra-conservative Oak Park? Did I choose for my country to make a civil war in South East Asia its own war, and send young men like me to kill and die for it? Had anything I'd done thus far in my life *really* been my own choice? Or had anything I'd done thus far in my life really *not* been my own choice? Or was it both? Or neither?

For an uprooted Oak Parker, life would never be the same after 1964 – or after 1968 either.

CHAPTER 7

Landed immigrants

When I got back to San Francisco, Jeanette and I had an awful lot to do. It wasn't just *what* was on our list; it was essential to do things in a certain *order* to avoid extra work. Jeanette had never undertaken a move before. From Oak Park to San Francisco, I had only moved a trunk and a suitcase – no moving vans were involved, no furniture, no termination of phone lines, meter readings of gas, electricity, and water, no logistical complications whatsoever. Moving to Daly City was a bit more complicated for me, but there was still no furniture (apart from my black trunk), nothing like this. We were now embarking on something entirely new, and moving to an entirely new country as well.

The suite awaiting us in Vancouver would be officially ours from the 1st of July, but since there was no old tenant to move out, Mario told me it would be fine if we wanted to start moving our stuff in a bit earlier. Jeanette was not going to leave her job at Bank of America until June 28th, in order to get the much-needed full month's salary. We confidently gave the required month's notice on our Pueblo Street apartment, and we were prepared to keep it after I got home from Vancouver, since we assumed we'd have to pay the full month's rent in San Francisco anyway. We didn't want to have to stay any longer than necessary with Jeanette's parents once our apartment was empty.

But when we talked over the situation with our San Francisco landlord, he told us that a new tenant was already lined up and eager to move in. He also told us that we'd only need to pay half the month's rent if we vacated our apartment by noon on Sunday, June 16th, which gave us nearly nine days to obtain empty cartons, fill them with everything that would fit in them, rent the van, load the cartons and furniture into the van, get the water and electricity meters read, then move our few plants, important papers and perishables to Jeanette's parents', for taking with us in our car when our final moving day came.

Michael had remained listlessly idle for over a year since coming home from Vietnam, but he said he could give me a hand moving our stuff up to Ross Street in the U-Haul. He understood our decision to leave the US, but he wouldn't discuss why. The mention of Vietnam continued to turn his skin clammy and pale. "*C'mon*," he would plead at any attempt to raise the subject. He still frequently remained holed up in his room for days on end, reading and listening to *The Sound of Silence* and other songs by Simon & Garfunkel. Yet he didn't mind accompanying me and helping with the move.

Michael and I picked up the U-Haul van late Saturday afternoon, June 15th. Over the 21 months we lived in our Pueblo Street apartment, we'd done a pretty good job of filling it with bulky furniture, my three paintings, well over a thousand books, plenty of clothes, a number of small Persian rugs, a cowhide, kitchen stuff, and all the other goods that seem to take no space at all in a household until it's time to move them. But since Jeanette and I had already packed everything, it took Michael and me just a couple of hours of intensive running up and down the two flights of stairs on the Sunday morning to load it all up. As soon as we finished, we said our good-byes and took off for Vancouver.

The U-Haul van had aluminum sides and orange trim. It swallowed everything we owned, and left plenty of room to spare for Michael and me to stretch out in sleeping bags in the back for a couple of hours somewhere in Oregon. Michael was tenser than anyone I've ever met, even when he claimed to be relaxed.

I was already making mental images of exactly where I'd try to fit the furniture once we got to Ross Street. There were few options. Fortunately, my two-track memories of the size of each piece of furniture and the size of each available space in our basement suite were of the same gauge. We would have to remove the lower shelves from one of my homemade bookcases, in order to place the armchair in a partially recessed position between the uprights in the living room, but as it turned out, there would even be room for a couple more bookcases, not yet built, in the room that was going to serve as the library and my study.

The rental fee for the van was by the 24-hour day. Our plan was to drive up to Vancouver as quickly as possible, unload everything and get the furniture arranged fairly well, leaving no heavy work for Jeanette. The fully loaded van was kind of sluggish, especially on the upgrades, but we pressed on. There were no customs problems at the border either; I showed them my Landed Immigrant card and documentation, and they waved us on through. We arrived in Vancouver in the late afternoon on June 17th. Mario was still at work. Maria was there to greet us and let us in, and Carmine, who had just come home from school, helped us carry a few things. Carmine was about 16 at the time, tall and dark. He was outgoing and seemed curious and amused about everything we did and everything we had in the van. His brother Semi, who was only about 10, was shy and always seemed to wear shorts, socks that slipped down around his ankles, and striped or argyle sweater-vests, giving him an old-world schoolboy look that might have been a reflection of Maria's ideals. Semi was kept out of the way of our busy moving by Maria's maternal arms.

Michael and I had already unloaded all the big stuff by the time Mario got home. He looked curiously about at everything, then after seeing that the library was full of cartons and no bed, and that the bedroom had a bed in it, he looked pleased to have new tenants. He explained that the former tenants hadn't worked out too well; they were noisy – a not-too-subtle hint that we shouldn't be.

As soon as we'd unloaded the truck, Michael and I went to an A&W drive-in we'd noticed on our way in. It was just a few blocks away. We had some burgers and root beer, then went back to the suite.

I spent a couple of hours trying to get as many cartons as possible unpacked and the contents put in dresser drawers and kitchen cabinets, in order to leave at least a little free floor space by the time Jeanette and I arrived to begin making it our new home two weeks later. I tried to get things in some semblance of order so as not to make too bad a first impression, but the physical and mental efforts soon caught up with me, and I flopped. Michael was already snoozing on the couch. I curled up on our bed, fully clothed, and fell asleep. We took off again for San Francisco early the next morning.

Our trip home with the empty van was a bit faster but just as uneventful. Again, we pulled over to the side of the road for a few hours' sleep somewhere just south of the Oregon border, realizing that we couldn't save any more day fees by hurrying, nor any more mileage fees. We talked quite a lot, which worked fine as long as the subjects were sports, food, popular music, comments on the scenery (beautiful) and the weather (also beautiful). But Michael's instant and severe nervousness made it quite clear that talk about politics, the war, the future (especially his own future) was off-limits. There were also extended periods of silence once we exhausted the safe subjects and the person not driving found it easier to sleep or to pretend to. We got back in the late afternoon on the 19th. We stopped by the house on Seville Street for Michael to pick up a car to follow me to U-Haul to turn in the van, and then we went back to Seville Street. I was incredibly eager to see Jeanette and tell her all about it.

I spent the next two weeks helping to paint the Minihane's house and do other odd jobs to earn our keep and keep me from getting too impatient. Jeanette was every bit as adventurous, impatient and excited as me, and thrilled about the prospect of seeing our suite in Vancouver. And she was bubbling when I picked her up at the big Bank of America building at Market and Van Ness on June 28th. I often picked her up there after work in the rush hour, circling the block while listening to Don Sherwood on KSFO, especially in those last months when I no longer had a job at The Emporium. Freedom was something I'd learned to appreciate, even before we set off for Canada.

We spent our last weekend in San Francisco (the last two days of June), at Mike and Rose's. The atmosphere was occluded. Jeanette and I suppressed our ebullience for their sakes, they suppressed their gnarled disapproval for ours. Beneath the surface, we were charging at each other, horns down; above the surface, we were astutely avoiding all confrontation. On Monday morning, July 1st, Jeanette and I started loading the Valiant with the last of our things. We, and possibly everyone else, felt a sense of considerable relief when we finally pulled away at around 2 PM. At least I did. Mike looked stern. His jaws were clenched, the muscles twitching.

On crossing the US side of the border in the evening of July 2nd, we let out a whoop of something that might have been liberation, or just as likely the sound of a huge new maple leaf turning over. The credit-card-sized "Landed Immigrant's Status" cards we'd been surprised to receive by mail two months earlier were in our hands and ready when we reached the Canadian side. The officer merely glanced at them, gave us a paper to sign, stamped it, and waved us on through. It was friendly enough, but there was no welcoming committee, no band playing, no motorcade. Shouldn't there have been *something*? A short speech? A little ceremony? Where does this urge for ceremony come from?

There are innumerable less-beautiful sights than the approach to Vancouver from the south on a clear July evening. The landscape from the border to the city is almost visibly the result of having been flattened by some geological steam roller. The temperate rain forest climate of the Pacific Northwest makes everything lush and verdant. Then suddenly, just beyond the city, and forming the boundary of its northern suburbs, the mountains rise up, the endless mountains, snow-capped purples and blues, starting with the Lions – twin mountain peaks that watch over the city (and would dwarf the hills called Twin Peaks in San Francisco). At the foot of them, the city with its modestly assertive skyline (this was 1968) towers over the plains to the south as if in revenge for being dwarfed by the mountains to the north. Off to the west, glimpses of water stretch towards the out-of-sight open waters of the Pacific. Above the water and land, the last traces of the oranges, yellows, pinks, and grays of twilight turned to dusk by the time we reached Ross Street.

Ross Street had the same kind of layout as Euclid Avenue: several feet of lawn between the street and the sidewalk, a sidewalk consisting of large concrete squares, and houses with yards in the front as well as in the back. But the streets of Oak Park were tightly dotted with elms (just as the streets of Elmwood Park were lined with oaks) in the part of the lawn between the sidewalk and the street. In Oak Park, the distance to the house opposite was much greater than it felt, because of the trees. Ross Street had no trees at all then, like a new housing tract, except that the houses hadn't been new for decades, and didn't look like one could be certain that they had ever been new; a few of them appeared to have been built with second-hand materials. (During the writing of *Hindsights*, Ross Street came to be lined with cherry trees!)

The Falcones were still up and about when we arrived. They all came out to greet us and meet Jeanette, who was always a bit uncomfortable meeting people for the first time, but masked it graciously. Mario and Maria were genuinely warm-hearted people. They had the good sense to keep the welcoming ceremony brief – or perhaps it was the lateness of the hour – and let us get settled in our new home.

Since I was pretty young at the time of my first marriage, I haven't been able to figure out whether it was because it was a first marriage, or because we were so young, or because that's how life is, or because that's how we were, but we were always convinced that we knew how the other one felt, because we thought we knew how we felt ourselves. We seldom came out and asked each other "How do you feel about this?" At the time it would have seemed as pointless as asking "Do you breath in and out or out and in?" We were mostly blithely unaware of each other's otherness. Jeanette was me, always there, often without my being aware of it, like my third toe, except when it hurts. I was excited and fidgety about moving to Canada. Jeanette behaved in a similar way, which I assumed was the same way. But we never asked. On the other hand, what choice did we have?

I was not quite 23 and Jeanette would turn 24 in less than three weeks. We lived in the kind of self-unconscious, self-assured blur that has all the answers only because it hasn't yet found the questions. But the undermining, soul-eroding questions were not at our command, being at once elusive and intrusive. *Don't call us, we'll call you.*

Had I not experienced living for two years in the jerrybuilt room at the back of Fred Bito's garage in Daly City, I probably would have fled from that basement suite the moment I first saw it. But now it seemed great – to Jeanette as well. It had its own entrance at the side of the house, down two steps to a greenish-gray landing. On the right-hand side of the landing was the gray-painted wooden staircase up to the Falcone's living quarters, with a closed door at the top of the stairs. A door to the right of the entrance and stairway led down a step to a small room that belonged to the suite. It was painted dusty blue, about eight by seven feet, and had a single small window. It would be perfect for the library and study.[9] We informed Mario of our intentions for this somewhat sensitive room, and he readily agreed; the sensitivity lay in the fact that their bedroom was directly above it, and he said with some emphasis and concern that we were *not* to use that room as a bedroom. He blushed as he said it, but with an expression as close to a leer as I ever saw him wear.

Straight ahead from the basement landing were facilities that belonged to the family's domains and were implicitly off-limits to us: their facilities for laundry, meat-curing, grape-juice fermenting, the furnace, and various tools, crates, trunks, and boxes that showed signs of having been taped and re-taped numerous times. In the farthest reaches of the basement there was also a three-by-five-foot bathroom that *was* part of our suite. Access to this tiny bathroom was via a big step up (as at Fred Bito's place) to accommodate the retrofitted drains and water pipes beneath the elevated floor. The shower was built into one corner, with the unfinished stones of the house's foundation itself serving as one wall. There was a tiny (about 6 x 8") grating-covered window in the shower, close to the low ceiling, that provided the only ventilation and a hint of natural light once the bathroom door was closed.

To the left of the entry landing was another door, and another step down, into a kitchen/living room combination. The ceilings were low everywhere, about six-four, and although that gave me half a foot to spare, and Jeanette even more, it added to the cramped impression. The kitchen half of this open-plan area, about ten by six feet, was partially separated from the living room half by a waist-high room divider covered in a slightly turquoise and mustard laminate, like the kitchen counter and cupboard doors. There would be room for our small kitchen table in the kitchen half, with a window above it. The kitchen was, in

---

9   See drawing of the suite in Appendix 1.

fact, the only part of the suite that almost seemed dimensioned for adults. There was ample counter space and cupboard space, as well as a stove and refrigerator of sizes we were used to. I guessed that Mario had done the refurbishing himself, picking up this bit here and that bit there. Mario was good at what he did.

The living-room half posed a few spatial and aesthetic problems. Apart from the low pink ceiling (which took three coats of cheap white paint to cover) and powder blue walls, the room was also only about ten by eight feet, but the long wall to the left was abbreviated to about eight feet by a diagonal fireplace in the corner – which turned out not to be a real fireplace at all, but a fake one with a flickering plastic-log lamp that might have suggested a real fire, but only to the person who designed it. In fact, apart from the differences, it was identical. We immediately replaced it with our wine rack. Above the mantelpiece, there was a cabinet built into the corner. It had glass doors covered on the inside with self-adhesive plastic film that may have been intended to make it look like stained glass but made it look a bit kitschy instead. That became our liquor cabinet. The straight part of the end wall was only about four feet long. A door in the middle of the other long wall led to a tiny room that, with a little imagination and a shoehorn, managed to hold all our bedroom furniture.

There was just room for our couch and an end table along the long wall of the living room after the kitchen divider. The armchair nestled perfectly into one of my bookcases after I removed the lower shelves, and just fit between the kitchen divider and the bedroom door opposite the couch, with another end table next to it. Forget a coffee table. The living room floor was an aisle, perfect for a couple of our small Persian throw rugs. In the far corner, opposite the fake fireplace, there was room for the only beautiful piece of furniture in our possession: a very old china cabinet with multi-paned, beveled-glass doors. We got it from Jeanette's parents; it might have pre-dated them. In the space between the cabinet and the fake fireplace, along the short wall closest to Ross Street, there was just enough room for my black trunk and our TV on top of it.

There were two windows in this open-plan kitchen/living room, both about a foot-and-a-half high and two-and-a-half feet wide. One was in the kitchen above the table, the other was along the far wall of the living room, along the front of the house. Relative to the height of the lot and its slightly downward slope from the street, you could only see the lower legs and feet of anyone passing just outside the living room window, but by the time they rounded the house and passed the kitchen on the slightly sloping lot, you could usually see who it was if you were seated at the table. It only took a few weeks for us to instantly recognize most of the owners of the legs as they passed the front window. The Falcones didn't have terribly many visitors.

The floors throughout the suite, except for the linoleum bathroom floor, were of painted concrete that was cool in the summer and cold in the winter, and were thus infinitely enhanced both aesthetically and thermally by our Persian throw rugs. Since the bedroom itself couldn't have been much more than nine by nine, excluding a built-in closet, it didn't matter much what the floor was made of: our furniture was wall-to-wall.

Our basement suite was clean enough, and it wouldn't be too long a commute for me to UBC. There was easy access to a Safeway grocery store and a laundromat, and it was only a brisk 5-10 minute walk over to Broadway and the bus to downtown Vancouver. The rent seemed to be as low as we could hope for. As for the landlords, one could do worse than Mario and Maria Falcone. It must have been a big step for the couple from the Old Country to become landlords to genuine Americanos. But it didn't feel like that small a step for us either.

Mario was a kind man, a butcher by trade only. He brought his wife Maria all the way from Cosenza in the ankle of Italy to Ross Street, smack dab in the middle of Vancouver's working-class residential area. His fairly small wiry build, bushy black eyebrows, hairy arms, and deeply and permanently tanned skin on his face, neck and lower arms fit my stereotype of someone from southern Italy. Mario would have to stand at least one step up the concrete front steps of the stucco Ross Street home before reaching the height of Carmine, his eldest teenage son, who spoke perfect, unaccented English, using half the syllables Mario needed, although their first names had an equal number.

Poverty, one of the principal chauffeurs in the migratory travels and travails of the human race through the ages, drove Mario and Maria from their meager home in Cosenza across the sea to the middle-class paradise of Vancouver. (In 1968, I had a different driver.) If people were born with shirts on, Mario's would have had the sleeves rolled up. His basement – except for the part that comprised the suite for Jeanette and me – was full of cottage rolls and sausages, smoked hams and curing racks of ribs, all products of Mario's charcuterian[10] skills, all hanging from the rafters. The smells of Mario's butchery were mingled with

---

10   I know, I do coin a word or two....

pungent, yeasty odors emanating from a dozen or so demijohns filled with the purplish juice Mario extracted by means of his own hand-cranked wine press every October. He would take a pick-up on a northeastward pilgrimage to a vineyard near Kamloops to buy grapes, stacking crate after crate of them under the back porch. Then he hurried to set up the press before anything went moldy. As the swollen grapes began to yield their juices with every turn of the screw, Mario's face would light up another notch. And by the time he straightened up and wiped his high brow and the rims of his filled demijohns, he would be grinning intensely.

I was happy to volunteer to lend a hand with any job Mario was up to on a Saturday or Sunday. The Falcones realized that we were on the run from the draft, and sympathized strongly with our situation. This was Canada; we no longer had to assume that strangers would be hostile to people who espoused humanitarian or even socialist ideas and ideals. Even though we never discussed politics much, it seemed clear that their centrist positions, by Canadian standards, would have been pretty far left even by the American standards of the late 1960s.

Maria spoke almost no English; Mario or the kids had to translate nearly everything she said or was told when body language and gestures proved insufficient. It was easiest for all concerned when Carmine was on hand. Maria smiled a lot, earnestly, and exuded kindness and compassion. She was also a terrific cook, as we would have occasion to experience about once a month, when we were invited upstairs to join the family for an amazing Italian Sunday dinner. In return, Jeanette would provide the Falcones with delicious, irresistible, freshly baked homemade bread or apple pies at about the same frequency. But there were barriers and limits, however friendly our landlords were. It was clear that we weren't part of the family (but they didn't seem to have much social life apart from us either). We used the laundromat, not Maria's laundry room. We took care not to make noise after 10 PM, and we tried to keep it down during the earlier part of the evening as well. But we weren't given to loud music or shouting anyway; perhaps it was just their proximity that made us feel inhibited.

Even though our living quarters were cramped, we both felt happier and freer than ever before. The painting of the rooms and the unpacking proceeded quickly. After putting up the bookshelves I'd made in the study, I found I had room for a desk with some additional shelves above it, so I made one. Mario helped me bring home boards and plywood from a lumber yard and he lent me his tools. He or Carmine were quick to lend a steadying hand when I had to saw a large awkward piece. Mario probably could have done the job ten times better and faster, and would gladly have done so, but he seemed to understand that I preferred to do things myself in order to learn. He therefore limited himself to being on hand to lend one when I needed it.

Jeanette and I managed to keep in pristine health and had set aside enough savings to see us through the first period of total uncertainty in Vancouver, when neither of us had any work, much less any income. We were both highly capable of being frugal, which might sound easy enough to be when you don't have much. Perhaps it would be more accurate to say that we shared a high level of aversion to spending money we didn't have. I wouldn't be getting any work until school started in September, when I hoped to earn a little by helping to correct undergraduate essays and exams for one of my professors. During the summer, I wanted to start tackling the long reading list of literature for my upcoming courses. The authors weren't new to me, but some of the titles were. Jeanette wanted to take a couple of weeks to get to know our surroundings before looking for a secretarial job. Anyway, we'd managed to save enough to see us through this initial period without duress. If he'd existed, Polonius would have been proud of us for having adopted his financial counsel.

We spent some weeks exploring Vancouver under the more relaxed conditions of having been married for nearly two years. The fact that it was now a warm summer rather than a rainy and nervous October made it easier. There was a lot to like about Vancouver, and about the smaller, slower pace of its late 1960s life. The city itself was squeaky clean; there seemed to be no slums and few shady parts. There were nice parks, particularly the spacious and gorgeous Stanley Park, which occupied its own peninsula in the northwest corner of the city and led to the Lion's Gate Bridge across the Burrard Inlet (a fjord linked to the Pacific) that opened into the harbor. The bridge crossed to the suburbs of North and West Vancouver, where the mountains began, and, if one continued beyond the first of them, there would reportedly be mountainous wilderness all the way north to the end of Canada, the North Pole and beyond. Driving west from West Vancouver, after rounding the inlet in the direction of the Whistler Mountain ski resort, led to Horseshoe Bay, with its spectacular mountain-and-fjord setting, and a vastly more scenic ferry terminal than Tsawwassen for trips to Vancouver Island. The westernmost part of the city of Vancouver consisted of another large park and forest area, which had one other particularly interesting feature for me: it was the location of the UBC campus.

Vancouver's public bus network was excellent, which made it fairly easy for whichever one of us didn't have or need the car to get around in. And the Falcone home was within easy walking distance of the nearest bus stop. The downtown area, the only area we explored on our honeymoon, had a good selection of unaffordable restaurants, but it wasn't long before we discovered a Chinatown district that almost blended into its surroundings by being low-key and non-touristy. Some of the most fabulous Chinese meals we'd ever tasted could be enjoyed here for loose change.

We would have stumbled onto the restaurant that instantly became our favorite, if it had been possible to stumble through a totally unassuming and poorly lit door bearing only a small sign in Chinese, and continue stumbling up a long, straight-and-narrow flight of dimly lit stairs opening onto a cavernous and noisy room that looked and sounded more like a warehouse, but whose real purpose was betrayed by the most wonderful smells, the clanging of pots and woks in the kitchen part, an array of well-worn tables, and a scurrying of staff members. We were the only Westerners in the industrial, high-ceilinged room; the staff and all the patrons were Chinese and spoke Chinese only (as far as we could hear). There was a small blackboard covered with Chinese characters that turned out to be the only menu – nothing was printed. Our sudden arrival caused about five seconds of total silence in the room, and then the food won out, and the noisy eating and conversational din resumed. Our only hope of getting a meal was to point at various dishes the people at our neighboring tables were digging furiously into.

We didn't need to order a beverage; immediately after showing us to a primitive table, the first thing our elderly waiter did was grab a metal teapot (which apparently already had tea leaves in it), fill it with boiling water directly from a tap, and place the pot on our table with two small cups without handles, two small plates, and two pairs of chopsticks. We'd never used chopsticks before, but we understood we wouldn't be offered anything else here. Gradually a few dishes that closely resembled the ones we'd pointed out began appearing on our table. The portions were enormous. They were beautiful. The smells were intoxicating. They were also amazingly delicious. And we hoped they'd please stop coming, because there was no way we could eat that much, no matter how inexpensive it was.

We had to keep checking our neighbors to get some clues about how to hold the sticks. And they kept checking us out to see how we were managing. They seemed to be enjoying the comedy show we hadn't realized we were putting on with our fumbling. But we eventually succeeded in getting full without getting too messy, and we would be back for more, many times over the ensuing months, reveling in the food each time. In the end, we were no longer putting on a show for our fellow patrons.

Vancouver also had a couple of nice beaches, and in that balmy summer of '68, Jeanette probably spent more time on the beach than in all her years in California combined.

That summer had little of the rain that the Pacific Northwest and BC were known for. During our frequent outings to the beach, we were introduced to the concept of having vinegar on French fries, which we liked, and being offered mayonnaise, which we declined.

I was also introduced to the concept of girls in bikinis. Due to the chilly winds, most people who went to Ocean Beach in San Francisco went there to walk or beachcomb, not to sunbathe or swim, although I did a lot of the latter. In Vancouver that summer, however, the beach was full of sunbathers, and since Jeanette and I seemed to be on the same wavelength in all other aspects, I somehow naively expected her to view the bikini-clad girls with the same titillation I felt. I could still be an excessively young 22 if I wasn't careful. Despite having lived in San Francisco from '64 to '68, I all but missed the sexual revolution, the Summers of Love, and all that I lustfully longed for. Perhaps I felt I missed out on something? Or perhaps I was only just beginning to become aware of the animal in me, like Hesse's Steppenwolf, the dark driving force of my libido that was not me, that did not define me, and yet was an irrepressible part of me.

Another feature of that summer of '68 in Vancouver was that suddenly our families and friends knew somebody living in a foreign country. Consequently, throughout that summer, we were invaded by brothers (Michael, John and family), a sister (Rosanne), two of Jeanette's "cousins" (they were actually an older cousin's daughters), various friends (Elsie, Dave Henderson, Albert LaValley and others) eager to visit and spend a night or two on our couch – or on the floor in the study when there wasn't enough couch, thus in contravention of Mario's explicit wishes. After the summer, we expected the stream of visitors to subside, and it did, but only slightly, during the early part of the autumn.

During the first few weeks in Canada, the similarities between Vancouver and San Francisco, and between Canada and the States, dominated our perceptions of our new environs. And there were many. Nearly all the foods were the same, most of the TV programs, the styles, the language (almost, apart from a few "funny" British spellings and a few "weird" words or usages, like *suite*), the music, the movies at the theaters/theatres. Most of the time Canada, or at least Vancouver, didn't feel foreign at all, which may have disappointed me a bit and certainly disappointed Jeanette a lot. But unlike her, I'd never been to Europe.

Gradually, we began to become aware of certain differences as well. One of the first unmistakable differences was when we saw the new Prime Minister addressing the nation on TV. Apart from the incredibly different attitude stemming from being the leader of a country having one-tenth of the US population, Pierre Elliott Trudeau was speaking to his people, not to the world. And, astonishingly, every few minutes he would switch between English and French – without repeating himself. As far as I could figure out, the only way one could understand the whole speech was to understand both languages. I'd heard that encouraging bilingualism was high on his agenda, as a way of preserving Canadian unity, parrying the appeal of the separatist René Lévesque – and creating a uniquely Canadian identity out of one that seemed to me to be more split between the US and Britain.

Differences in American and Canadian attitudes slowly began to emerge from the fog over the summer: the humility of being a small country not necessarily having all the answers, not a braggadocious superpower; a peaceful country, not one waging war all over the globe; a straightforward country, not playing so many hypocritical games like bashing Cuba while supporting Saudi Arabia; not claiming to be biggest and best at everything. At the same time, disappointingly, we sensed a little-brother complex towards the US, with not entirely unsuccessful efforts to imitate aspects where I felt that going one's own way would have been both stronger and better.

Canadians – the general public, the media, the politicians – all seemed to be constantly aware of what was happening in the United States, following nearly every story, adopting nearly every trend and fad. Most Americans, by contrast, seemed only to have heard somewhere that there was a country called Canada up north, probably populated by a few people, many of them hockey players and lumberjacks, most of whom undoubtedly aspired to be "real" Americans, whether they were aware of it or not. Trudeau certainly had his work cut out for him to influence attitudes on both sides of the continent-wide border.

There were also differences, positive and negative, in many other areas that began to ooze up to our awareness: the chromatically distinct denominations of the paper money, the beautifully simple flag, the government-run booze shops (although Washington and Oregon also had them) with their higher prices, the less-biased and more global news on TV, and government-subsidized healthcare. But there were also the many and incomprehensible (to us) vestiges of the British Empire and monarchy.

Subsidized healthcare was the tip of a new and particularly interesting iceberg, reflecting Canada's fundamentally different version of democracy. Canada had three major parties, not two. I always found it difficult to understand why hundreds of millions of Americans were presumed to be unable to handle more than two parties, two choices. Yet here was Canada, with only 10% of the US population, but with 150% of the number of major political parties. Not only that, but Canada had a parliamentary system; or perhaps that was why. At first I just thought that "Parliament" was the Canadian word for "Congress", until I realized that the parliament chooses the prime minister, which tends to prevent the kinds of logjam impasses that arise when a president is from one party, while the congressional majority is from another.

And then I discovered that Canada's Liberal party was in the middle, with the other two parties on the right and left, respectively. We – still meaning the US – had only middle and right, notwithstanding the fact that for most Americans, "liberal" meant "left", even though the American liberals' positions would place them in the middle in Canada.

For all its professed founding principles of Christianity, the US soundly rejected (thanks to massive lobbying by the AMA and others) any attempts to follow the numerous injunctions of Jesus by actually caring for the sick instead of just preaching about it. All attempts to introduce universal, affordable healthcare in the States were met with howls of "*Socialism!*" as though that word were automatically a pejorative and required blind rejection of anything and everything associated with it. Canada, which seemed to me to be every bit as free as the US, and a whole lot freer in the sense of not fomenting war here and there throughout the world, simply took the view that universal affordable healthcare is a basic *human right* – that it is the duty of the people to choose a good government that helps to ensure the health of the governed.

My curiosity was aroused, so I began reading up on what "socialism" was instead of allowing the mere utterance of the word to shut down my brain and cause my mouth to froth. I quickly discovered highly varied and complex definitions. Some people – proponents and detractors alike – equated it with multiple varieties of communism, others with an array of philosophies commonly labeled liberalism. It was clearly not a word that could be discussed meaningfully before agreeing on which definition to use. A central principle of socialism – *"from each according to his ability, to each according to his need"* – is commonly attributed to Marx, who popularized that pre-existing ideal. To me, that simple principle sounded awfully civilized and reflected every good thing that Jesus nagged about; he was (by most definitions) a true socialist, at least in what he preached about caring for others, yet the word "socialism" itself was enough to make Americans rabid, including (or especially) "Christian" Americans.

It seemed to me that the opponents of "socialism" I'd heard of were using a very different definition from mine – and making an equivocation fallacy. For one thing, they claimed that it would mean a lot of "handouts" (preferably pronounced with a sneer) to lazy people. How did they figure? The central principle of socialism starts with "from each according to his ability", i.e. everyone has to contribute in whatever way they can – no room for freeloaders! Nor does it claim that everyone has to be the same or have the same. What it did imply, at least to me, was that the basic needs of everyone in a society have to be met *first*, that there should be no opulence for anyone *at the expense of* anyone else being destitute. Canada seemed to have taken quite a few more steps towards it than the US. Canada was thus making a lot of sense.

Other differences between the US and Canada took longer for us to recognize. Some of them were identified only by their absence, the kind one perhaps notices last (*"Hey, look at that bear that isn't there!"*). There were no slums, at least not by America's urban standards. No "big-league" baseball (the Montreal Expos were launched a year later, in 1969), basketball or American football teams. (George Bork, my once-upon-a-time college quarterback hero, went on to play Canadian football and was never heard from again in the US; the rules were slightly different and thus unacceptable to American TV broadcasters and viewers.)

Some American brands of certain products were unavailable in Canadian grocery stores, having been substituted by other, Canadian brands of the same products that I initially and unconsciously regarded as inferior, *a priori*. How many of our value judgments – *my* value judgments – are based on erroneous preconceptions? How do we come to realize that a preconception *is* a preconception? And if and when we ever do, how about our willingness to revisit and possibly modify our values?

Within a few weeks of moving into our basement suite, I sent a letter to my draft board, duly notifying them of my change of address. I still retained some optimism that I could keep getting student deferments until the goddamn War was over, or until I was disqualified due to age or other reasons. If that should happen, I didn't want to have exposed myself unnecessarily to the risk of being charged with the additional offense of failing to report my change of address.

It wasn't long before I received a new classification, 1-A, which I immediately appealed on the basis of already being registered as a full-time graduate student at UBC. My first appeal was rejected and I immediately appealed that decision to the next higher level, sending them a copy of a previous letter in which I was given an unqualified promise of a student deferment until the end of the academic year, provided I was registered as a full-time student, which I was. While that appeal was still being processed, I received another particularly chilling letter from the Selective Service: my induction notice! I was ordered to report for military service in Forest Park, Illinois, early one morning a couple of weeks later. Although we were "safe" in Canada, failing to follow the order would mean I'd never be able to cross the border again unless my still-pending appeal went through. It felt final, sickening, monumental, life-changing, disheartening, numbing, dizzying, infuriating, chaotic. But then a few days later, before the actual induction date arrived, I got another letter: I'd been reclassified with a new kind of temporary student deferment, a *non-renewable* deferment until the end of the current academic year only, June 1969.

My induction order was thus cancelled; I had a reprieve. The notification also stated that when the temporary, non-renewable reclassification expired in June 1969, I would be reclassified 1-A. And in the fine print it said, contrary to the information about the non-renewable aspect of my latest classification, that *any* reclassification would automatically entail reopening my right to appeal.

Jeanette found herself a part-time job as the secretary to the head of a small trade union with a catchy name: the Economic Security Employees' National Association. Their office was on the eastern edge of the downtown area, 101 E. Hastings, just a few blocks from our favorite Chinese restaurant. By joining that office she doubled the number of employees there. But she seemed content with the work, her boss and her pay, and we were somehow able to live on that and even save a bit; anything I earned would be gravy.

Mostly out of curiosity, Jeanette went to a Catholic Church once during our time in Vancouver, at Christmas, and found it pathetic. Her religion was only 1% faith and 99% tradition to start with, or at least by the time I met her. The tradition part was deeply tied to those San Francisco churches that played a role in her childhood. Now that she no longer had to go through the motions of placating her parents or revisiting childhood venues, her interest quickly faded, spurred by her moral objections to belonging to an organization that promised eternal torment to all those who didn't measure up to and abide by its teachings. Although Jeanette would have been more than willing to scorn the Pope's watershed encyclical banning birth control, issued in late July that year, she still feared the possible medical side-effects of the Pill. My unholy alliance with the condom would have to remain.

For a while, we vaguely considered joining the Quakers because of our perceptions of them as non-dogmatic pacifists, combined with the last fading vestiges of our inculcated need to belong to something of a religious nature. But we never got around to it; it wasn't important enough. We were both pretty fed up with religion, once we began thinking about it, although at this stage we were only fed up with *organized* religion, not its foundations as far as we understood them (or were motivated to explore).

Jeanette's response to our new life in Canada – or perhaps it was more her response to the inexorable development that can come with additional life experience – seemed to be much more complex than mine (and mine wasn't all that simple). Certain comments she would make, and certain expressions that would cross her face, indicated that she felt something like relief to be *away* from the old place, a feeling that seemed stronger than the joy of being in the new one. Was it the US? California? The Bay Area? Her family? Had the glimpses of moodiness I noticed the first time I met her begun appearing more frequently now, or was I just getting a little bit better at recognizing them? She never wanted to talk about what was going on in her mind when she got that way – she made it clear that it was her secret, private world that I had no access to and simply had to respect. She hadn't exactly been raised to talk about her feelings. But her restlessness – and whatever else might have been behind any sense of relief in leaving the past behind her and moving to Canada – began to return within months, once the novelty, the wonder of the newness, began to subside.

It was also becoming apparent to me that Jeanette's ties with her family were not nearly as close, or as trouble-free, as I'd originally assumed. She seemed to fear her father; her attitude when she spoke of him was openly contemptuous, but she would never say why.

Rose played the leading role in Jeanette's childhood, as mothers tend to do, but there were few outward signs of affection in either direction. The only term of endearment (if that was how it was intended) I ever heard Rose use towards her was when she occasionally called her "Jenny Wren" (a species of wren; also a sentimental character from Dickens' *Our Mutual Friend* – a poor, disabled little girl with a drunken father. I never understood the reference, but I picked up the "Jenny" part and sometimes called her that). Rose tended to present as facts her opinions on how things ought to be done, with all the unwavering, unswerving conviction of people who are dedicated to ignoring the possibility of other versions or interpretations of how they see the world. Jeanette never confronted her mother, but churned inside instead.

Jeanette's bond with her twin brother was most noticeable to me when Michael was in Vietnam – her letters, gifts, and all the thoughtfulness and anxiety behind them caught me completely by surprise, since I'd never seen any signs of such a bond before he left. If Michael returned any of the thoughtfulness, I knew nothing of it, which is not to say he didn't; it would take me most of my life to realize that my capacity for failing to observe the subtle, let alone the obvious, has few limits.

Jeanette and Rosanne spoke to each other in English with a sarcastic accent. I have no memory of any of the big-sister-little-sister playfulness and affection that I might have expected if I added what was absent to my perceptions of what was present. There was clearly some of that, however, in Jeanette's interaction with her older sister. But although Marilyn had "settled down" – with a home, a husband, and a couple of kids – at an early age, Jeanette seemed not to envy any of that, but to look upon it as chains, something she would find suffocating.

Sometime in 1968, someone in my family read a new book by a newly published Christian apologist named Francis Schaeffer. It could have been Dad who first read it and tipped off my brothers about this new guru (or vice-versa). Whoever came first, Al sent me a copy of *The God Who Is There*, urging me to read it and comment on it. I read it diligently, religiously. And then I wrote an extensive letter of reply in which I analyzed Schaeffer's logic, or lack thereof. Taking it apart was an enormously eye-opening exercise, since it was the first time I devoted anywhere near that amount of analytical thought and observation to the Bible or religious matters since leaving Oak Park. By giving me my first taste of the writings of a full-fledged Christian apologist, Dad and my brothers inadvertently made me more aware than ever before just how much Christianity – and religion in general – had to apologize for.

To my surprise (I would get used to it) and disappointment (I never got used to it), Al totally ignored my long, diligent, detailed and sincere reply. I got no response at all. I spent many dull days scrutinizing that damn book and many long hours outlining my objections based on the numerous and obvious fallacies. Not a word in reply. I finally had to phone Al to make sure he'd received my letter. Oh yes, he said. And he'd "get back to me" when his busy schedule permitted. He never did. Eventually, he claimed that all the painstaking research behind my diligently composed, multi-page response had been "mislaid". Or maybe the dog ate it. That didn't stop him from sending additional similar books for me to consider, thereby giving himself new opportunities to ignore my responses. Apart from these book-report assignments, my correspondence with Al consisted largely of me writing long letters to him, and Nancy replying with short, only obliquely related letters to Jeanette. Al didn't seem to understand the highly corrosive effect on our brotherly bonds wrought by his taking the liberty both to send me his religious teachings for my edification and his corresponding self-awarded freedom ignore my responses.

This led to an increasing awareness on my part of every instance of my brothers' appending their religious messages to me and their howls of protest when I openly challenged such messages – another playing field that would never be level.

There was a three-week postal strike in Canada starting July 18th, just a couple of weeks after we arrived, but I'd already had time to send my parents an account of our move and a sketch with a detailed floor plan of our suite. The strike only contributed marginally to the growing infrequency of communication between us. The pattern was unchanged: every letter from Mom was filled with Bible quotes and pre-Elizabethan clichés that left me little to respond to. That's not quite true; her letters gave me a great deal I would have loved to respond to, but I was trying to consider my parents' feelings. I wasn't, however, inclined to let my brothers off the hook so easily.

The end of the Canadian postal strike coincided with the nomination of Nixon at the Republican National Convention, just a couple of weeks before the USSR invaded Czechoslovakia, brutalizing the Prague Spring into the harshest of winters. Then came the corrupt Democratic National Convention in Chicago, where Mayor Daly barred the entry of most of those who opposed Humphry (opponents who made it through the gantlet had their microphones turned off). It made Jeanette and me sick, and strengthened our feelings that choosing exile was the right decision for us.

That Russian-led, Warsaw Pact invasion of Czechoslovakia dealt a severe and much-needed blow to my naiveté concerning certain definitions of socialism, as well as other *-isms*, all of which were labels in a world without truth-in-labeling restrictions. Countries calling themselves socialist were not. Countries calling themselves democratic were not. My distrust of the inherent ambiguity of *-isms* of every variety was slowly awakening; surely they tend to obfuscate more than they explain?!

I came to hate being put into boxes or being labelled in any way. It seemed to me the boxers and labelers are just looking for an excuse to over-simplify the world and the people they meet: whack on a label, then ignore everything that doesn't fit it, don't bother about the nuances, subtleties, contradictions, etc that make up *real* people.

The same applies to the grand abstractions: peace, justice, freedom, and a host of others. Freedom is what everybody says they want, but freedom without limitations is anarchy, which nobody wants, although a few say they want it until someone freely clobbers them. Everyone claims to want peace, but they define it as the unconditional surrender of the other side. The justice white people *want* is not necessarily the justice they want to *give* to people of other epidermal colorations.

To my still-too-innocent horror, people were hiding their selfish ambitions and greed behind grand words like these, facilitated by the fact that each such word represents a continuum with no clear lines of demarcation between each such word and its antithesis. Yet the words were being used as if they represented absolute truths. "Truth" – there's another! Thinking clearly is never going to be easy; no wonder the wholesale or even blind acceptance of someone else's definitions (particularly those of an institution, with the added force of group pressure behind it) seems like such a safe and easy way out.

During the summer I met one of my professors, Dr Lee Whitehead, who would become both my thesis supervisor and my paramount professorial role model. He did his best to shove a little paid work my way: correcting undergraduate papers and looking up some stuff at the library for him. I even had a little work from the summer school session he was teaching. I was told I might be able to get a teaching assistantship, which would have eased the pressure on our budget considerably, but that fell through. As a result, I decided that I would just have to bear down and try to complete my Master's in 12 months, by August 1969, then hope to get a grant for a doctoral program for the following autumn.

I acquired the reading lists for my courses for the academic year, and spent most of my time that summer reading – getting a head start. Fortunately for our budget, my old Emporium habit of simply taking whatever books were available by any author I liked turned out to serve me well in graduate school. I'd already amassed nearly all the works of Faulkner, Conrad, D.H. Lawrence, F. Scott Fitzgerald, Virginia Woolf, and numerous others – many of which were on the long reading lists for my graduate studies. I would have been hard pressed to afford them all on my paltry income.

The term started in September, and I was pleased to learn that I would primarily be working with Dr Whitehead. He was a tall, slender, mild-mannered guy, in his mid-30s, looking every bit the professor with his tweed jackets, sweater vests, and pipe. He was originally from Idaho, but had been living in Canada for quite a few years already, on the posher (compared to Ross Street) western side of Vancouver, in a tastefully pleasant home with beautiful wood paneling. He sometimes held the seminars at his home in the evening once the term started, rather than in the classroom during the day, as he felt the home environment was more conducive to open discussion of symbolism and meaning in early 20th century English literature. The home setting made it feel much more personal and relaxed.

Another of my professors, Dave Powell, was the polar opposite of Lee in many ways. Dave, also American, was built like an inside linebacker, and had a gregarious temperament and a watch-out-world-here-I-come approach to his environs. He had a beautiful, gentle golden retriever, unusually large, that he named Tank, and taught it reverse commands: "*Charge, Tank!*" caused the dog to sit. Dave was active in campus politics and protests, and corralled me into drawing a few cartoons for the student newspaper to accompany controversial articles he'd written.

The courses in my Master's work spanned both the autumn and spring terms, unlike my undergraduate courses that were one term only. There would also be other differences. One of the courses was entitled "English Drama to 1642", and I was greatly looking forward to a much deeper dive into the likes of Shakespeare, Marlowe and Ben Johnson, as well as learning about the works of other less-well-known playwrights of that age. Although the course was interesting, I was disappointed that the focus was more on the biographies of the playwrights than on their works. There was also a great deal of attention paid to what various critics had to say about the authors and their works. I began to wonder whether the doctoral program would cover the critics of the biographies of the critics of the playwrights.

Another course, under Dave Powell, covered 19th century literature, but again, more attention seemed to be given to theories of the Enlightenment and Romanticism movements than to the literature itself. The time we spent getting into Shelley, Coleridge and Wordsworth, however, compensated for a lot of the academic babble.

I also had two graduate seminars that overlapped quite a bit. One was entitled "Innovators of the Novel", under the prolific Dr Elliot B. Gose, Jr., and involved in-depth analysis of selected works from a number of my favorite authors: Joseph Conrad, Ford Madox Ford, James Joyce, Virginia Woolf, William Faulkner and F. Scott Fitzgerald. The other seminar, under Lee Whitehead, focused entirely on Joseph Conrad. This was the seminar that Lee held in his home one evening a week, and it was the seminar that epitomized everything I'd looked forward to in graduate school.

Both seminars were enjoyable and meaningful in many ways; I loved getting at what the authors were saying on different levels and how they used language. For each seminar, we had to write several extensive and well-researched papers that required a lot of critical thinking. But at the same time, Dr Gose's seminar was making it clear that we were being groomed for a lifetime of producing papers – academic papers analyzing the literary works of others, analyzing the critics of the literary works of others, and creating careful bibliographies of the works of the critics who analyzed the literary works of others. It was like pulling a heavy, smothering blanket over the pleasure I derived from literature. Had it not been for the Conrad seminar, I might have walked out of graduate school then and there. But then I couldn't, could I? There was the draft....

One of the papers I wrote for Lee purported to show a parallel between the actions of the chief mate Jukes in chapters four and five of Conrad's *Typhoon* on one hand, and the Biblical story of Jonathon the other hand. My upbringing was paying an unforeseen academic dividend in providing me a topic for my work, which the good professor praised highly, telling me it would be "worth trying to publish". My first reaction was elation – *I'm on track to an academic career; Professor Erisman, here I come!* And then, with the full weight of my other graduate courses bearing down on me, I thought, who gives a shit whether there's a parallel between Jukes and Jonah? What difference could it possibly make to anybody? *What's he to Hecuba?* Is this what I want to do with my life? I quickly fled from such thoughts, because in fact I was enjoying this seminar greatly. But since the rest of my courses were nothing like this, I was unable to give my dark thoughts the slip.

The most noxious part of the rest of my graduate work was the worst course I ever took, including all my under-graduate courses. It was a deal-breaker and ball-crusher, entitled "Bibliography and Methods". It was led by the worst professor I'd ever had, Dr W.E. Fredeman, a totally humorless (in my classroom experience) former US military officer who behaved like one. It and he were so exquisitely boring and beside the point of literature that it nearly made me cry – or vomit. Imagine Shelley making *ibid* and *op cit* his be-all-and-end-all! My spontaneous aversion to rigidity, conformity, orders, regulations, following the mindless crowd, dogma and other demotivators involving "that's the way it's done" was kicking in. The tremendous waves of freedom I experienced in my first years at university and in Lee's seminar were breaking on the rocks of nit-picking academe.

The shock of having seen my life so close to going down the drain when those detectives got hold of me in February had all but quenched my kleptomaniacal flames. Crossing the border to Canada finished the job; there would be no further filching, pilfering, thieving, stealing *et al, op cit, ad nauseum*. At the same time, I failed utterly to feel any real guilt about keeping my loot. I knew that what I had done was wrong and illegal, but not *evil*. For one thing, as far as I could see (and I looked), *I hadn't hurt any other person*. Nobody was suffering because of my actions. There was no victim. Nor had I been *trying* to harm any other human being (or animal). The Emporium undoubtedly got some tax write-offs and insurance claims, the fat cats hadn't even been obliged to tighten their belts, go hungry, or lose a minute of sleep. Yet if I tried to give it all back, they would have realized that my operations were on a much grander scale than they'd ever imagined, and the police would certainly have been called in, and then quite a few people would have been hurt and made to suffer, not just me.

On the other hand, I realized that any legal, moral or philosophical attempt to justify my actions would be totally indefensible, and thus such actions must therefore cease forthwith and forever. They couldn't be set up as a norm or a universal standard. They had, in fact, been irresponsible and reprehensible. *Foolhardy* seemed to me to be the best word for what I'd done. Like my death-defying runs across North Avenue, about which I would later shake my head with a wan, snorting smile – *stupid youthful bravado!* – there was no excuse. But it was time to move on.

Our transition to life in Canada was about as short as any transition period people normally experience when changing to a new school, job or apartment. The time during which Canada felt like a foreign country to us could in most respects be measured in weeks, and in some respects in days. It wasn't so much that Canada *ever* felt new; it was more the school (for me), the job (for Jeanette) and the suite (for us) that were new, and that the sum of those newnesses had a name: Canada.

It's quite possible that the brevity of the transition period was at least partly due to the rapid adaptability and agility of our youth, a condition that still defined us, although we were of course unaware of it at the time, since we were older than we'd ever been and only slightly the wiser for it. I'd almost immediately felt at home on arriving in San Francisco in 1964, despite an even greater upheaval in my life than the move to Vancouver. Jeanette and I had already spent the better part of four years together, with almost daily contact even prior to marriage, which then accounted for half of that time.

We were still restless, but now we were at least restless *together*, a little island unto ourselves.

CHAPTER 8

Mario's dilemma

"Eh, Estanley, we tink you anna Jeanette-a isa very nice-a pippel." (This is an attempt to faithfully render how Mario actually spoke, not to mock him or his accent. I have nothing but admiration for his ability to learn a new language as well as he did!) Mario had a nervous smile on his face when I came out the door of our suite on the side of the house on that crisp autumnal Saturday afternoon, October 12th, four days after our second wedding anniversary. Jeanette and I were sitting at our kitchen table having a leisurely lunch that was extra leisurely because it was Canada's three-day Thanksgiving weekend. It was also the day when a few Italian-Americans in the US were celebrating the day that Christopher Columbus "discovered" an entire hemisphere that was discovered by others a dozen millennia or so before, and who were soon to have it violently taken from them. (For the Indians, whose land was stolen, Columbus Day was a day of mourning.) And it was Norm's birthday.

We'd noticed that Mario was pacing back and forth on the walkway outside our door. We found it strange. I went out to see if anything was the matter. He started when he saw me, as if I'd interrupted some sort of dress rehearsal. I smiled inquisitively at him and he placed a hairy arm on my shoulder, continuing his attempts to smile, although he appeared to be in great pain. He had the same burdened expression on his face that Dad used to have when he came home from work after the ordeal of having to let someone go who wanted to stay. Dad's brow could take hours to unwrinkle. His breathing would be a series of fitful sighs. Dad wouldn't have been emotionally cut out for work in an abattoir.

That pained smile notwithstanding, there was little physical similarity between Mario Falcone and Maurice Erisman, other than the usual two-of-those, one-of-those similarities resulting from all *homo sapiens* sharing 99.99% of their genes (which apparently is not enough, considering the wars and bloodshed over the differences that the 0.01% entail).

I doubted that Mario's comment on our congeniality was intended to be a general observation and assessment of us as his tenants; his ill-disguised agitation suggested there was something more to follow, in the way that some compliments give the feeling that a "but" is just around the corner. Mario's smile was not a relaxed one, and it failed to mask his growing discomfort. I now felt certain he had something else to say, something he didn't want to, but had to. I lingered.

"*Thanks, Mario, we really like you too,*" I replied, just in case I was inferring something he hadn't implied. But he caught his breath and went on, starting over from the beginning of the little speech he seemed to have rehearsed many times.

"*You anna Jeanette-a, you nice-a, and we like-a you, butta whena we arenta deesa suite, we teenka we arenta to <u>two</u> pippel – butta you alwaysso <u>mainy</u>!!*"

I blanched. Of course he was right. Although we hadn't been excessively noisy, we'd had overnight visitors as often as 10 nights a month. Worse, on a couple of those nights of multiple guests, we'd let one of them sleep on a mattress on the floor in the study directly beneath the Falcone's marital bed. I smiled wincingly and sighed bravely yet sheepishly.

"*Yes, I know, Mario, you're right. I get what you mean. I'm very sorry, we didn't mean to let it get this way. We'll take care of it, I promise you. We're really very sorry. We won't let it happen again.*"

I could see how much Mario hated having to complain. And I knew that his claim was perfectly legitimate. I also hated causing such a nice guy any discomfort or disrespecting his wishes. Clearly we had to do something. I went back inside, sat down at the table and related my conversation with Mario to Jeanette. We looked at each other and both sighed deep, *this-is-it* sighs. We had a problem that wasn't going to melt away; we'd have to find a solution. And it couldn't wait.

We knew from the start that our spartan accommodations as Mario's tenants, however nice he was and however spartanly we could deal with them, were never going to be a long-term solution. We just hadn't expected to need to deal with the problem this soon. Looking at our situation analytically, we found that the core of the problem – no, not necessarily, but the deal-breaker – was that we couldn't go on having multiple visitors, and we definitely could not allow the licit library to be used as an illicit guest bedroom. We could put up two visitors in our living room – one on the couch and the other on the floor, using the back cushions from the couch to sleep on, even though it would create an obstacle course between the kitchen and our bedroom, and offer no privacy for anybody. Three other options were left: (1) tell friends and family they couldn't come to see us; (2) tell friends and family that if they came to see us, they'd have to stay elsewhere; or (3) we would have to move to a proper and larger apartment that was not squeezed into someone's already-small family home.

Emotionally, (1) was not an option, even though in some cases we might not have had a problem reducing the number of visitors and duration of their stay; (2) would only be an option for those who could afford other accommodations, which wouldn't include many of those who expressed their interest in coming to see us; and (3) would have been the best solution apart from the fact that proper apartments cost two to three times as much as we could afford. Long-term we would have to choose (3), but use some combination of (1) and (2) short-term until we could alter our circumstances in such a way as to be able to afford (3).

So how could we afford a bigger, better place to live? I had next to no income due to my full-time studies. And since graduate school, with all its requirements for producing academic-style papers, was much more demanding than San Francisco State ever was, working part-time wasn't an option either. The tiny union office that was Jeanette's employer had no opportunity to offer her full-time work, and it turned out that Jeanette had been kind of lucky to get that job at all; worse, full-time positions turned out to be scarce everywhere in Vancouver.

Although apartments and suites were at least twice as expensive in Vancouver as in San Francisco, we found out that buying a house in 1968 would for some reason only cost about half the prices in most of the Bay Area. That would be the ideal solution, but again, only if we had steady jobs that would entitle us to an affordable mortgage. As far as I knew, Dad and Mom helped both John and Al with low- or no-interest loans in connection with buying their first homes, but my parents never said anything to indicate that I would ever get such an offer. They made all their previous offers contingent upon my acceptance of and adherence to their beliefs. I knew there would be a price to pay for my apostasy, and I preferred to pay that price rather than deal with blackmail or bribery on their part, or hypocrisy on mine. As a result, I didn't ask. Jeanette and I felt that we were being impaled on the horns of Mario's dilemma.

Surely there must be other options? I was probably facing three or so more years of graduate school before I could get my doctorate and begin to work my way towards the kind of university position I was striving for. But by now I'd already begun wondering whether that was what I wanted after all. Apart from Lee's course and seminar sessions, I wasn't enjoying graduate school all that much. (We'd seen Albee's play *Who's Afraid of Virginia Woolf?*, as well as the movie.) The obligatory course in bibliography was making me gag. I had to jog my memory to recall how I'd once been looking forward to graduate school, to delve ever deeper into the works of the English writers of the late 19th and early 20th centuries, to examine how they used language and what messages they were conveying, what symbolism they used, to get into the philosophies that lay behind their work. But that was not to be. Instead it was goddamn bibliographies and the rules for structuring them. It was the prospect of having to engage in endless, esoteric research drudgery in the world of nit-picking academe. It was churning out specialized academic papers for specialized academic journals to be read solely by specialized academics, full of words and fury, signifying very little of consequence. I felt it was maybe not what I'd signed up for.

In the sciences, to my understanding, graduate school opens the door to the student's passion for learning more and in greater depth about the discipline in question (instead of what the critics have to say about it) – to solve problems and pioneer into the heretofore unknown, to contribute to mankind's body of knowledge in the respective scientific disciplines, and ultimately to help lay expanded foundations of learning that have the potential to benefit everyone.

Even though Lee did his bit to uphold and encourage the quest for meaning, I still felt that the overall focus of graduate school was archeological. In most of my courses, we weren't using our studies of earlier literature as a springboard for writing new literature, creating beauty and meaning and understanding of the human condition. We were simply writing about the writings of others, supporting our writings with references to the writings of others about the writings of the others who once upon a time created beauty, meaning, and understanding: picking as many nits as we could to enhance our standing among our colleagues. I'd already begun to learn the game, and picked an appropriate subject for my master's thesis: the use of circles and lines as symbolism in the work of Joseph Conrad. Although Lee encouraged me greatly in this pursuit, I was already totally disillusioned about the idea of continuing in academia and began thinking of leaving it at the end of the academic year in June, Master's or no Master's.

Suddenly Jeanette and I saw another option on the table. I could finish the current academic year – I was convinced I could complete my Master's degree during the coming summer, even if it meant holding my nose for months in order to achieve a passing grade in that damn bibliography course – and then take a job teaching high school English, trying to open young minds to the joys of literature without the need to use that literature to create endless hair-splitting papers to fill obscure academic journals. The rent level for ordinary apartments (or suites) would be money down the drain even if I were working and we could cover it. Purchasing a home would make the most sense. Then we could find ourselves a house, get our 30-year mortgage, make the house our home, and have all the damn visitors we pleased.

Jeanette gulped audibly when I outlined all this. She turned pale at the part about the 30-year mortgage. (I probably gulped when I said it.) The thought of tying a 30-year millstone around our 24- and 23-year-old necks was admittedly about as attractive to us as getting a root canal with a jack hammer and without Novocain.

Then she had a suggestion. She had by no means forgotten her trip to Europe with Michael during the summer of '65 and how much it thrilled her. "*I'd love to show you Europe before we settle down like that,*" she said, and I could tell she felt the way I did about the 30-year bondage. I was reluctant to make any big decisions, but Jeanette's enthusiasm and playful mocking of my timidity soon won me over.

But how could we manage it, in practical terms? Our modest savings might possibly allow us to live over there – in Europe! – for half a year at most, provided we continued to maintain our spartan lifestyle, but since that lifestyle would allow us very little travelling once we got there, what would be the point? Cranial wheels were turning. We'd need to work over there somewhere, at something or other, but for how long? How long would it take us to see what we wanted to see in Europe without being able to know what we would want to see until we got over there and began seeing it? Jeanette had a possible ultimate answer to that question too, in the form of another question: "*What if we just move there, then work and travel according to what we can afford?!*" That sounded wonderful, but wouldn't that require a base somewhere? And where might that be?

It was getting to be late afternoon. We hauled out and unfolded a big National Geographic map of Europe and covered the kitchen table with it like a tablecloth, with parts of Finland and Greece and all of Malta hanging over the edges. Jeanette had only been to Ireland (Shannon Airport, her relatives in County Cork, a night or two in Dublin), England (London only), France (Paris only), and Italy (Rome and Florence only), which was four more European countries than I'd ever visited. We suddenly realized how incredibly little we knew about Europe, and would have to use some sort of process-of-illumination[11] criteria to come up

---

11   *sic*

with a few reasonable choices in a matter this big.

Having endured the first round of the scare of an imminent induction notice, we both felt that a NATO country would be too risky to use as a base; we didn't want any more hassle or cat-and-mouse games with the Selective Service, nor did we want to face the risk of extradition, if indeed that might be a risk over there. That left just a handful of neutral Western European countries: Spain, which we immediately ruled out because of Franco's right-wing dictatorship; Ireland, off our list because of the poor job opportunities and its rigid Catholic worldview; and Finland, whose remoteness up in the corner next to the USSR would defeat the main purpose of having easy access to the whole of Europe (plus an impossible language that was not even in the Indo-European group).

There were still three neutral countries to consider. We might have found Switzerland attractive, with its spectacular mountains and long-standing reputation as a sanctuary to many people from wars of various kinds, plus the fact that I reportedly had a renegade cousin named Robert living there. And my surname came from there. But they also had some extremely anachronistic and discriminatory laws relating to women, and in recent years they were known to have a highly restrictive immigration policy that required proof of possession of the kind of wealth we didn't even dare or want to dream of. Only two countries now remained: Austria and Sweden. My mom's side of the family were all from Sweden. I'd seen nearly all of Ingmar Bergman's films, and in Canada we'd both seen the hauntingly beautiful Swedish film *Elvira Madigan* with its ethereal theme music from Mozart's 21st piano concerto. To us, Sweden gave every impression of being a modern, secular country. People from their government had recently demonstrated against the Vietnam War. They'd been in the news a number of times about granting asylum to American deserters. And Orr fled to Sweden at the end of *Catch-22*. Sweden became our clear first choice.

The next step was finding where we might live once we got there. Sweden was a country whose geography we knew next to nothing about when we began our perusal of that part of the National Geographic map on our table. We'd both been city people all our lives – neither of us had lived anywhere other than a major urban area – and thus we naturally gravitated towards big cities. We'd heard of Sweden's capital city, Stockholm, which was where they awarded the Nobel Prizes, but after looking closely at the map, we felt that Stockholm would be too far from our primary goal: to live in Europe. A bit farther south, along the west coast, was another city. We'd heard the name Göteborg (Gothenburg), but had thought it was in Germany, probably because we confused the name with Gutenberg, the 15th century German inventor of moveable type.

And then there was a place called Malmö (Malmoe), in southernmost Sweden. We'd never heard of it, but it was just across a narrow strait from Copenhagen (which we'd heard of) in Denmark. That would at least put us close to a major European city that was fairly close to the heart of Europe, and we'd still be in a friendly, progressive, neutral country.

We made the decision, right there and then, within a few hours of Mario having expressed his concerns about our many overnight guests: we would move our worldly goods, our lives, hopes and dreams to the entirely unknown, over-the-cliff place called Malmö, Sweden, with the ostensible aim of having it as our base for exploring Europe for an indefinite period of time.

It wasn't even dusk yet. In one afternoon, from a starting point that life would continue creeping its petty pace from day to day, we came to a decision that would change the direction of our lives, completely, profoundly and forever. In Vancouver we created a home out of a dingy little basement suite. We'd now made a monumental decision together to cross the ocean to find something we knew almost nothing about, externally or internally, another undiscovered country. It was scary. It was daunting. And yet we felt so close to each other, so part of each other, so completely and mutually in love. And suddenly I wanted to paint again.

CHAPTER 9

Inconclusive anticipation

The evening passed. Questions were sweeping down upon us in purple and gold. Answers were only coming in ones, at best. We were highly charged, terrified and thrilled at the same time. It wasn't just the change in whatever long-term view we had of our *future*; the perspective on everything in our *now* had also been jolted violently from its moorings and was adrift, altered beyond recognition. And yet it felt right. This was what both of us truly wanted to do.

We'd wait a couple of months before we broke the news of our intentions to anyone; we thought it best to first make sure we felt the same about a decision of this magnitude when we woke up, tomorrow and the next day and in the weeks to come. We also had to look into as many of the daunting practical ramifications as we could possibly figure out ourselves. For one thing, the decision wasn't entirely ours to make (few decisions in life ever are or would be); the Swedish authorities, for example, might have a thing or two to say about allowing us in. Furthermore, we had no idea of the costs an intercontinental move might entail, and thus we had no way of knowing whether or how we could even afford it financially. In fact, the move was far more major than any other undertaking we'd ever attempted, and covered just about every aspect of our lives. Then there was the small matter of entering a complete unknown, and thus not being able to know what we were getting into before we were in it, possibly without any way of getting back.

During the remainder of the autumn, we continued to have occasional house guests from South of the Border, but those who couldn't fit on our living room couch and floor had to find accommodations elsewhere; we were *not* going to upset Mario again.

Other events Down South continued to fuel our desire to put a greater distance between ourselves and the country of our birth. The Olympics in Mexico City in late October were not only memorable to me for Bob Beamon's fantastic long jump and Dick Fosbury's fascinating flop, but also for the raised fists of Tommy Smith and John Carlos at their medal ceremony. The resulting public outcry in much of the US media was literally incredible – not only because so few white people could see how justifiable and desperate those brilliant athletes' silent protest was, but because it also stood in such stark contrast to the *lack* of an equivalent outcry on the part of white people over all the generations of lynchings, miscarriages of justice, racist laws and discriminatory practices and behavior that had been and still were infinitely more threatening to black people than two raised, black-gloved, non-violent fists were to any white people.

And then, just a few weeks later, the American voters elected Richard Nixon to be their President, and he appointed Henry Kissinger to be his National Security Advisor.

My attitude towards graduate school changed quickly and drastically following our tentative decision to move to Sweden. I retained my growing disaffection with the whole idea of being a graduate student and heading for a career in academe, but at the same time I became more relaxed and less stressed. I could laugh at the abstruseness of some of the titles of the academic papers I was constantly encountering, especially in the bibliography course, because they no longer represented anything like a goal towards which I had any desire to strive. I was suddenly an outsider looking in (not an entirely unusual role for me), a window shopper whose views of what was on offer had squelched all interest in making purchases. Paradoxically, that new attitude enabled me to start thoroughly enjoying graduate school again, because I could focus solely on learning about the literature I was reading, not on impressing anyone, not on performing like a trained seal. The one big, bottlenecking, revolting exception in the enjoyment of my studies was that fascist bibliography professor.

Jeanette and I both felt that living in Canada was almost like living in a 51st state, largely because of the burden of so many similarities to the US, while facing the rapidly approaching probability that the other 50 would soon be off-limits to me. Therein lay the problem. We *really* liked Canada. In one sense it was the US without the crap: the politics and most of the macho-jingo-gung-ho bullshit. But it still seemed to us like a *version* of the US; it was *too* familiar, it didn't feel like a new enough or different enough country, and that was probably what we were in search of, or at least Jeanette was. I was in search of what might make Jeanette happy. I'm sure that if Canada were located in Europe, we would never have thought of leaving Canada. (Maybe if San Francisco were located in Canada *or* Europe, we might not have thought of leaving San Francisco either. Maybe if we'd been born chickens we'd have flown the coop.)

In many ways, what we read about Sweden sounded like a north-south slice of Canada. The climate there was supposedly rather like British Columbia: mild winters in the south, frozen ones in the north, almost no extreme heat. In terms of population, Sweden sounded like anywhere in Canada: the densest parts were in the south, while the north remained sparsely settled. Sweden also had a parliamentary system of a kind I as yet knew little about, and "socialism" seemed not to be a swear word there – it was possibly even a watchword for many. The level of education was high and it would reportedly be possible to communicate in English just about everywhere. The standard of living was also high; and like Canada's high standard, it was available to everyone.

The decision to move to Europe, to Sweden, changed Jeanette. There was a whole new spark, an enthusiasm I hadn't seen in her before to such an extent. This would be her emancipation, like leaving Oak Park was mine. How could we know whether we were primarily going *to* something or *from* something? To her it seemed to be the pursuit of a dream; to me it was a step – an incredibly long step – into the unknown.

As mid-December was approaching, Jeanette was talking to her mom about a possible visit from Rosanne and Maureen to spend Christmas with us, and she mentioned our plans to move to Sweden. Her mom was too flabbergasted, flustered, upset, outraged and confused to formulate a cogent response, but she was clearly not supportive.

On December 17th, I wrote to my parents that "*Next year you may be wanting to take a European vacation. Jeanette and I plan to move to Sweden in August.*" By this time my letters had outgrown the pre-Elizabethan language and the even-older ideas; I used no Meeting or Biblical clichés whatsoever.

Mom's response was to ask whether they could send us a Swedish Bible. I replied politely that it would be fine. They sent us a Swedish Bible. Jeanette replied to thank them politely for thinking of us. I don't remember which of the numerous translations of the Swedish Bible they sent us; they all remained illegible to us for years until our Swedish was sufficiently sophisticated to enable us to read what it said, and largely unintelligible after that.

When Rosanne and Maureen arrived for their week-long visit, they shared our tiny living room with our tiny Christmas tree, next to our tiny bedroom. They seemed excited about our plans to move to Europe, perhaps mostly about the prospect of having a future European destination to crash at. But they didn't ask much about anything: our reasons, why Sweden, what we'd do there, any of the things that were racing through our minds day and night.

Jeanette made a fabulous roast goose for our non-traditional (for either of us) Christmas dinner. We had some fun showing the two giggly teenagers around Vancouver, which felt a bit strange now that we knew we'd be leaving it. They were obviously there to see Jeanette; I was pretty much an invisible chauffer, which was no surprise to anyone involved.

What did surprise us was that Vancouver, normally and allegedly temperate even in the winter, was hit by a major Chicago-style blizzard. The locals assured us that this was most unusual for Vancouver; they claimed that the city seldom got more than an inch of snow during the winter, but now we had more like a foot. It made a strikingly beautiful blanket of purest fleece on everything, but also caused considerable traffic inconvenience and some concern.

The day of our guests' departure was approaching, and neither Jeanette nor I was eager to prolong their stay, but very few buses were still running, and it the heavy snowfall continued. We phoned the airport to check that flights were still taking off, which they were, but with some delays. There was far too much snow to make it possible for us to drive to the airport. We had no snow tires or chains, and the only people who seemed to have them were those who made frequent trips into the mountains to ski.

Fortunately, one of the only bus lines still running was the one to the airport, but the nearest stop was a couple of miles away, at the corner of Granville and 41st. We all struggled off on foot, laughing and cursing and shivering through the deep snow, me carrying the two heaviest suitcases. Our human convoy stretched out further and further behind me as we battled our way to the bus stop, with the girls lagging more than a block behind Jeanette and me by the time we got there. Then we had to wait until we were all thoroughly frozen, but not in vain. The bus was surprisingly close to schedule. We said our goodbyes, and Jeanette and I again had each other to ourselves.

The unusually heavy winter weather remained throughout most of January, and I was already beginning to doubt that I could complete my Master's thesis before leaving for Sweden – or that I could be bothered to. My heart was no longer in it. I had to paint. And the prospect of visiting and possibly moving to Europe was also much more exciting than further studies, now totally overshadowed by that damn bibliography course, which had assumed a symbolic role of dread and drudgery, and its professor that of an archetypal villain.

We discovered in the Yellow Pages that there was a Swedish consulate just east of the downtown area, not far from where Jeanette worked. Surely they would have all the information we needed to confirm the wisdom – or at least the feasibility, or the theoretical possibility – of our decision to move to Sweden? Of course we thought they would also offer us unlimited assistance and support in effecting it.

I decided to make the first contact by undertaking a solo visit. The consulate turned out to be an "honorary consulate", which meant that the Honorary Consul himself was not an official member of the Swedish diplomatic corps, but for some reason was entrusted with certain consular duties in Vancouver on behalf of Sweden. I don't think he was Swedish. His main line of work was as an insurance broker, which seemed to be (like the consulate itself) a one-man operation. It was located in the Dominion Building, Canada's first "skyscraper" (13 stories), at 207 West Hastings Street.

The office was upstairs, along a dark and dingy corridor lined with frosted glass doors with lettering stenciled onto them, in the old Detective Marlowe fashion. One door had the name of an insurance brokerage. The next door was for the Swedish Honorary Consulate. Both doors opened onto the same room, with a single large desk, behind which was a large opened newspaper with fingertips visible along the two vertical sides, holding it up. Two legs emerged from beneath the paper, ending in two well-worn, well-filled crossed shoes lethargically parked on the desk.

I cleared my throat and the paper dropped instantly to reveal a bored-looking, somewhat disheveled, upper-middle-aged man peering at me over glasses that were parked towards the end of his reddish nose. He asked if he could help me, but sounded and looked more like he wondered what on earth had compelled me to disturb his morning paper-reading session. I asked if this was indeed the Swedish Consulate, which I was genuinely unsure of, in addition to wishing to preclude a possible sales pitch for some form of insurance. He grunted and nodded in assent.

"*My wife and I are thinking of moving to Sweden,*" I ventured. "*You'll have to get a work permit first,*" he grunted somewhat brusquely after a brief pause. I considered that minimalist reply for a moment while he stared at me. Then I continued. "*OK, how do we go about getting a work permit?*" With no hesitation this time, but with equally bored brusqueness, he picked up his paper again and said from behind it, "*You'll have to get a job first.*" Since we had not quite come full circle, I again paused to consider the implications and came up with a new and insightful question: *"OK, how do we see about getting a job?"* Again, he had no need to weigh his answer, but dipped his paper just enough to reveal his bored yet piercing eyes and replied at once, triumphantly, *"You'll have to get a work permit first!"*

Now he'd come full circle, so fast that it almost made me dizzy. My strongest impulse was to burst out laughing, but somehow, finding myself in a genuine, real-life Kafkaesque or Helleresque situation left me speechless. His interest in helping me was clearly far less than his interest in whatever he was reading in the paper; he stuck to that with full concentration while I continued to stand there trying to figure out what questions I should have asked, or should now ask, in order to get some information that would be useful for Jeanette and me to know how to proceed.

I have no idea how long I stood there. His newspaper prevented visual contact, apart from my view of the soles of his shoes, until I finally decided to ask for some printed matter relating to immigration or Sweden. As long as it was printed, it wasn't coming from him. I was convinced that he was anti-social at best and stark-raving mad at worst. Without speaking, but with a barely audible groan and snort, he put his paper down, reached over to a shelf behind him, plucked out a few leaflets, and handed them to me. Then he went back to his paper as I left the auspicious office of Sweden's Honorary Consul.

The leaflets raised more questions than they answered, but there was enough information to raise *specific* questions, and to wipe out most of the unfairly negative first impressions of the country conveyed by the somewhat bizarre occupant of the office I visited. We were not confident, however, that the cantankerous Honorary Consul would be willing or able to take the trouble to provide any answers. But at least the printed matter gave us the impression that our aims were not hopelessly unrealistic.

I also contacted the American consulate in Vancouver to see about getting a passport. (Jeanette already had hers from her trip to Europe in '65.) The person I spoke to there, even gruffer and unfriendlier than the Honorary Consul, told me they would certainly *not* be able to help me – I'd have to go to the passport office in Seattle. Although entering the US still made me nervous, it had to be done. I found out exactly which documents and photos I would need so I could make a day trip of it. I don't remember whether they mailed me my passport, or if I had to go to Seattle a second time to pick it up. But it felt good to have one less problem.

I told Lee Whitehead about our plans to move to Sweden, and he put me in touch with one of his colleagues, Grove Powell (no relation to Dave), who'd lived in Sweden for a year. Mr Powell advised me to learn Swedish as soon as possible, which was sound enough advice, but possibly less altruistic than I first imagined; it also enabled him to sell me his Swedish primer and cassette tapes. The only Swedish words I'd previously known were *tack så mycket* (thank you so much), *jag kan inte förstå dig* (I can't understand you), *sju hundra sjuttio sju* (seven hundred and seventy seven) and *en sådan pojk* (such a boy). The latter of these phrases was what my Grandpa Larson sometimes said to me when I sat on his lap as a small boy. I thought it sounded so funny. The others I learned from my mom. I realized that we'd need to learn a bit more.

Mr Powell told me that he liked Sweden a lot, although his own efforts to learn Swedish were not terribly successful, since nearly everyone he met preferred to practice their English with him. He also claimed that some towns in Sweden "adopted" artists, essentially hiring them, provided them a livable income, and purchased or exhibited their works in public places. That sounded amazing to me, particularly since I'd just set up my rickety easel in my study, and had stretched and primed a few canvases. In other words, I was about to do what I began doing between nine and two months before leaving Oak Park and hadn't done since: I was going to paint again.

Jeanette was incredibly enthusiastic about my decision to paint again; it was as if she would do anything to make it happen, and would allow nothing to interfere. I had a few clear ideas, and these would be the subjects of my first paintings. My messages and symbolism were conscious and they were clear in my mind.

It wasn't so much a question of *wanting* to paint again; I *needed* to paint, in order to synthesize the monumental changes that were taking place in my life (and ours) and my mind (and ours) since I put down my brushes a month or so before Norm and I got on that bus to San Francisco. I certainly had plenty to come to terms with. And Jeanette, nearly three and a half years after I fell in love with her, nearly a year and a half after we married, told me that she had at last truly fallen in love with me. The hateful *I wish you love* had been replaced by Chaplin's *Eternally*, as well as Jo Stafford's version of *No Other Love*, with music taken from Chopin. Those were now her songs for me, she said. And with that, I not only needed to paint; I *could* paint.

So in our cramped studio/library/study beneath the Falcone's bedroom on

Ross Street, I started out with a fairly large canvas and with a fully formed idea in my head: to resolve the inner conflict that both Jeanette and I felt about rejecting organized religion, but not all the teachings of Jesus. Jesus was pretty much OK, we still felt, but churches were cynical institutions for amassing power and wealth by preying on human imperfection and fear of the unknown and unknowable, turning it into the strongest possible guilt feelings, thereby enabling the church to amass the maximum of said power and wealth by offering "atonement" or "salvation".

Using a fairly large canvas, I made a charcoal sketch directly on the cloth from the image in my head. I wanted to depict our view of the organized religions of Christianity as businesses. This painting represents a first major milestone in my liberation from religion. Leaving Oak Park was my liberation from the Meeting, but the withdrawal symptoms from all religion were still too strong.

Stylistically, it was in this painting that I was first fully conscious of using not only the "building blocks" or geometrical planes of color I had stumbled onto in my first painting, but also the *void* – which would go on to play a significant role in nearly all of my subsequent paintings. In studying a little astronomy, I'd been astounded by the emptiness of space, and the feeling that matter is just sprinkled onto or into an incredible void – the ultimate background. The same feeling of a void struck me when studying a little biology and chemistry – the empty space between atoms and sub-atomic particles, tiny flecks of matter randomly strewn upon nothingness. I found it mind-boggling that with just 100+ elements we get an entire universe, or with just 26 letters we get the entire body of English literature.

I finished the painting in the early part of 1969 and called it *"Hurry up with the Lumber, for Christ's Sake!"*[12] In my view (as I'm the artist, I'm allowed to have this view), it is one of the best paintings I would ever create.

Since Jeanette was going to be the Maid of Honor at the wedding of her friend Carol in San Francisco on February 1st, 1969, we flew down there for an extended weekend – which turned out to be our last trip to San Francisco prior to our move in August. As always, we both felt a little nervous and paranoid about entering the US, even though I was not yet officially on the wrong side of the law where the draft was concerned.

---

12   Painting #9 (see Appendix 2)

Being "at home" with Jeanette's family was also strange and stiff, but we did our best to keep it light – clowning and joking and trying to promote laughter, or provoke it if needed. By this time, our still-tentative plans to move to Sweden were known by all, but had not been met with anything remotely resembling enthusiasm. Only Michael seemed to understand why we were thrilled, but then he was the only one who'd been to Europe as an adult. Perhaps that explained it. He also said that once we were settled, he might want to come over and spend some time with us. He was clearly having difficulty adjusting at home, which Jeanette seemed to understand on a level I was ill-equipped to grasp. Maybe there were things in their childhood or family life that nobody would talk about. Jeanette certainly didn't, and became nervous when I asked. That particular kind of not-entirely-suppressible nervousness in the face of deeply troubling topics seemed to run in the family.

My latest non-renewable 1-S(C) draft classification was due to expire at the end of the school year, in June, at which time I knew that my appeal rights would be reopened (although I didn't expect the draft board to remind me). Since official "peace" talks among American and Vietnamese adversaries had just commenced in Paris, I hoped that the War would come to an end soon, that the draft board would get off the backs of America's young men, and that our trip to Europe would be nothing more than an entirely voluntary trip. But that no longer seemed the most likely outcome to us, nor did it in any way affect Jeanette's desire to show me Europe and get back there herself. Our tentative plans would remain intact: we'd remain in Europe indefinitely.

Jeanette wore a long wine-red velvet bridesmaid's dress to the wedding. She looked stunningly beautiful. Neither of us knew more than a handful of the people at the entirely predictable Catholic wedding, and I'm assuming it was not terribly memorable, or I might have had more memories to write about it. It was primarily an excuse to visit San Francisco again. It also made us realize that we now had an entirely new definition of "home", a very clear meaning: *wherever we were together*. Our closeness had become completely natural and self-evident. A sense of belonging together flowed dreamlike across our daily lives, just beyond our horizon of awareness, just below the radar of our understanding.

It was strange being back in the US, staying at the Minihanes. Rose and Michael seemed genuinely glad to see us; Mike seemed resentful; Marilyn seemed somewhat irritated; and Rosanne seemed mostly bored, as though we'd interrupted something she wasn't doing.

On the Sunday, after a midday family dinner in the kitchen, with Marilyn and family also present, Mike got up to go and have a look at the news on TV. He was dressed in his California State Highway Patrol uniform, as he was about to go on duty. He was carrying little Victor on his arm as he left the kitchen. I followed him out, since the news in early 1969 was profoundly important to me in many ways: there was the War, and the anti-war demonstrations, possibly something about peace talks, the Civil Rights movement and more demonstrations and battles with the police, who were frequently referred to by the demonstrators as *pigs*, partly due to the predilection many cops had for swinging their truncheons viciously and causing as much injury as possible, with particular preference shown to those whose skin color was considered too dark.

When I entered the living room, Mike was standing in the middle of the living room floor, in front of the TV, still holding the little boy, glaring at the screen that showed Blacks marching in protest against the failure of their country to disregard the color of their epidermis. Then Mike turned and looked straight at Victor, pointed at the TV and snarled, "*Look, Victor. Niggers! Niggers!*" The blood drained from me. Adrenalin started pumping. *Not again*, I thought. *Not yet another generation to be infused with this disgusting bigotry!!!* I was so angry, so incensed, I could hardly think, but I *had* to do something. "*Look, Victor!*" I hissed loudly, pointing at my uniformed father-in-law. "*Look, Victor, a pig!!*" Mike twitched involuntarily, then glared at me as if I'd hit him and he'd like nothing better than to knock me into the next county. I glared right back because he *had* hit me: a sharp blow to my sense of human decency. He saw instantly that my fury was far greater than his. Maybe he could also see that he had no defense whatsoever for his racist comment. In any case, he said nothing, but whirled around and left the room without looking back. I remained standing there, alone, for a while.

Later, I told Jeanette about the incident. She was shocked – and extremely proud of me. Mike never mentioned it, not ever. I don't think anyone else in the family ever knew what happened there in less than half a minute. I understood from Jeanette that Mike could be quite a bully and that *nobody* ever got away with talking to him like that.

Mom came to visit us for a couple of days in mid-February, in connection with visiting Al and Nancy in Seattle. By that time, we were already making our move mentally, and decided to sell everything we couldn't take with us (or didn't want to), and to give away whatever we couldn't sell. Since we'd received a lot of nice electrical appliances as wedding presents, none of which would work in Europe due to the different voltage, we saw selling them all as a way to supplement what we needed to pay for our move.

Just after Mom's brief visit, I wrote to Dad, telling him we wished he'd come along. I also told him that I'd probably make up my mind by April as to whether I would be pursuing my Master's any further. If I didn't think there was a realistic chance of completing it before August, I probably wouldn't bother, I told him. "*I'm beginning to take my painting more seriously now, and I hope to do that full-time, at least to start, in Sweden. If after six months to a year I decide I can't support us that way, I'll have learned Swedish anyway, so I could teach English* [there] *part- or full-time.*" Like many monolingual people I'd met and would continue to meet, we had no doubts that we could more or less effortlessly learn a new language; it would just happen simply by being there, wouldn't it? Some kind of osmosis? No big deal or anything like that!

We didn't, however, get far in the project to teach ourselves some Swedish before leaving. I read (or looked at) the book and listened to (or looked at) the tapes, but somehow things like "*Vi flog över en öde ö i Söderhavet*" neither spurred us a lot nor succeeded in teaching us how to pronounce the Swedish letter ö.[13] It's a sound that doesn't exist in English, and therefore simply doesn't register in ears trained only to hear English sounds. We would encounter many more of those.

Our initial moving plans were still sketchy and tentative, as they were likely to remain, in view of the paucity of information that our local Honorary Consul could be bothered to provide. From the leaflets, however, we were able to ascertain that work permits would be a prerequisite for getting jobs in Sweden, but it seemed equally obvious that we would have to go to Sweden to find jobs. So that's what we decided to do. If, however, I was going to work as an artist and maybe get "adopted" by some Swedish community, I would be self-employed. Would we then need work permits at all if I were going to work as an artist?

When I look back at our moving plans as I write this nearly five decades later, it becomes clear that our lack of information and insight created a kind of vacuum that was readily filled by whatever rumors and misinformation came to our attention, particularly if such information was what we wanted to believe in

---

13   The sentence means "We flew over a remote island in the South Seas." The closest approximation of the pronunciation of the Swedish letter ö might be in the French pronunciation of the last part of the French word "adieu", but not as it's pronounced in English!

the first place. We presumed that learning the language was virtually automatic. Getting permission to stay was a certainty. Finding work and a place to live would be a walk in the park. Any other adjustments that might be required wouldn't be any more difficult than adjusting a thermostat to achieve perfect comfort. Maybe naiveté is how things get done. All we really knew was that we had an awful lot to anticipate. But what it was we had to anticipate – as well as when, where and how – was totally inconclusive.

I paid another visit to said consulate, where the totally bored HC had a new newspaper and made a note of my new question, for which he had no answer, but said he would contact someone "higher up". I don't know whether he meant the Swedish Embassy in Ottawa or the Swedish Foreign Office in Stockholm, or his barber or tailor, or his neighbor's cousin, but a couple of weeks later, he phoned to say he'd received a reply and I could come down and pick it up. It was in the form of a telegram (in Swedish) stating (he claimed, as he translated) that if I were working as an artist, I would not be subject to the requirement for a work permit. That seemed to open the door for us, and we began looking into how we would get there and when we would leave Vancouver.

Since my plan at that point was still to complete my Master's during the summer, our search for travel options would be limited to alternatives in August, thus giving me June and July to complete the thesis work. Lee offered me as much flexibility and support as anyone could reasonably hope for to expedite my Master's, but since we would be leaving Vancouver and Canada indefinitely anyway, it would probably be prudent to sell our furniture; then if we did have to come back, it would be to look for a house, and we might as well start with a blank slate for the furniture. And we would sell our car.

But there were lots of things we didn't want to part with – clothing, books, dishes and a few other wedding presents, bedding and rugs; it added up quickly. Despite the telegram, we were still uncertain about whether we would be allowed to stay in Sweden, yet the fact that we would be arriving there in late August meant that even with a minimum stay of just a few months, we would need to have both summer and winter clothing along with us on the trip. All the rest of our possessions could be put into storage.

It would, however, still be difficult to travel light. We didn't want to have to buy a lot of things we already had and couldn't afford over there soon after we arrived. Moreover, because of the indefinite nature of our trip (or move?!), we'd probably have to get one-way tickets – either by plane or by boat from some eastern port city (after taking a train there first). But the baggage allowance on planes was pretty limited, and the charges for excess luggage were steep. Ocean liners were far too costly, but perhaps we could find a freighter that would be cheaper? (Remember that there was no internet back then; searching through travel agencies was time-consuming, frustrating and often futile – and they wouldn't have had any information about possible passage on freighters.)

We got lucky. We somehow discovered that there was a passenger ship called the *Stefan Batóry*, belonging to the Polish Ocean Lines, that would be sailing from Montréal on August 14th, stopping in Southampton in England, then arriving in Copenhagen on August 24th, where we would disembark before the ship sailed on to its final destination, Gdynia, along the Baltic coast in northern Poland. From Copenhagen we would then have just a short ferry ride across a strait to Sweden, to Malmö.

The cost of the trans-Canadian train ride, plus the fare for the ship, turned out to be only slightly more than the one-way plane fare, but there was a nearly unlimited baggage allowance. The fare also seemed to include the breakfasts. And since we weren't in any particular hurry – we had no deadlines to meet or appointments to keep – we figured that this might be a once-in-a-lifetime opportunity to enjoy a 10-day voyage across the Atlantic.

We'd amassed seven suitcases over the years, five of them Jeanette's. We filled them with both summer and winter clothing to last for several months, either until we could send for our things from storage or until we returned, chastened, to Vancouver to look for a home, jobs and that 30-year mortgage. On the storage question, we got lucky again. There was a Vancouver branch of the Johnson Line, a huge international shipping company with storage facilities where we could rent the required number of cubic feet of space[14] at an affordable $25 a month and, if it turned out that we were able to stay in Sweden or elsewhere, we could simply notify them of our address and they would arrange sea transport from Vancouver to our door, wherever that might turn out to be, also at a reasonable price. Otherwise, we could collect our things on returning to Vancouver.

Since we'd be needing all our suitcases for the trip, we had to pack our goods for storage in trunks and cartons. We still had my big black trunk, the one I used when Norm and I moved to San Francisco from Oak Park, but it was far from enough. I located a place in Vancouver where they could build us three more

---

14   We estimated a need for 150 cu.ft. (about 4.25 m^3).

such trunks, slightly larger (and blue, for some reason). They would be ready in plenty of time, in the beginning of June, giving us the chance to pack them carefully to distribute weight and protect fragile things.

We also discovered that we could get as many reasonably sturdy liquor cartons as we wanted, free of charge, from the government liquor stores. Designed for holding 12 bottles each, they were also perfect for packing books; a trunk fully loaded with books would have not be possible to lift manually, but liquor-bottle cartons were strong enough and large enough to hold quite a few books without becoming too heavy for me to lift without risking back injury (except when trying to carry two at a time up five flights of stairs…).

The second of my four Vancouver canvases was underway, with Jeanette cheering me on. It was somewhat larger than the previous one, and was a reaction to the nearly total male dominance that was making wars all over the place and otherwise fucking up the planet. Maybe I had some pipe-dream that if women were to dominate instead, it might be about music and not war. I call it *Matriarch*.[15]

Painting transported me, transfigured me. The world around me had become a blur, and I was in a room so secret that only Jeanette knew about it and could flit in and out to keep me going and keep all manner of practical distractions and disruptions at bay. A number of people I'd met said things like "Oh, so you paint to relax?" For me, painting was by no means relaxing! It took all my energy, both physically and mentally. On completion of a painting I would flop, exhausted. And again, Jeanette would be there to revive me and get me going again.

One of the few personal contacts I made with my fellow students at UBC was with a guy named Mike Barbour who, like me, was planning to become a university professor someday – unless he became a racing driver instead. He had his own race car (Formula 2? 3?) and said he sometimes participated in races. He'd seen the *Matriarch* painting during a brief visit to our place and was extremely enthusiastic about it. In the early summer, he brought his wife around to see the painting, and they ended up buying it, making a much-needed contribution to our travel funds.[16]

---

15 Painting #10 (see Appendix 2)

16 I unfortunately lost all contact with Mike after moving to Sweden, and have been unable to locate him since. I've learned he got divorced, but I have no idea what has happened him after that – or to the painting.

The third Vancouver painting was a self-portrait – *The Animal in Me*[17] – in which I also used a palette knife to create multiple layers, predominantly shades of orange. I was trying to come to terms with Dionysian impulses I recognized in myself – notably from my libido – which I neither desired nor could fully control, even though I'd still been successful in stopping myself from acting on them. It's one of several paintings I did on primed linen souvenir dishtowels (we urgently needed to save money). In this case it was a kitschy souvenir dishtowel promoting Chicago. I don't remember how it came to be in my possession; perhaps it came in a package from Mom.

I went back to the brushes for my final Vancouver painting, a small, iconographic, and exaggeratedly simple farewell to North America. I call it *Landscape: Retrospect*.[18]

I didn't dare to paint any more after that, because I would soon have to remove all my paintings from their stretchers, roll them up and insert them into a robust cardboard tube I'd acquired to withstand the long trip ahead. (Since the layered palette-knife technique I used in *Matriarch* wouldn't have survived the rolling up, I was glad to have found a buyer; *The City* got slightly damaged, but *The Animal in Me* came out surprisingly unscathed, as it was small enough not to require rolling tightly.)

In all four of my Vancouver paintings, Jeanette was the new dimension. While I was painting, she would bring me coffee, fruit, chocolate, wine, sandwiches, anything to reduce the need for me to stop or interrupt my work and get such things myself. She had an uncanny way of anticipating what would suit me at any moment. I was totally absorbed in my work, sometimes painting far into the night, and when Jeanette brought me things, she took great pains not to disturb my concentration (or to bring to Mario's attention that there was someone in the room beneath the conjugal bed). She would just sit quietly and look at what I'd painted or what I was still in the act of painting. Few of our visitors gave me a clue as to what they thought of my work; she gave me all the feedback I needed, even when she said nothing. I was painting for her.

Michael came to spend a week or so with us in early April, during my Easter break, and the three of us took some fairly adventurous camping trips together.

---

17   Painting #11 (see Appendix 2)
18   Painting #12 (see Appendix 2)

Inconclusive anticipation

One was into the wilderness beyond Horseshoe Bay, beyond Whistler Mountain, where there was still quite a bit of snow, lots of rain and no other people at all. The "roads" were not meant for a Valiant. They were presumably intended only for big logging trucks, of which we saw none. The scenery was magnificent despite the rain and except for some areas of ugly clear-cutting. We created shelter under our plastic sheeting – and added mosquito netting after the first night. We hadn't been expecting mosquitoes since there was still a great deal of snow around, but they seemed to be expecting us.

A second camping trip together started with the ferry from Horseshoe Bay across to Vancouver Island, where we were determined to get a look at the west coast of the island – and the open waters of the Pacific – even though our map indicated that the only roads were still under construction. Our car was appropriately named. When we arrived on the island, we took Highway 19 to the junction of Highway 4 as far as a hamlet called Great Central. Soon after the turnoff, we spotted a sign for the Englishman River Falls Provincial Park. Since waterfalls always held the greatest fascination for Jeanette and me since our first ascent of the Yosemite Falls on an outing while we were living in San Francisco, we decided to take a look. We were all alone when we got to a campsite in a deep forest of cedars and towering Douglas firs, with lush giant green ferns and a soft thick carpet of needles.

As soon as we got out of the car, we heard the roar of the falls and took a trail heading in that direction. There were lots of similarities to the Rogue River, but these narrow falls were even more spectacular. The river not only made a deep vertical drop while taking a 90° left turn, blasting at the rock along one side before crashing to the bottom some 100 feet below. A timber footbridge crossed the roaring river almost on top of the falls and high above the river below. It was slippery as grease due to the constant spray, which soon curtailed any impulses we might have had to clown around there. Few views have ever thrilled me more than that one.

When we got back to the car, we found that it was being inspected by four youths who seemed as surprised to be interrupted by our approach as we were to see them. I have no idea what their intentions were, but their gang-style posturing suggested certain aspirations to leave their mark. They looked us over; their body language was challenging. When Michael and I responded in kind, they seemed to decide quickly that we might not be worth it. Their leader or spokesman asked if we knew somebody whose name we'd never heard before. We said no, and then they left.

The next day, after we reached Great Central, the remaining vehicles on Highway 4 – or what was in the process of becoming Highway 4 – consisted entirely of two or three big earth-movers, miles apart, and then we were on our own entirely, often driving along what seemed to be more like riverbeds than roads, although there was enough rain and snowmelt to fill any real riverbeds. We concluded that they must have been areas that had been blasted in preparation for laying roadbeds and then roads. Our trip may have been foolhardy, but the tougher the conditions, the more the three of us seemed to enjoy surmounting them.

After traveling for some time in the general direction of Ucluelet (which we never saw), without meeting any other cars or seeing anyone, we finally reached the Pacific Ocean, and of course went clambering out to the farthest extension of the rocky promontories we could find to watch the waves and peer across a different ocean from the one Jeanette and I would soon be crossing. The rocks below the high-water mark were covered in layers of barnacles with fairly large starfish (about a foot across) clinging to them. The waves were not terribly high that day, but were roaring and foaming enough to limit our communications to gestures whenever we were more than a couple of paces from each other. The view was vast, up and down the coast and of course out to the world's biggest ocean. Except for our car parked in the distance, and ourselves, there were no signs of human presence in any direction. Somewhere on our camping trips with Michael, I sadly left behind my beautiful Bowie knife (sad despite it having been a gift from guess where).

We had a good time with Michael. For Jeanette it was as if he was at last showing signs of landing – coming home from Vietnam – but that was more likely her wishful thinking at work. He continued to drift, living with his parents, not working, not studying, not socializing. We were concerned about him and told him we hoped he would make good on his earlier musing that he might come over to Europe and spend some time with us once we'd found a place to stay, and maybe we could do some travelling together, or maybe he could use our place in Malmö as a base for some travels on his own. We were surprised at how quickly he jumped at our suggestion. He seemed eager to get out of his parents' house, but he hadn't been able to figure out where to go instead. We presumed he had no income, unless he was getting something from the Army.

After the Easter break, with Jeanette and me on our own again and me back in school, I at last made that big Decision: screw the Master's degree. If I truly wanted one, which seemed most unlikely at the time, I could maybe get one from a Swedish university, or resume my academic work at UBC if our European venture failed. I got two A's and two B's in my coursework. Apart from the F (for Fascism?) in bibliography, my grade-point average gave me lots of options.

But now it was time to shift from moving plans into moving actions, no longer just theoretical musings. First I had to get a smallpox vaccination. When Jeanette got hers in '65, she hadn't reacted with more than mild discomfort for a day or two, but mine gave rise to painful swelling and a high fever for nearly a week.

We turned our earlier travel inquiries into confirmed bookings, and made our first payments on tickets for the Trans-Canadian Railway and for passage on the *Stefan Batóry*. The sailing date, August 14th, gave us a fixed point in time on which to base all other plans, working backwards. We'd visit Dad and Mom for a number of days in Oak Park en route to Montréal, which meant we would need to take the eastbound train from Vancouver on August 1st, a Friday. Al and Nancy kindly offered to come up to take us to the train, where we'd say good-bye to them. Jeanette would retain her job until Friday, July 18th. We'd have the month of July to devote to selling our stuff, packing what we were taking, preparing what we were leaving behind for storage, and seeing that it got picked up.

Although my watershed talk with Mario in October resulted in our having fewer visitors, I was frequently painting late into the night – in the library. But Mario never said another word about it. I suspected he would have if he liked Jeanette and me any less than he did, or if he'd been any less kind than he was. During the spring I mentioned a thing or two about our looking into moving to Europe for a while, and he reacted with delight – probably not only for our sakes. Thus, as soon as our August 1st departure date by train from Vancouver was confirmed, I informed him.

In July, Jeanette's parents drove up to see us, in what Jeanette said was the first trip in her memory that the two of them ever made together. The atmosphere was tense, except when it was terse, or when it was both. Marilyn and family also drove up for a few days, and again the conversation was tense. Although Jeanette and Marilyn had been pretty close, there was a definite redshift, as Marilyn remained stationary while Jeanette was moving faster and farther away in many more respects than the geographical ones. I seem to remember that Marilyn and Vic drove up in a pickup in order to be able to take our glass china cabinet back with them to San Francisco; Jeanette was told (by Marilyn or Rose) that it was a family heirloom, not ours to sell. Fair enough.

John and family also came up from California for a few days and we had a nice time. Jeanette seemed to get along better with them than with the other relatives, including her own. John said he might want to buy *Hurry up with the Lumber, for Christ's Sake!*, but since he didn't want to pay the $100 I was asking, he dropped it. I was glad. It was my personal favorite and I didn't want to part with it for less.

In the beginning of July we took delivery of the three new blue trunks to complement my old black one, and I started filling a couple of liquor cartons with books, in order to determine how many cartons we would need for the whole collection. I estimated 60; we ended up needing 67, and it took many trips to the booze shop to bring them all home. Since I'd catalogued all my books and arranged all the fiction alphabetically by author, I packed them roughly in the order they were arranged on the shelves, then numbered all the cartons, to be able to unpack them someday, somewhere, and put them directly into place with minimal disorder.

With just two weeks to go before departure, we sold our small black-and-white TV and our radio, which meant that we would have missed witnessing the first manned moon landing on July 20th (two days before Jeanette's 25th birthday), but for the kindness of the Falcones, who invited us upstairs for the historic occasion. From our perspective at that moment, our European landing was far more momentous, and we were probably too wound up to have taken in anything lunar anyway.

Then we began offering all our visitors – locals and those from afar – our remaining electrical goods, mostly lamps. After filling three trunks with things we'd eventually want in a new home somewhere but had no need for now, we began separating the remaining things into three categories: what we needed to use until we left, but still wanted to put into storage (the fourth trunk was reserved for that purpose); what we needed to have on the trip and for our first few months in Europe (mostly clothing); and what we could do without.

We found that there weren't all that many of our dishes or glassware that we liked. We thus packed only the ones we did like and still had enough to see to our needs until we left. And we adjusted and re-adjusted our "keep" criteria to match the available remaining space, ending up with just enough to fill the 67 cartons and four trunks for storage. I purchased a small collapsible dolly to stack our seven suitcases on, and a sturdy strap to hold them in place. We also had a rigid, rugged cardboard tube for my paintings, and my guitar case. In other words, we'd be traveling with nine pieces of luggage.

Mario suggested that any dishes or other things we couldn't sell and wanted to leave behind could remain in the kitchen cupboards for the next tenant. I seem to remember that he gave us a decent sum of money for much of the furniture as well; he said he'd be renting out the suite furnished. The only thing left was our valiant Valiant.

The good deal we got on our car from Jim Gillingham's father-in-law in September '66, combined with the considerably higher prices for cars in Canada, enabled us to get a sizeable addition to our savings. We put an ad in the paper in mid-July, asking the same $2200 price we paid for it nearly three years earlier,[19] and were astonished to get an immediate response. A young Chinese guy named Lyman Lai came out to our place the same day, cash in hand, and the deal was done. We left a little money in our Vancouver bank account and converted the rest to traveler's checks to see us through until we found jobs in Sweden, provided we continued to live extremely frugally – up to about six months.

But the unexpectedly quick sale of the car left us in the lurch for transportation during the final week or so. Al kindly offered us the use of their extra car – a VW Beetle – so I took the train down to pick it up. I'd never driven a stick shift before, and needed a quick lesson (I declined the offer of a crash course…). There was a whole lot of jerking going on before Al felt comfortable about releasing the car into my temporary custody, although he felt certain I would learn it quickly. I did my utmost to avoid stopping on upgrades.

The day after I got back to Vancouver with it, I discovered that I'd probably imported it illegally. I was terrified that the Canadian authorities would impound it or even confiscate it. I used it as little as possible and held my breath until our departure on Friday, August 1st, when Al and family came up to see us off and bring their VW back to where it belonged.

The farewell from the Falcones was warm and heartfelt. They'd always been wonderful, and apart from Mario's dilemma, we never had any problems at all. The whole day was extremely hectic, however, and there was quite a lot of pressure, tension and sweat during the course of the send-off at the train station.

---

19   Albeit not in US dollars, which were worth around 25% more than Canadian dollars at the time.

Al's kids, Mike and Andy, were around five and three respectively, and restless; it was an unusually warm day. Everything was awkward and uncomfortable. We were all just waiting for the train to pull out of the station.

The scenery through British Columbia, following the Fraser River and its whirlpools through the Fraser River Canyon, was spectacular. The next morning we were told that we were passing Mount Robson (the highest peak in the Canadian Rockies), but unfortunately it was shrouded in fog. However, when we reached Jasper, the views were again breathtaking, which Jeanette described as *"shaped white granite like a mountain chiseled by its parents."* (This quote, and others pertaining to the trip, are from the travel diary Jeanette kept.)

Not long after Jasper, where we had a little time to walk around, we began leaving the mountains behind us and entering the rolling plains of the ranchers and farmers. *"Such a contrast was almost earth-shaking,"* Jeanette wrote, *"like man & woman beside each other so close, and so different."* On and on we rolled, through seemingly unending fields of golden wheat, towards Saskatoon. *"What a feeling of vastness ... fields after fields, quite a world!"*

On Sunday morning we had a delay due to a burnt-out bridge. We didn't reach Winnipeg until the following afternoon (instead of the scheduled morning arrival), where we had to wait a few hours for a later connection to Chicago. *"We travel very well together,"* Jeanette wrote. *"We seem to get along nicely with life, but are unable to adjust to people."*

We arrived at the station in Chicago with all nine pieces of luggage on August 6th. I don't think we brought it all with us out to Oak Park; I seem to remember stashing most of it at the station, in storage lockers or at a freight office, which would have made sense (not that we were always sensible). Anyway, we had six days to spend with Dad and Mom, and we were determined to make the best of it; and so, it seemed, were they.

It was difficult to find common ground, but with all four of us struggling to do so, we managed pretty well. There was even less to say when we visited Grandma Erisman in her specially built room at my parental home; she'd never had anything personal to say to me, even when I was a child, and she offered little more than her wan smile. But now her silence could at least be partly attributed to her advancing muscular dystrophy. It was the first time I'd met her since just before Grandpa Erisman died. Perhaps a lifetime under his holy thumb had stilled her voice beyond repair.

Jeanette truly loved my dad; she said she saw much of what she loved in me in him. She and my mom were the only ones who'd ever said something like that to me; most people thought I took after Mom.

Dad showed us some slides, and Jeanette was particularly interested in seeing those of me when I was younger. We also saw slides of my parent's trip to Europe (a business trip for Dad) that spring, when they made a side trip to Basel, Switzerland, where they tried unsuccessfully to look up my renegade cousin Robert. His renegade nature consisted of his having left the Meeting and apparently turning from the Lord. He was also *divorced!* My parents had been eager to persuade him to return to the Fold. Dad took a couple of slides of the building where Robert lived and where they fruitlessly rang his doorbell numerous times. I said we might like to try to look him up one day, he being my only relative in Europe. Mom gave me his address; they didn't have his phone number.

I phoned Carroll Anderson, my old high school homeroom teacher, to see how he was – and how my first painting was. He was delighted to hear from me, and immediately invited Jeanette and me to their place for dinner. Jeanette and I were glad to have a break from the prayerful mealtimes at 1231, which my dad used as a cover to get in a little preaching. (Fortunately, protocol left it solely to my dad to say the pre-meal prayer.) I was particularly pleased to see my painting prominently displayed on the Andersons' living room wall. He'd had it tastefully framed, and seemed proud to own it. He also said he was thrilled to hear I'd been doing well academically. But the conversation was rather vacuous and free from controversy; the war in Vietnam was never mentioned. It was an enjoyable, largely superficial evening.

One hot sunny day, Dad took us all on an outing to Starved Rock State Park, along the Illinois River about halfway to Peoria, where we went hiking along the cliff trails, sweating profusely in the sweltering Midwest summer heat. Dad grilled some hot dogs and we had a fun time. The most awkward moments during our stay with them were the incessant mealtime speeches to their Invisible Friend to *beseech* Him contritely about one thing and another concerning our spiritual welfare. They couldn't understand (and most likely didn't feel they needed to) how they were lambasting our ears with things that generated in us a powerful urge either to laugh, to gag or to issue a stern rebuttal. There was no honest response we could give that would not be hurtful to them, so we just remained silent.

One evening we were invited to dinner at the home of my cousin Howard (no longer Howie) and his wife Carolyn in Evanston. Howard now had a degree in biology, yet somehow managed to retain his literal belief in the biblical creation myth and to disavow evolution and claims of anything older than 6000 years as evil lies. It was another example of the principle that logic doesn't tell you whether your premise is correct, only what conclusions you can validly draw from it. Howard's starting point was that the Bible is Truth, and to hell with evidence to the contrary, to hell with the need for evidence for any belief one holds.

However, we didn't discuss anything controversial there either. After dinner, Howard needed to make a brief visit to Abbott Labs, his place of work. I tagged along. In the lab where he worked, he showed me cage after cage of dogs and other animals grotesquely disfigured by implants and other horrendous-looking vivisectionist procedures. I found myself grappling with the moral issue of ends justifying means, preventing human suffering through animal trials, means justifying ends, the whole moral morass, standing first on one foot, then on the other. Absolutely no absolute clarity was forthcoming – and never has been.

Our last day in Chicago was Monday, August 11th. Jeanette described it as a pleasant last day, and that Mom and Dad *"held up nicely"* when they took us to the station in the Loop. The train departed at 9 PM for Montréal via Toronto, where we and our nine pieces of luggage would have to change trains for the final leg. (If I include the lunch hamper Mom kindly sent along, we had 10 pieces of luggage.)

The train from Toronto was fast but noisy and we didn't get much sleep. We arrived in Montréal on Tuesday afternoon, and found a fairly clean and reasonably adequate rooming house for $6 a night. It was there we finally enjoyed most of Mom's lunch box. Our brief exploration of the harbor area revealed a surprise: our vessel was already there, ready and waiting; we got our first look at the *Stefan Batóry* from dockside. We also found out that we could leave off our luggage the next morning, Wednesday. After breakfast, I and most of our luggage filled a taxi back to the dock and where I checked in all the bags we wouldn't be needing on the voyage itself. Our ship was far bigger than any vessel we'd ever been on, but it would have been dwarfed by ships like the *Queen Elizabeth* and other major ocean liners. It looked well worn. The paint wasn't flaking, but had lost all of its gloss. It looked well-cared-for, in the manner of patients in a well-run geriatric ward. It was nothing to get excited about, but it was something to get to Europe on, and that was incredibly exciting. After I got back to our rooming house, I found that Jeanette had bought a loaf of French bread and other stuff. We had our final meal on North American soil in a lovely park on a summery Montréal hillside with a fine view.

The next morning, August 14th, we checked out of the rooming house and found ourselves some breakfast before boarding the ship, not realizing that we would be offered a vastly more substantial breakfast for free as soon as we were on board. We only had one suitcase each in our cabin during the voyage, but since I wasn't comfortable about putting the paintings and guitar in the ship's hold, we kept them in our tiny windowless stateroom too. We'd chosen the cheapest possible accommodations, which meant we were pretty far down in the hold and pretty far from anything resembling a porthole – nothing posh about it. After we got settled, we went up to one of the decks where we could go outdoors and look at the surroundings before the ship sailed.

We got a good view of *Habitat*, the imaginative housing complex built for Expo67 two years earlier. It was a sunny day, not too suffocatingly hot, and we were impatient to get going, but we could see that there was still an awful lot of loading to be done. They were loading much more than the passengers and their belongings; perhaps they were using all available space to load goods bound for Poland as well, or perhaps some Polish travelers were bringing cars and more back with them.

At noon, not terribly long after we'd finished our second breakfast, there came an announcement inviting all passengers to report to the dining room for lunch. We were shown to an assigned round, white-linen-covered table for four, the other two being a young couple. We never figured out whether they were Danish or Dutch, or Dutch living in Denmark, or maybe one of each, or maybe they weren't a couple at all. They didn't seem terribly interested in conversing, despite the prospect of spending 10 days sharing that table with us three times a day. Jeanette described the guy as a "photo maniac" and her as a "sun goddess".

Our waiter looked to be in his late sixties at least, short, weary and wizened, but with a kind smile. He brought us huge menus: tall and narrow booklets, with a two-page spread each for salads, soups, fish, poultry, meat, desserts, and cheeses. There was another page for soft drinks, and a separate wine list for alcoholic beverages. Only the wine list showed prices, which we immediately decided were beyond our budget. Although we were both young and ravenous, we were uncertain about how to proceed. Our attempts to strike up conversations with the other couple at our table had hitherto fallen flat. They also appeared uncertain; after all, we were all facing multiple choices.

When the waiter came to our table take our orders, he started with Jeanette and me. We thought we'd play it safe and go for a meat dish. This was a Polish ship, and we were cautious; we'd never eaten Polish food before. The only thing I knew about it was that they ate carp for Christmas, which didn't sound too appetizing. The waiter looked at me. "*But what kind of salad would you like?*" he asked. "*Do we get salad too?*" I asked, surprised. "*Of course! It's all included. A salad, a soup, a fish dish, then a poultry dish....*" I had to interrupt him. "*But how much is it?*" I asked, afraid that his answer would blow our budget to bits. "*It's all included,*" he replied with a grin, "*everything but alcohol. That you have to pay for yourself.*" Our eyes grew wide, our mouths began to water; we hurried back to the salad page, picked something there, then picked a soup, and asked for more time to decide about the rest. We were grinning from ear to ear, and our tablemates were too, possibly because of their own appetites, possibly because our reactions amused them; they were quite a lot older – in their thirties?

The food was absolutely fabulous. And this was just lunch. We hadn't even set sail yet. The more we ordered, the more our waiter seemed to enjoy serving us. After taking plenty of time to enjoy the massive lunch, we went back out on deck to enjoy the sunshine. Finally, at around 4 PM, the gangways were hauled in, the ropes were loosened, the engines began roaring and belching smoke, the horn was blaring, and we slowly slid away from the dock, the water churning beneath us, the boat trembling. It was finally real. Jeanette and I were leaving North America, heading for a European adventure, into the unknown, and possibly to a whole new life.

END OF BOOK TWO

Appendix

APPENDIX 1 – My homes, 1964-69

Stan & Norm's apartment at 450 Ellis, San Francisco, July 1-November 30, 1964

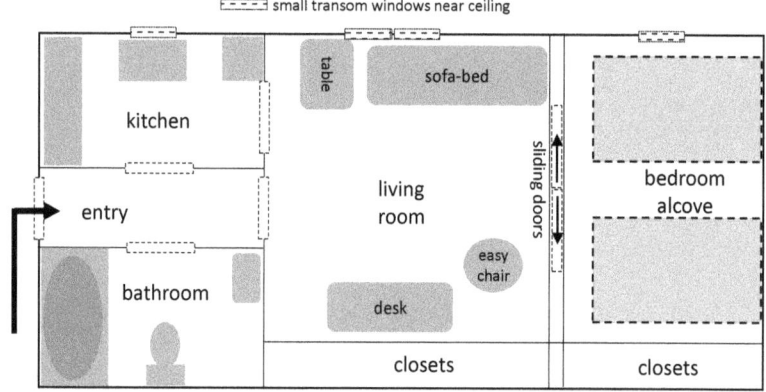

Stan's apt, 574 Evergreen, Daly City, Dec 1964-Sept 1966

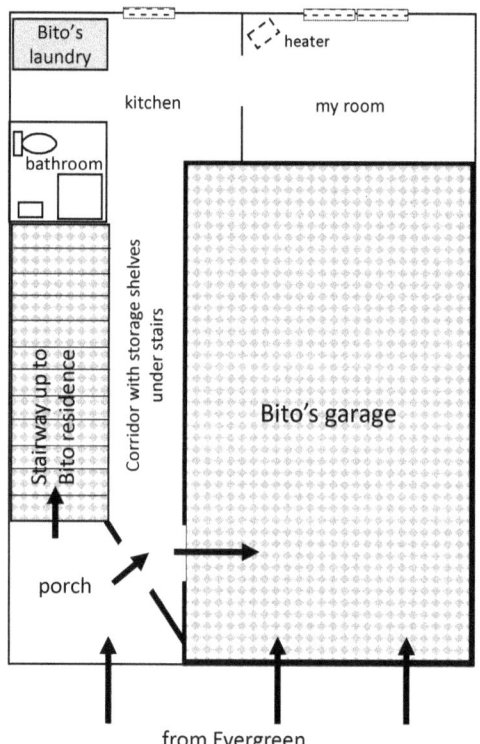

Stan & Jeanette's apartment, 110 Pueblo, San Francisco, October 1966-June 1968

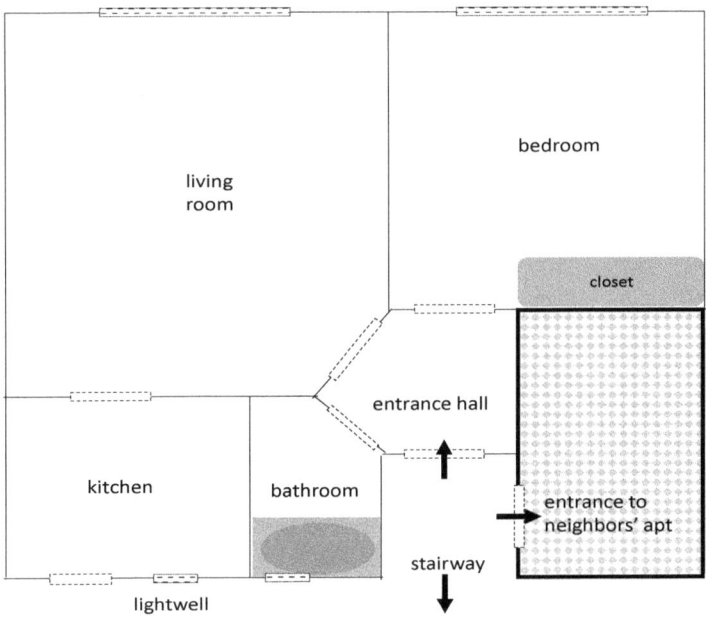

Stan & Jeanette's basement suite, 4520 Ross St., Vancouver, July 1968-August 1969

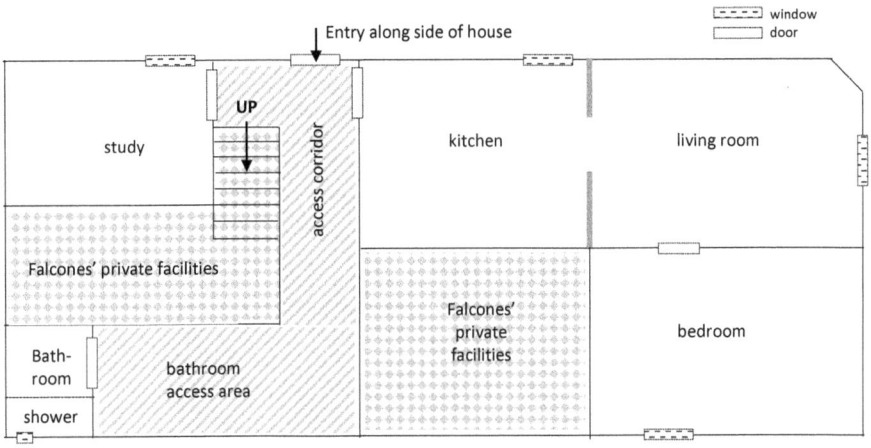

APPENDIX 2 – Paintings 9-12

These paintings were painted in 1969, while we were living in Vancouver BC.

#9 Hurry up with the Lumber, for Christ's Sake!

#10 Matriarch

Appendix 2

#11 The Animal in Me

#12 Landscape: Retrospect

Hindsights
the six-part autobiography of an unknown artist

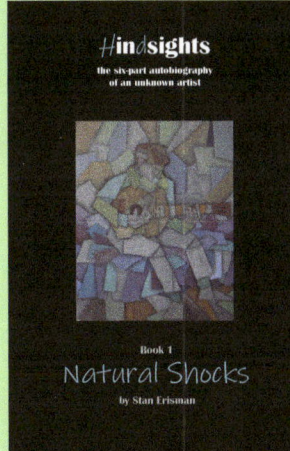

Book 1
Natural Shocks
by Stan Erisman

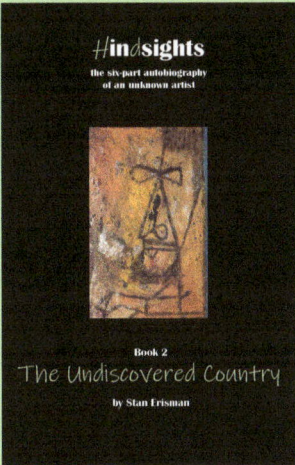

Book 2
The Undiscovered Country
by Stan Erisman

Book 3
No Traveller Returns
by Stan Erisman

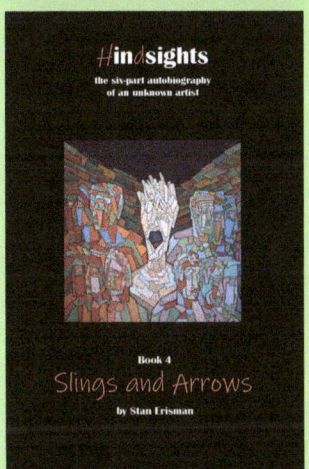

Book 4
Slings and Arrows
by Stan Erisman

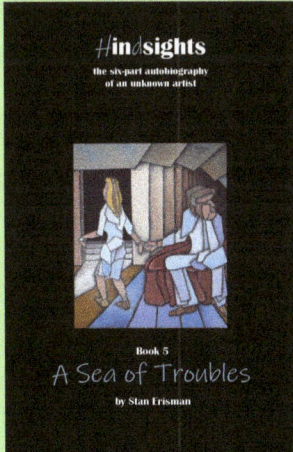

Book 5
A Sea of Troubles
by Stan Erisman

Book 6
Perchance to Dream
by Stan Erisman

www.ingramcontent.com/pod-product-compliance
Lightning Source LLC
Chambersburg PA
CBHW040252170426
43191CB00019B/2391